EDWARDS

ON THE

FREEDOM OF THE WILL.

AN INQURY

INTO

THE MODERN PREVAILING NOTIONS

OF THAT

FREEDOM OF THE WILL

WHICH IS SUPPOSED TO BE ESSENTIAL TO

MORAL AGENCY, VIRTUE AND VICE, REWARD AND PUNISHMENT, PRAISE AND BLAME

BY THE LATE

REV. JONATHAN EDWARDS
PRESIDENT OF THE COLLEGE OF NEW JERSEY

"It is not of him that willeth." Romans 9:16

Soli Deo Gloria Publications
...for instruction in righteousness...

Soli Deo Gloria Publications
P.O. Box 451, Morgan, PA 15064
(412) 221-1901/FAX 221-1902

*

This edition of *The Freedom of the Will* was taken
from the edition published by Thomas Nelson
in London in 1845. This Soli Deo Gloria
reprint is 1996. Printed in the USA.

*

ISBN 1-57358-033-3

PREFACE.

MANY find much fault with the calling professing
Christians, that differ one from another in some matters of opinion, by distinct *names;* especially calling
them by the names of particular men, who have distinguished themselves as maintainers and promoters
of those opinions: as the calling some professing
Christians Arminians, from Arminius; others Arians,
from Arius; others Socinians, from Socinus, and the
like.   They think it unjust in itself; as it seems to
suppose and suggest, that the persons marked out by
these names received those doctrines which they entertain, out of regard *to*, and reliance *on*, those men
after whom they are named, as though they made
them their rule; in the same manner as the followers
of Christ are called Christians, after his name, whom
they regard and depend upon as their great head and
rule,—whereas, this is an unjust and groundless imputation on those that go under the fore-mentioned
denominations.   Thus (say they) there is not the
least ground to suppose, that the chief divines who
embrace the scheme of doctrine which is, by many,
called Arminianism, believe it the more, because Arminius believed it: and that there is no reason to
think any other, than that they sincerely and impar-

tially study the holy Scriptures, and enquire after the
mind of Christ, with as much judgment and sincerity
as any of those that call them by these names; that
they seek after truths, and are not careful whether
they think exactly as Arminius did; yea, that in
some things they actually differ from him. This
practice is also esteemed actually injurious on this
account, that it is supposed naturally to lead the
multitude to imagine the difference between persons
thus named and others to be greater than it is; yea,
as though it were so great, that they must be, as it
were, another species of beings. And they object
against it as arising from an uncharitable, narrow,
contracted spirit, which, they say, commonly inclines
persons to confine all that is good to themselves and
their own party, and to make a wide distinction between themselves and others, and stigmatise those
that differ from them with odious names. They say,
moreover, that the keeping up such a distinction of
names has a direct tendency to uphold distance and
disaffection, and keep alive mutual hatred among
Christians, who ought all to be united in friendship
and charity, however they cannot in all things think
alike.

I confess, these things are very plausible. And I
will not deny, that there are some unhappy consequences of this distinction of names, and that men's
infirmities and evil dispositions often make an ill improvement of it. But yet I humbly conceive these
objections are carried far beyond reason. The generality of mankind are disposed enough, and a great
deal too much, to uncharitableness, and to be censo-
rious and bitter towards those that differ from them

in religious opinions; which evil temper of mind will take occasion to exert itself from many things in themselves innocent, useful, and necessary. But yet there is no necessity to suppose, that the thus distinguishing persons of different opinions by different names, arises mainly from an uncharitable spirit. It may arise from the disposition there is in mankind (whom God has distinguished with an ability and inclination for speech) to improve the benefit of language, in the proper use and design of names, given to things which they have often occasion to speak of, or signify their minds about; which is to enable them to express their ideas with ease and expedition, without being encumbered with an obscure and difficult circumlocution. And the thus distinguishing persons of different opinions in religious matters may not imply, nor infer, any more than that there is a difference, and that the difference is such as we find we have often occasion to take notice of, and make mention of, that which we have frequent occasion to speak of (whatever it be that gives the occasion), this wants a name: and it is always a defect in language, in such cases, to be obliged to make use of a description instead of a name. Thus we have often occasion to speak of those who are the descendants of the ancient inhabitants of France, who were subjects or heads of the government of that land, and spake the language peculiar to it; in distinction from the descendants of the inhabitants of Spain, who belonged to that community, and spake the language of that country. And therefore we find the great need of distinct names to signify these different sorts of people, and the great convenience of those distin-

guishing words, *French* and *Spaniards;* by which
the signification of our minds is quick and easy, and
our speech is delivered from the burden of a continual reiteration of diffuse descriptions, with which it
must otherwise be embarrassed.

That the difference of the opinions of those who,
in their general scheme of divinity, agree with these
two noted men, Calvin and Arminius, is a thing
there is often occasion to speak of, is what the practice of the latter itself confesses; who are often, in
their discourses and writings, taking notice of the
supposed absurd and pernicious opinions of the former sort. And therefore the making use of different
names in this case cannot reasonably be objected
against, or condemned, as a thing which must come
from so bad a cause as they assign. It is easy to be
accounted for, without supposing it to arise from any
other source than the exigence and natural tendency
of the state of things; considering the faculty and
disposition God has given to mankind, to express
things which they have frequent occasion to mention.
by certain distinguishing names. It is an effect that
is similar to what we see arise, in innumerable cases
which are parallel, where the cause is not at all
blameworthy.

Nevertheless, at first, I had thoughts of carefully
avoiding the use of the appellation *Arminian* in this
treatise. But I soon found I should be put to great
difficulty by it; and that my discourse would be so
encumbered with an often-repeated circumlocution,
instead of a name, which would express the thing intended as well and better, that I altered my purpose.
And therefore I must ask the excuse of such as are

apt to be offended with things of this nature, that I
have so freely used the term *Arminian* in the following discourse. I profess it to be without any design
to stigmatise persons of any sort with a name of reproach, or at all to make them appear more odious.
If, when I had occasion to speak of those divines
who are commonly called by this name, I had, instead of styling them Arminians, called them *these
men*, as Dr Whitby does Calvinistic divines, it probably would not have been taken any better, or thought
to show a better temper or more good manners. I
have done as I would be done by in this matter.
However, the term *Calvinistic* is, in these days,
among most, a term of greater reproach than the
term *Arminian*, yet I should not take it at all amiss
to be called a Calvinist, for distinction's sake; though
I utterly disclaim a dependence on Calvin, or believing the doctrines which I hold, because he believed
and taught them, and cannot justly be charged with
believing in every thing just as he taught.

But, lest I should really be an occasion of injury
to some persons, I would here give notice, that though
I generally speak of that doctrine, concerning free
will and moral agency, which I oppose, as an Arminian doctrine; yet I would not be understood as asserting, that every divine or author whom I have
occasion to mention as maintaining that doctrine,
was properly an Arminian, or one of that sort which
is commonly called by that name. Some of them
went far beyond the Arminians; and I would by no
means charge Arminians in general with all the corrupt doctrine which these maintained. Thus, for
instance, it would be very injurious, if I should rank

Arminian divines in general with such authors as Mr
Chubb. I doubt not many of them have some of his
doctrines in abhorrence; though he agrees, for the
most part, with Arminians in his notion of the freedom of the will. And, on the other hand, though I
suppose this notion to be a leading article in the Arminian scheme, that which, if pursued in its consequences, will truly infer, or naturally lead to all the
rest; yet I do not charge all that have held this doctrine with being Arminians. For whatever may be
the consequences of the doctrine really, yet some that
hold this doctrine may not own nor see these consequences; and it would be unjust, in many instances,
to charge every author with believing and maintaining all the real consequences of his avowed doctrines.
And I desire it may be particularly noted, that though
I have occasion, in the following discourse, often to
mention the author of the book, entitled "An Essay
on the Freedom of the Will in God and the Creature," as holding that notion of freedom of will which
I oppose; yet I do not mean to call him an Arminian, however in that doctrine he agrees with Arminians, and departs from the current and general opinion of Calvinists. If the author of that Essay be
the same as it is commonly ascribed to, he, doubtless,
was not one that ought to bear that name. But
however good a divine he was in many respects, yet
that particular Arminian doctrine which he maintained is never the better for being held by such an one,
nor is there less need of opposing it on that account;
but rather is there the more need of it; as it will be
likely to have the more pernicious influence, for being
taught by a divine of his name and character; sup-

posing the doctrine to be wrong, and in itself to be of
an ill tendency.

I have nothing further to say by way of preface,
but only to bespeak the reader's candour and calm
attention to what I have written. The subject is of
such importance as to *demand* attention, and the
most thorough consideration. Of all kinds of knowledge that we can ever obtain, the knowledge of God,
and the knowledge of ourselves, are the most important. As religion is the great business for which we
are created, and on which our happiness depends;
and as religion consists in an intercourse between
ourselves and our Maker, and so has its foundation
in God's nature and ours, and in the relation that
God and we stand to each other; therefore a true
knowledge of both must be needful, in order to true
religion. But the knowledge of ourselves consists
chiefly in right apprehensions concerning those two
chief faculties of our nature, the *understanding* and
will. Both are very important; yet the science of
the latter must be confessed to be of greatest moment; inasmuch as all virtue and religion have their
seat more immediately in the will, consisting more
especially in right acts and habits of this faculty.
And the grand question about the freedom of the
will, is the main point that belongs to the science of
the will. Therefore, I say, the importance of this
subject greatly *demands* the attention of Christians,
and especially of divines. But as to my manner of
handling the subject, I will be far from presuming to
say, that it is such as *demands* the attention of the
reader to what I have written. I am ready to own
that in this matter I depend on the reader's *courtesy*.

But only thus far I may have some colour for putting in a *claim;* that if the reader be disposed to pass his censure on what I have written, I may be fully and patiently heard, and well attended to, before I am condemned. However, this is what I would humbly *ask* of my readers, together with the prayers of all sincere lovers of truth, that I may have much of that Spirit which Christ promised his disciples, which guides into all truth: and that the blessed and powerful influences of this Spirit would make truth victorious in the world.

CONTENTS.

PART I.

PART II.

PART III.

WHEREIN IS INQUIRED WHETHER ANY SUCH LIBERTY
OF WILL AS ARMINIANS HOLD BE NECESSARY TO
MORAL AGENCY, VIRTUE AND VICE, PRAISE AND
DISPRAISE, &C.

PART IV.

WHEREIN THE CHIEF GROUNDS OF THE REASONINGS OF ARMINIANS, IN SUPPORT AND DEFENCE OF THEIR NOTIONS OF LIBERTY, MORAL AGENCY, ETC., AND AGAINST THE OPPOSITE DOCTRINE, ARE CONSIDERED.

INQUIRY,

PART I.

WHEREIN ARE EXPLAINED AND STATED VARIOUS TERMS AND THINGS BELONGING TO THE SUBJECT OF THE ENSUING DIS-COURSE.

SECTION I.

CONCERNING THE NATURE OF THE WILL.

It may possibly be thought, that there is no great need of going about to define or describe the *will;* this word being generally as well understood as any other words we can use to explain it: and so, perhaps, it would be, had not philosophers, metaphysicians, and polemic divines brought the matter into obscurity by the things they have said of it. But since it is so, I think it may be of some use, and will tend to the greater clearness in the following discourse, to say a few things concerning it.

And therefore I observe, that the *will* (without any metaphysical refining) is plainly, *that by which the mind chooses any thing.* The faculty of the *will* is that faculty or power, or principle of mind, by which it is capable of *choosing :* an act of the *will* is the same as an act of *choosing* or *choice.*

If any think it is a more perfect definition of the will to say, that, It is that by which the soul either *chooses* or *refuses,* I am content with it; though I think that it

B

is enough to say, It is that by which the soul chooses:
for in every act of will whatsoever, the mind chooses
one thing rather than another; it chooses something
rather than the contrary, or rather than the want or
non-existence of that thing. So, in every act of refusal,
the mind chooses the absence of the thing refused; the
positive and the negative are set before the mind for its
choice, and it chooses the negative ; and the mind's
making its choice in that case is properly the act of the
will; the will's determining between the two is a voluntary determining, but that is the same thing as making
a choice. So that whatever names we call the act of
the will by, *choosing, refusing, approving, disapproving,
liking, disliking, embracing, rejecting, determining, directing, commanding, forbidding, inclining,* or being *averse,*
a *being pleased* or *displeased with;* all may be reduced
to this of *choosing.* For the soul to act *voluntarily,* is
evermore to act *electively.*

Mr Locke* says, " The will signifies nothing but a
power or ability to *prefer* or *choose ;*" and in the foregoing page says, "The word *preferring* seems best to
express the act of volition;" but adds, that " it does it
not precisely ; for (says he) though a man would prefer
flying to walking, yet who can say he ever wills it?"
But the instance he mentions does not prove that there
is any thing else in *willing* but merely *preferring ;* for
it should be considered what is the next and immediate
object of the will, with respect to a man's walking, or
any other external action; which is, not being removed
from one place to another, on the earth or through the
air—these are remoter objects of preference—but such
or such an immediate exertion of himself. The thing
nextly chosen or preferred when a man wills to walk,
is, not his being removed to such a place where he
would be, but such an exertion and motion of his legs
and feet, &c., in order to it. And his willing such an
alteration in his body in the present moment, is nothing
else but his choosing or preferring such an alteration in

* Human Understanding.   Edit. 7, vol. i. p. 197·

his body at such a moment, or his liking it better than the forbearance of it. And God has so made and established the human nature, the soul being united to a body in proper state, that the soul preferring or choosing such an immediate exertion or alteration of the body, such an alteration instantaneously follows. There is nothing else in the actions of my mind, that I am conscious of while I walk, but only my preferring or choosing, through successive moments, that there should be such alterations of my external sensations and motions, together with a concurring habitual expectation that it will be so; having ever found by experience, that on such an immediate preference, such sensations and motions do actually, instantaneously, and constantly arise. But it is not so in the case of flying; though a man may be said remotely to choose or prefer flying, yet he does not choose or prefer, incline to, or desire, under circumstances in view, any immediate exertion of the members of his body in order to it, because he has no expectation that he should obtain the desired end by any such exertion; and he does not prefer or incline to any bodily exertion or effort under this apprehended circumstance, of its being wholly in vain. So that if we carefully distinguish the proper objects of the several acts of the will, it will not appear, by this and such like instances, that there is any difference between *volition* and *preference*; or that a man's choosing, liking best, or being best pleased with a thing, are not the same with his willing that thing; as they seem to be according to those general and more natural motions of men, according to which language is formed. Thus, an act of the will is commonly expressed by *its pleasing a man* to do thus or thus; and a man doing as he *wills*, and doing as he *pleases*, are the same thing in common speech.

Mr Locke* says, " The will is perfectly distinguished from desire, which in the very same action may have a quite contrary tendency from that which our wills set us upon. A man (says he,) whom I cannot deny, may

* Human Understanding, vol. i. pp. 203, 204.

oblige me to use persuasions to another, which, at the same time I am speaking, I may wish may not prevail on him. In this case, it is plain the will and desire run counter." I do not suppose that *will* and *desire* are words of precisely the same signification: *will* seems to be a word of a more general signification, extending to things present and absent. *Desire* respects something absent. I may prefer my present situation and posture, suppose sitting still, or having my eyes open, and so may will it. But yet I cannot think they are so entirely distinct, that they can ever be properly said to run counter. A man never, in any instance, wills any thing contrary to his desires, or desires any thing contrary to his will. The forementioned instance, which Mr Locke produces, does not prove that he ever does. He may, on some consideration or other, will to utter speeches which have a tendency to persuade another, and still may desire that they may not persuade him; but yet his will and desire do not run counter at all; the thing which he wills, the very same he desires; and he does not will a thing, and desire the contrary, in any particular. In this instance, it is not carefully observed what is the thing willed, and what is the thing desired : if it were, it would be found that will and desire do not clash in the least. The thing willed on some consideration, is to utter such words; and certainly, the same consideration so influences him, that he does not desire the contrary; all things considered, he chooses to utter such words, and does not desire not to utter them. And so as to the thing which Mr Locke speaks of as desired, viz. that the words, though they tend to persuade, should not be effectual to that end ; his will is not contrary to this; he does not will that they should be effectual, but rather wills that they should not, as he desires. In order to prove that the will and desire may run counter, it should be shown that they may be contrary one to the other in the same thing, or with respect to the very same object of will or desire: but here the objects are two; and in each, taken by themselves, the will and desire agree.

And it is no wonder that they should not agree in different things, however little distinguished they are in their nature. The will may not agree with the will, nor desire agree with desire, in different things. As in this very instance which Mr Locke mentions, a person may, on some consideration, desire to use persuasions, and at the same time may desire they may not prevail; but yet nobody will say, that *desire* runs counter to *desire*, or that this proves that *desire* is perfectly a distinct thing from *desire*. The like might be observed of the other instance Mr Locke produces, of a man's desiring to be eased of pain, &c.

But not to dwell any longer on this, whether *desire* and *will*, and whether *preference* and *volition*, be precisely the same things or no; yet, I trust it will be allowed by all, that in every act of will there is an act of choice; that in every volition there is a preference, or a prevailing inclination of the soul, whereby the soul, at that instant, is out of a state of perfect indifference, with respect to the direct object of the volition. So that in every act, or going forth of the will, there is some preponderation of the mind or inclination one way rather than another; and the soul had rather *have* or *do* one thing than another, or than not to have or do that thing; and that there, where there is absolutely no preferring or choosing, but a perfect continuing equilibrium, there is no volition.

SECTION II.

CONCERNING THE DETERMINATION OF THE WILL.

By *determining the will*, if the phrase be used with any meaning, must be intended, *causing that the act of the will or choice should be thus, and not otherwise:* and the will is said to be determined, when, in consequence of some action or influence, its choice is directed to, and fixed upon, a particular object. As, when we speak of the determination of motion, we mean causing the motion of the body to be such a way, or in such a direction, rather than another.

To talk of the determination of the will, supposes an effect which must have a cause. If the will be determined, there is a determiner. This must be supposed to be intended even by them that say the will determines itself. If it be so, the will is both determiner and determined; it is a cause that acts and produces effects upon itself, and is the object of its own influence and action.

With respect to that grand inquiry, *What determines the will?* it would be very tedious and unnecessary at present to enumerate and examine all the various opinions which have been advanced concerning this matter; nor is it needful that I should enter into a particular disquisition of all points debated in disputes on that question, *Whether the will always follows the last dictate of the understanding.* It is sufficient to my present purpose to say, *It is that motive which, as it stands in the view of the mind, is the strongest, that determines the will:* but it may be necessary that I should a little explain my meaning in this.

By *motive,* I mean the whole of that which moves, excites, or invites the mind to volition, whether that be one thing singly, or many things conjunctly. Many particular things may concur and unite their strength to induce the mind; and when it is so, all together are, as it were, one complex motive. And when I speak of the *strongest motive,* I have respect to the strength of the whole that operates to induce to a particular act of volition, whether that be the strength of one thing alone, or of many together.

Whatever is a motive, in this sense, must be something that is *extant in the view or apprehension of the understanding,* or perceiving faculty. Nothing can induce or invite the mind to will or act any thing, any further than it is perceived, or in some way or other in the mind's view; for what is wholly unperceived, and perfectly out of the mind's view, cannot affect the mind at all. It is most evident, that nothing is in the mind, or reaches it, or takes any hold of it, any otherwise than as it is perceived or thought of.

And I think it must also be allowed by all, that every thing that is properly called a motive, excitement, or inducement, to a perceiving willing agent, has some sort and degree of *tendency* or *advantage* to move or excite the will, previous to the effect, or to the act of the will excited. This previous tendency of the motive is what I call *the strength of the motive.* That motive which has a less degree of previous advantage or tendency to move the will, or that appears less inviting, as it stands in the view of the mind, is what I call a *weaker motive.* On the contrary, that which appears most inviting, and has, by what appears concerning it to the understanding or apprehension, the greatest degree of previous tendency to excite and induce the choice, is what I call the *strongest motive.* And in this sense, I suppose the will is always determined by the strongest motive.

Things that exist in the view of the mind, have their strength, tendency, or advantage, to move or excite its will, from many things appertaining to the nature and circumstances of the *thing viewed,* the nature and circumstances of the *mind that views,* and the degree and manner of its *view;* which it would perhaps be hard to make a perfect enumeration of. But so much I think may be determined in general, without room for controversy, that whatever is perceived or apprehended by an intelligent and voluntary agent, which has the nature and influence of a motive to volition or choice, is considered or viewed *as good;* nor has it any tendency to invite or engage the election of the soul in any further degree than it appears such. For to say otherwise, would be to say, that things that appear have a tendency by the appearance they make to engage the mind to elect them some other way than by their appearing eligible to it, which is absurd; and therefore it must be true, in some sense, that *the will always is as the greatest apparent good is.* But only, for the right understanding of this, two things must be well and distinctly observed.

1. It must be observed in what sense I use the term *good:* namely, as of the same import with *agreeable.* To appear *good* to the mind, as I use the phrase, is the same as to *appear agreeable* or *seem pleasing* to the mind. Certainly nothing appears inviting and eligible to the mind, or tending to engage its inclination and choice, considered as *evil* or *disagreeable;* nor indeed as *indifferent,* and neither agreeable nor disagreeable. But if it tends to draw the inclination and move the will, it must be under the notion of that which *suits* the mind. And therefore that must have the greatest tendency to attract and engage it, which, as it stands in the mind's view, suits it best and pleases it most; and in that sense is the greatest apparent good: to say otherwise, is little, if any thing, short of a direct and plain contradiction.

The word *good,* in this sense, includes in its signification the removal or avoiding of evil, or of that which is disagreeable and uneasy. It is agreeable and pleasing to avoid what is disagreeable and displeasing, and to have uneasiness removed. So that here is included what Mr Locke supposes determines the will. For when he speaks of uneasiness as determining the will, he must be understood as supposing that the end or aim which governs in the volition or act of preference, is the avoiding or removal of that uneasiness; and that is the same thing as choosing and seeking what is more easy and agreeable.

2. When I say the will is as the greatest apparent good is, or (as I have explained it) that volition has always for its object the thing which appears most agreeable, it must be carefully observed, to avoid confusion and needless objection, that I speak of the *direct* and *immediate* object of the act of volition and not some object that the act of will has not an immediate, but only an indirect and remote, respect to. Many acts of volition have some remote relation to an object that is different from the thing most immediately willed and chosen. Thus, when

a drunkard has his liquor before him, and he has to choose whether to drink it or no, the proper and immediate objects about which his present volition is conversant, and between which his choice now decides, are his own acts in drinking the liquor or letting it alone; and this will certainly be done according to what, in the present view of his mind, taken in the whole of it, is most agreeable to him. If he chooses or wills to drink it, and not to let it alone, then this action, as it stands in the view of his mind, with all that belongs to its appearance there, is more agreeable and pleasing than letting it alone.

But the objects to which this act of volition may relate more remotely, and between which his choice may determine more indirectly, are the present pleasure the man expects by drinking, and the future misery which he judges will be the consequence of it: he may judge that this future misery, when it comes, will be more disagreeable and unpleasant than refraining from drinking now would be. But these two things are not the proper objects that the act of volition spoken of is nextly conversant about. For the act of will spoken of, is concerning present drinking or forbearing to drink. If he wills to drink, then drinking is the proper object of the act of his will; and drinking, on some account or other, now appears most agreeable to him, and suits him best. If he chooses to refrain, then refraining is the immediate object of his will, and is most pleasing to him. If in the choice he makes in the case, he prefers a present pleasure to a future advantage, which he judges will be greater when it comes, then a lesser present pleasure appears more agreeable to him than a greater advantage at a distance. If, on the contrary, a future advantage is preferred, then that appears most agreeable, and suits him best. And so still the present volition is as the greatest apparent good at present is.

I have rather chosen to express myself thus, *that the will always is as the greatest apparent good,* or *as what appears most agreeable is,* than to say that the will *is determined by the* greatest apparent good, or by what seems most agreeable; because an appearing most agreeable or pleasing to the mind, and the mind's preferring and choosing, seem hardly to be properly and perfectly distinct. If strict propriety of speech be insisted on, it may more properly be said, that the *voluntary action,* which is the immediate consequence and fruit of the mind's volition or choice, is *determined* by that which appears most agreeable, than the preference or choice itself; but that the act of volition itself is always determined by that, in or about the mind's view of the object, which *causes it to appear* most agreeable. I say *in or about the mind's view* of the object, because what has influence to render an object in view agreeable, is not only what appears *in* the object viewed, but also *the manner* of the view, and *the state and circumstances* of the mind that views. Particularly to enumerate all things pertaining to the mind's view of the objects of volition, which have influence in their appearing agreeable to the mind, would be a matter of no small difficulty, and might require a treatise by itself, and is not necessary to my present purpose. I shall therefore only mention some things in general.

I. One thing that makes an object proposed to choice agreeable, is the *apparent nature* and *circumstances of the object.* And there are various things of this sort, that have a hand in rendering the object more or less agreeable; as,

1. That which appears in the object, which renders it *beautiful* and pleasant, or *deformed* and irksome to the mind, viewing it as it is *in itself.*

2. The apparent degree of pleasure or trouble *attending* the object, or the *consequence* of it. Such concomitants and consequents being viewed as circumstances of the objects, are to be considered as belonging to it, and as it were parts of it; as it stands in the mind's view, as a proposed object of choice.

3. The *apparent state* of the pleasure or trouble that appears, with respect to *distance of time;* being either

nearer or farther off.   It is a thing in itself agreeable to
the mind, to have pleasure speedily, and disagreeable to
have it delayed; so that if there be two equal degrees of
pleasure set in the mind's view, and all other things are
equal, but only one is beheld as near, and the other far
off; the nearer will appear most agreeable, and so will
be chosen.   Because, though the agreeableness of the objects be exactly equal, as viewed in themselves, yet not
as viewed in their circumstances: one of them having the
additional agreeableness of the circumstance of nearness.

II. Another thing that contributes to the agreeableness of an object of choice, as it stands in the mind's
view, is the *manner of the view*.   If the object be something which appears connected with future pleasure, not
only will the degree of apparent pleasure have influence,
but also the manner of the view, especially in two respects.

1. With respect to the degree of *judgment*, or firmness
of *assent*, with which the mind judges the pleasure to be
future.   Because it is more agreeable to have a *certain*
happiness than an *uncertain* one ; and a pleasure viewed
as more probable, all other things being equal, is more
agreeable to the mind than that which is viewed as less
probable.

2. With respect to the degree of the *idea* of the future
pleasure.   With regard to things which are the subject
of our thoughts, either past, present, or future, we have
much more of an idea or apprehension of some things
than others; that is, our idea is much more clear, lively,
and strong.   Thus, the ideas we have of sensible things
by immediate sensation, are usually much more lively
than those we have by mere imagination, or by contemplation of them when absent.   My idea of the sun when
I look upon it, is more vivid than when I only think of
it.   Our idea of the sweet relish of a delicious fruit is
usually stronger when we taste it, than when we only
imagine it.   And sometimes the idea we have of things
by contemplation is much stronger and clearer than at
other times.   Thus, a man at one time has a much

stronger idea of the pleasure which is to be enjoyed in
eating some sort of food that he loves than at another.
Now, the degree or strength of the idea or sense that
men have of future good or evil, is one thing that has
great influence on their minds to excite choice or volition. When of two kinds of future pleasure, which the
mind considers of, and are presented for choice, both are
supposed exactly equal by the judgment, and both
equally certain, and all other things are equal, but only
one of them is what the mind has a far more lively sense
of than of the other ; this has the greatest advantage by
far to affect and attract the mind, and move the will.
It is now more agreeable to the mind to take the pleasure it has a strong and lively sense of, than that which
it has only a faint idea of : the view of the former is attended with the strongest appetite, and the greatest uneasiness attends the want of it ; and it is agreeable to
the mind to have uneasiness removed, and its appetite
gratified.   And if several future enjoyments are presented together, as competitors for the choice of the mind,
some of them judged to be greater, and others less, the
mind also having a greater sense and more lively idea of
the good of some of them, and of others a less ; and some
are viewed as of greater certainty or probability than
others, and those enjoyments that appear most agreeable in one of these respects, appear least so in others ;
in this case, all other things being equal, the agreeableness of a proposed object of choice will be in a degree
some way compounded of the degree of good supposed
by the judgment, the degree of apparent probability or
certainty of that good, and the degree of the view or
sense, or liveliness of the idea the mind has of that good ;
because all together concur to constitute the degree in
which the object appears at present agreeable ; and accordingly, volition will be determined.

I might further observe, the state of the mind that
views a proposed object of choice, is another thing that
contributes to the agreeableness or disagreeableness of
that object : the particular temper which the mind has

by nature, or that has been introduced and established
by education, example, custom, or some other means, or
the frame or state that the mind is in on a particular
occasion. That object which appears agreeable to one,
does not so to another ; and the same object does not always appear alike agreeable to the same person at different times. It is most agreeable to some men to follow
their reason, and to others to follow their appetites : to
some men it is more agreeable to deny a vicious inclination than to gratify it, others it suits best to gratify the
vilest appetites. It is more disagreeable to some men
than others to counteract a former resolution. In these
respects, and many others which might be mentioned,
different things will be most agreeable to different persons ; and not only so, but to the same persons at different times.

But possibly it is needless and improper to mention
the frame and state of the mind, as a distinct ground of
the agreeableness of objects from the other two mentioned before; viz. the apparent nature and circumstances
of the objects viewed, and the manner of the view : perhaps, if we strictly consider the matter, the different
temper and state of the mind makes no alteration as to
the agreeableness of objects any other way, than as it
makes the objects themselves appear differently beautiful or deformed, having apparent pleasure or pain attending them; and, as it occasions the manner of the
view to be different, causes the idea of beauty or deformity, pleasure or uneasiness, to be more or less lively.

However, I think so much is certain, that volition, in
no one instance that can be mentioned, is otherwise than
the greatest apparent good is, in the manner which has
been explained. The choice of the mind never departs
from that which, at that time, and with respect to the
direct and immediate objects of that decision of the mind,
appears most agreeable and pleasing, all things considered.   If the immediate objects of the will are a man's
own actions, then those actions which appear most
agreeable to him he wills. If it be now most agreeable

to him, all things considered, to walk, then he now wills
to walk. If it be now, upon the whole of what at
present appears to him, most agreeable to speak, then
he chooses to speak ; if it suits him best to keep silence,
then he chooses to keep silence. There is scarcely a
plainer and more universal dictate of the sense and experience of mankind, than that, when men act voluntarily, and do what they please, then they do what suits
them best, or what is most *agreeable to them.* To say
that they do what they please, or what pleases them,
but yet do not *do* what is *agreeable* to them, is the
same thing as to say they do what they please, but do
not act their pleasure ; and that is to say, that they do
what they please, and yet do not do what they please.

It appears from these things, that in some sense *the
will always follows the last dictate of the understanding;*
but then the *understanding* must be taken in a large
sense, as including the whole faculty of perception or
apprehension, and not merely what is called *reason* or
judgment. If by the dictate of the understanding is
meant what reason declares to be best, or most for the
person's happiness, taking in the whole of its duration,
it is not true that the will always follows the last dictate of the understanding. Such a dictate of reason is
quite a different matter, from things appearing now
most *agreeable ;* all things being put together which per-
tain to the mind's present perceptions, apprehensions,
or ideas, in any respect; although that dictate of reason, when it takes place, is one thing that is put into
the scales, and is to be considered as a thing that has
concern in the compound influence which moves and
induces the will ; and is one thing that is to be considered in estimating the degree of that appearance of good
which the will always follows ; either as having its influence added to other things, or subducted from them.
When it concurs with other things, then its weight is
added to them, as put into the same scale ; but when it
is against them, it is as a weight in the opposite scale,
where it resists the influence of other things : yet its re-

sistance is often overcome by their greater weight, and so the act of the will is determined in opposition to it.

The things which I have said, may, I hope, serve in some measure to illustrate and confirm the position I laid down in the beginning of this section, viz. that *the will is always determined by the strongest motive*, or by that view of the mind which has the greatest degree of *previous* tendency to excite volition.   But whether I have been so happy as rightly to explain the thing wherein consists the strength of motives, or not, my failing in this will not overthrow the position itself, which carries much of its own evidence with it, and is the thing of chief importance to the purpose of the ensuing discourse ; and the truth of it I hope will appear with great clearness before I have finished what I have to say on the subject of human liberty.

SECTION III.

CONCERNING THE MEANING OF THE TERMS, NECESSITY, IMPOSSIBILITY, INABILITY, &C., AND OF CONTINGENCE.

The words *necessary, impossible,* &c. are abundantly used in controversies about free-will and moral agency; and therefore the sense in which they are used should be clearly understood.

Here I might say, that a thing is then said to be *necessary,* when it must be, and cannot be otherwise. But this would not properly be a definition of necessity, or an explanation of the word, any more than if I explained the word *must,* by there being a necessity.   The words *must, can,* and *cannot,* need explication as much as the words *necessary* and *impossible;* excepting that the former are words that children commonly use, and know something of the meaning of, earlier than the latter.

The word *necessary,* as used in common speech, is a relative term, and relates to some supposed opposition made to the existence of the thing spoken of, which is overcome, or proves in vain to hinder or alter it.   That is necessary, in the original and proper sense of the

word, which is, or will be, notwithstandin all supposable opposition. To say that a thing is necessary, is
the same thing as to say that it is impossible it should
not be: but the word *impossible* is manifestly a relative
term, and has reference to supposed power, exerted to
bring a thing to pass, which is insufficient for the
effect ; as the word *unable* is relative, and has relation
to ability or endeavour, which is insufficient; and as
the word *irresistible* is relative, and has always reference
to resistance which is made, or may be made, to some
force or power tending to an effect, and is insufficient to
withstand the power, or hinder the effect. The common
notion of necessity and impossibility implies something
that frustrates endeavour or desire.

Here several things are to be noted:—

1. Things are said to be necessary in *general*, which
are or will be, notwithstanding any supposable opposition *from us or others*, or from whatever quarter. But
things are said to be necessary *to us* which are or will be
notwithstanding all opposition supposable in the case
from us. The same may be observed of the word *impossible*, and other such like terms.

2. These terms, *necessary, impossible, irresistible*, &c.
do especially belong to controversy about liberty and
moral agency, as used in the latter of the two senses
now mentioned; viz. as necessary or impossible *to us*,
and with relation to any supposable opposition or endeavour *of ours.*

3. As the word *necessity*, in its vulgar and common
use, is relative, and has always reference to some supposable insufficient opposition ; so, when we speak of
any thing as necessary *to us*, it is with relation to some
supposable opposition of *our wills*, or some voluntary
exertion or effort of ours to the contrary. For we do
not properly make opposition to an event, any otherwise
than as we *voluntarily* oppose it. Things are said to be
what must be, or *necessarily* are, *as to us*, when they
are, or will be, though we desire or endeavour the contrary, or try to prevent or remove their existence ; but

such opposition of ours always either consists in, or implies, opposition of our wills.

It is manifest, that all such like words and phrases, as vulgarly used, are used and accepted in this manner. A thing is said to be *necessary*, when we cannot help it, let us do what we will. So any thing is said to be *impossible* to us, when we would do it, or would have it brought to pass, and endeavour it; or at least may be supposed to desire and seek it; but all our desires and endeavours are, or would be, vain. And that is said to be *irresistible*, which overcomes all our opposition, resistance, and endeavour to the contrary. And we are said to be *unable* to do a thing, when our supposable desires and endeavours to do it are insufficient.

We are accustomed, in the common use of language, to apply and understand these phrases in this sense : we grow up with such a habit, which by the daily use of these terms, in such a sense, from our childhood, becomes fixed and settled; so that the idea of 'a relation to a supposed will, desire, and endeavour of ours, is strongly connected with these terms, and naturally excited in our minds, whenever we hear the words used. Such ideas, and these words, are so united and associated, that they unavoidably go together—one suggests the other, and carries the other with it, and never can be separated as long as we live. And if we use the words as terms of art, in another sense, yet unless we are exceeding circumspect and wary, we shall insensibly slide into the vulgar use of them, and so apply the words in a very inconsistent manner. This habitual connexion of ideas will deceive and confound us in our reasonings and discourses, wherein we pretend to use these terms in that manner, as terms of art.

4. It follows from what has been observed, that when these terms, *necessary, impossible, irresistible, unable,* &c. are used in cases wherein no opposition, or insufficient will, or endeavour, is supposed, or can be supposed, but the very nature of the supposed case itself excludes and denies any such opposition, will, or endeavour,—

c

these terms are then not used in their proper signification, but quite beside their use in common speech. The
reason is manifest; namely, that in such cases we cannot use the words with reference to a supposable opposition, will, or endeavour. And therefore, if any man
uses these terms in such cases, he either uses them nonsensically, or in some new sense diverse from their
original and proper meaning. As, for instance, if a man
should affirm after this manner—That it is necessary
for a man, and what must be, that a man should choose
virtue rather than vice, during the time that he prefers
virtue to vice; and that it is a thing impossible and irresistible, that it should be otherwise than that he should
have this choice, so long as this choice continues,—such
a man would use the terms, *must, irresistible*, &c. with
perfect insignificance and nonsense, or in some new
sense, diverse from their common use ; which is with reference, as has been observed, to supposable opposition,
unwillingness, and resistance; whereas, here, the very
supposition excludes and denies any such thing|: for the
case supposed is that of being willing, and choosing.

5. It appears from what has been said, that these
terms, *necessary, impossible*, &c., are often used by philosophers and metaphysicians in a sense quite diverse
from their common use and original signification : for
they apply them to many cases in which no opposition
is supposed or supposable. Thus, they use them with
respect to God's existence before the creation of the
world, when there was no other being but He : so with
regard to many of the dispositions and acts of the Divine
Being, such as his loving himself, his loving righteousness, hating sin, &c. So they apply these terms to
many cases of the inclinations and actions of created
intelligent beings, angels, and men ; wherein all opposition of the will is shut out and denied, in the very supposition of the case.

Metaphysical or *philosophical* necessity is nothing different from their certainty. I speak not now of the certainty of knowledge, but the certainty that is in things

themselves, which is the foundation of the certainty of
the knowledge of them; or that wherein lies the ground
of the infallibility of the proposition which affirms them.

What is sometimes given as the definition of philosophical necessity—namely, *That by which a thing cannot
but be*, or, *whereby it cannot be otherwise*, fails of being
a proper explanation of it, on two accounts ; first, the
words *can* or *cannot*, need explanation as much as the
word *necessity;* and the former may as well be explained
by the latter, as the latter by the former. Thus, if any one
asked us what we mean, when we say, a thing *cannot but
be*, we might explain ourselves by saying, we mean, It
must necessarily be so ; as well as explain necessity, by
saying, It is that by which a thing cannot but be.   And
secondly, this definition is liable to the forementioned
great inconvenience : the words *cannot* or *unable*, are
properly relative, and have relation to power exerted, in
order to the thing spoken of; to which, as I have now
observed, the word *necessity*, as used by philosophers,
has no reference.

Philosophical necessity is really nothing else than the
full and fixed connexion between the things signified by
the subject and predicate of a proposition, which affirms
something to be true.   When there is such a connexion,
then the thing affirmed in the proposition is necessary,
in a philosophical sense, whether any opposition or contrary effort be supposed, or supposable in the case, or
no.   When the subject and predicate of the proposition,
which affirms the existence of any thing, either substance, quality, act, or circumstance, have a full and
certain connexion, then the existence or being of that
thing is said to be necessary, in a metaphysical sense.
And in this sense I use the word *necessity* in the following discourse, when I endeavour to prove *that necessity
is not inconsistent with liberty.*

The subject and predicate of a proposition which
affirms existence of something, may have a full, fixed,
and certain connexion several ways.

1. They may have a full and perfect connexion *in*

and of themselves, because it may imply a contradiction or gross absurdity to suppose them not connected.
Thus, many things are necessary in their own nature.
So, the external existence of being, generally considered,
is necessary *in itself;* because it would be, in itself, the
greatest absurdity to deny the existence of being in general, or to say there was absolute and universal nothing;
and is as it were, the sum of all contradictions, as might
be shown, if this were a proper place for it. So, God's
infinity and other attributes are necessary. So, it is necessary, *in its own nature,* that two and two should be four;
and it is necessary that all right lines, drawn from the
centre of a circle to the circumference, should be equal.
It is necessary, fit, and suitable, that men should do to
others as they would that they should do to them. So,
innumerable metaphysical and mathematical truths are
necessary *in themselves;* the subject and predicate of the
proposition which affirms them are perfectly connected
of themselves.

2. The connexion of the subject and predicate of a
proposition which affirms the existence of something,
may be fixed and made certain ; because the existence
of that thing is already come to pass, and either now is
or has been, and so has, as it were, made sure of existence.   And therefore the proposition which affirms
present and past existence of it, may by this means be
made certain, and necessarily and unalterably true; the
past event has fixed and decided the matter, as to
its existence, and has made it impossible but that existence should be truly predicated of it.   Thus, the existence of whatever is already come to pass, is now become necessary ; it is become impossible it should be
otherwise than true, that such a thing has been.

3. The subject and predicate of a proposition which
affirms something to be, may have a real and certain
connexion *consequentially;* and so the existence of the
thing may be consequentially necessary, as it may be
surely and firmly connected with something else that is
necessary in one of the former respects; as it is either

fully and thoroughly connected with that which is absolutely necessary in its own nature, or with something which has already received and made sure of
existence. This necessity lies *in*, or may be explained *by*, the connexion of two or more propositions one
with another. Things which are perfectly connected
with other things that are necessary, are necessary themselves, by a necessity of consequence.

And here it may be observed, that all things which
are future, or which will hereafter begin to be, which
can be said to be necessary, are necessary only in this
last way: their existence is not necessary in itself ; for
if so, they always would have existed. Nor is their existence become necessary by being made sure, by being
already come to pass. Therefore, the only way that
any thing that is to come to pass hereafter, is or can be
necessary, is by a connexion with something that is necessary in its own nature, or something that already is,
or has been ; so that the one being supposed, the other
certainly follows. And this, also, is the only way
that all things past, excepting those which were from
eternity, could be necessary *before they came to pass*, or
could come to pass necessarily ; and therefore the only
way in which any effect or event, or any thing whatsoever that ever has had or will have a beginning, has
come into being necessarily, or will hereafter necessarily
exist. And therefore *this* is the necessity which especially belongs to controversies about the acts of the
will.

It may be of some use in these controversies, further
to observe, concerning *metaphysical* necessity, that
(agreeable to the distinction before observed of necessity,
as *vulgarly* understood) things that exist may be said to
be necessary, either with a *general* or *particular* necessity. The existence of a thing may be said to be necessary with a *general* necessity, when, all things whatsoever being considered, there is a foundation for certainty
of their existence ; or when, in the most general and universal view of things, the subject and predicate of the

proposition, which affirms its existence, would appear with an infallible connexion.

An event, or the existence of a thing, may be said to be necessary with a *particular* necessity, or with regard to a particular person, thing, or time, when nothing that can be taken into consideration in or about that person, thing, or time, alters the case at all, as to the certainty of that event, or the existence of that thing; or can be of any account at all, in determining the infallibility of the connexion of the subject and predicate in the proposition which affirms the existence of the thing; so that it is all one, as to that person or thing, at least, at that time, as if the existence were necessary with a necessity that is most *universal* and *absolute.* Thus, there are many things that happen to particular persons, which they have no hand in, and in the existence of which no will of theirs has any concern, at least at that time ; which, whether they are necessary or not, with regard to things in general, yet are necessary to them, and with regard to any volition of theirs at that time, as they prevent all acts of the will about the affair. I shall have occasion to apply this observation to particular instances in the following discourse. Whether the same things that are necessary with a *particular* necessity, be not also necessary with a *general* necessity, may be a matter of future consideration. Let that be as it will, it alters not the case, as to the use of this distinction of the kinds of necessity.

These things may be sufficient for the explaining of the terms *necessary* and *necessity,* as terms of art, and as often used by metaphysicians and controversial writers in divinity, in a sense diverse from and more extensive than their original meaning in common language, which was before explained.

What has been said to show the meaning of the terms *necessary* and *necessity,* may be sufficient for the explaining of the opposite terms *impossible* and *impossibility;* for there is no difference, but only the latter are negative, and the former positive. *Impossibility* is the same as

necessity, or a necessity that a thing should not ... it is used as a term of art, in a like diversity ... the original and vulgar meaning with necessity.

... he same may be observed concerning the words *un-* ... and *inability*. It has been observed, that these ... ms, in their original and common use, have relation ... will and endeavour, as supposable in the case, and as ... insufficient for the bringing to pass the thing willed and endeavoured; but as these terms are often used by philosophers and divines, especially writers on controversies about free-will, they are used in a quite different and far more extensive sense, and are applied to many cases wherein no will or endeavour for the bringing of the thing to pass is or can be supposed, but is actually denied and excluded in the nature of the case.

As the words, *necessary, impossible, unable,* &c., are used by polemic writers in a sense diverse from their common signification, the like has happened to the term *contingent.* Any thing is said to be contingent, or to come to pass by chance or accident, in the original meaning of such words, when its connexion with its causes or antecedents, according to the established course of things, is not discerned; and so is what we have no means of the foresight of. And especially is any thing said to be contingent or accidental with regard to us, when any thing comes to pass that we are concerned in, as occasions or subjects, without our foreknowledge, and beside our design and scope.

But the word *contingent* is abundantly used in a very different sense ; not for that whose connexion with the series of things we cannot discern, so as to foresee the event, but for something which has absolutely no previous ground or reason, with which its existence has any fixed and certain connexion.

SECTION IV.

OF THE DISTINCTION OF NATURAL AND MORAL NECESSITY, AND INABILITY.

THAT necessity which has been explained, consisting in an infallible connexion of the things signified by the subject and predicate of a proposition, as intelligent beings are the subjects of it, is distinguished into *moral* and *natural* necessity.

I shall not now stand to inquire whether this distinction be a proper and perfect distinction; but shall only explain how these two sorts of necessity are understood, as the terms are sometimes used, and as they are used in the following discourse.

The phrase *moral necessity* is used variously; sometimes it is used for a necessity of moral obligation. So, we say a man is under necessity, when he is under bonds of duty and conscience, which he cannot be discharged from. So, the word *necessity* is often used for great obligation in point of interest. Sometimes, by moral necessity is meant that apparent connexion of things which is the ground of *moral evidence;* and so is distinguished from *absolute necessity,* or that sure connexion of things that is a foundation for *infallible certainty.* In this sense, moral necessity signifies much the same as that high degree of probability which is ordinarily sufficient to satisfy, and be relied upon by mankind, in their conduct and behaviour in the world, as they would consult their own safety and interest, and treat others properly as members of society. And sometimes by moral necessity is meant that necessity of connection and consequence which arises from such *moral causes,* as the strength of inclination, or motives, and the connection which there is in many cases between these, and such certain volitions and actions. And it is in this sense that I use the phrase *moral necessity* in the following discourse.

By *natural necessity,* as applied to men, I mean such necessity as men are under through the force of natural causes; as distinguished from what are called moral causes, such as habits and dispositions of the heart, and moral motives and inducements. Thus, men placed in certain circumstances are the subjects of particular sensations by necessity; they feel pain when their bodies are wounded; they see the objects presented before them in a clear light when their eyes are opened: so, they assent to the truth of certain propositions as soon as the terms are understood; as that two and two make four, that black is not white, that two parallel lines can never cross one another; so, by a natural necessity, men's bodies move downwards when there is nothing to support them.

But here several things may be noted concerning these two kinds of necessity.

1. Moral necessity may be as absolute as natural necessity: that is, the effect may be as perfectly connected with its moral cause as a natural necessary effect is with its natural cause. Whether the will in every case is necessarily determined by the strongest motive, or whether the will ever makes any resistance to such a motive, or can ever oppose the strongest present inclination, or not; if that matter should be controverted, yet I suppose none will deny, but that, in some cases, a previous bias and inclination, or the motive presented, may be so powerful, that the act of the will may be certainly and indissolubly connected therewith. When motives or previous bias are very strong, all will allow that there is some *difficulty* in going against them. And if they were yet stronger, the difficulty would be still greater. And therefore, if more were still added to their strength, to a certain degree, it would make the difficulty so great, that it would be wholly *impossible* to surmount it; for this plain reason, because whatever power men may be supposed to have to surmount difficulties, yet that power is not infinite; and so goes not beyond certain limits. If a man can surmount ten degrees of difficulty of this kind with twenty degrees of strength, because the degrees of strength are beyond the degrees of difficulty ; yet, if the difficulty be increased to thirty, or a hundred, or a thousand degrees, and his strength not also increased, his strength will be wholly insufficient to surmount the difficulty. As, therefore, it must be allowed, that there may be such a thing as a *sure* and *perfect* connexion between moral causes and effects ; so this only is what I call by the name of *moral necessity.*

2. When I use this distinction of *moral* and *natural* *necessity*, I would not be understood to suppose, that if any thing comes to pass by the former kind of necessity, the *nature* of things is not concerned in it, as well as in the latter. I do not mean to determine, that when a *moral* habit or motive is so strong, that the act of the will infallibly follows, this is not owing to the *nature of* *things*. But these are the names that these two kinds of necessity have usually been called by; and they must be distinguished by some names or other; for there is a distinction or difference between them, that is very important in its consequences, which difference does not lie so much in the nature of the *connexion* as in the two terms *connected*. The cause with which the effect is connected is of a particular kind ; viz. that which is of a moral nature; either some previous habitual disposition, or some motive exhibited to the understanding. And the effect is also of a particular kind; being likewise of a moral nature, consisting in some inclination or volition of the soul or voluntary action.

I suppose, that necessity which is called *natural*, in distinction from *moral* necessity, is so called, because *mere nature*, as the word is vulgarly used, is concerned, without any thing of *choice*. The word *nature* is often used in opposition to *choice;* not because nature has indeed never any hand in our choice; but this probably comes to pass by means that we first get our notion of nature from that discernible and obvious course of events, which we observe in many things that our choice has no concern in; and especially in the material world, which, in very many parts of it, we easily perceive to be in a settled course; the stated order and manner of succession being very apparent. But where we do not readily discern the rule and connexion, (though there be a connexion, according to an established law, truly taking place,) we signify the manner of event by some other name. Even in many things which are seen in the material and inanimate world, which do not discernibly and obviously come to pass according to any settled course, men do not call the manner of the event by the name of *nature*, but by such names as *accident, chance, contingent,* &c. So, men make a distinction between nature and choice, as though they were completely and universally distinct. Whereas, I suppose none will deny but that choice, *in many cases,* arises from nature, as truly as other events. But the dependence and connexion between acts of volition or choice, and their causes, according to established laws, is not so sensible and obvious. And we observe, that choice is as it were a new principle of motion and action, different from that established law and order of things which is most obvious, that is seen especially in corporeal and sensible things; and also the choice often interposes, interrupts, and alters the chain of events in these external objects, and causes them to proceed otherwise than they would do, if let alone, and left to go on according to the laws of motion among themselves. Hence, it is spoken of as if it were a principle of motion entirely distinct from nature, and properly set in opposition to it;—names being commonly given to things, according to what is most obvious, and is suggested by what appears to the senses without reflection and research.

3. It must be observed, that in what has been explained, as signified by the name of *moral necessity*, the word *necessity* is not used according to the original design and meaning of the word : for, as was observed before, such terms—*necessary, impossible, irresistible,* &c. in common speech, and their most proper sense, are always relative; having reference to some supposable voluntary opposition or endeavour that is insufficient. But no such opposition, or contrary will and endeavour, is supposable in the case of moral necessity; which is a certainty of the inclination and will itself, which does not admit of the supposition of a will to oppose and resist it. For it is absurd to suppose the same individual will to oppose itself in its present act, or the present choice to be opposite to and resisting present choice ; as absurd as it is to talk of two contrary

motions in the same moving body at the same time. And therefore the very case supposed never admits of any trial, whether an opposing or resisting will can overcome this necessity.

What has been said of natural and moral necessity, may serve to explain what is intended by natural and moral *inability*. We are said to be *naturally* unable to do a thing, when we cannot do it if we will, because what is most commonly called *nature* does not allow of it, or because of some impeding defect or obstacle that is extrinsic to the will; either in the faculty of understanding, constitution of body, or external objects. *Moral* inability consists not in any of these things; but either in the want of inclination, or the strength of a contrary inclination, or the want of sufficient motives in view to induce and excite the act of the will, or the strength of apparent motives to the contrary. Or both these may be resolved into one; and it may be said in one word, that moral inability consists in the opposition or want of inclination. For when a person is unable to will or choose such a thing, through a defect of motives, or prevalence of contrary motives, it is the same thing as his being unable, through the want of an inclination, or the prevalence of a contrary inclination, in such circumstances, and under the influence of such views.

To give some instances of this *moral inability*.—A woman of great honour and chastity may have a moral inability to prostitute herself to her slave. A child of great love and duty to his parents may be unable to be willing to kill his father. A very lascivious man, in case of certain opportunities and temptations, and in the absence of such and such restraints, may be unable to forbear gratifying his lust. A drunkard, under such and such circumstances, may be unable to forbear taking of strong drink. A very malicious man may be unable to exert benevolent acts to an enemy, or to desire his prosperity: yea, some may be so under the power of a vile disposition, that they may be unable to love those who are most worthy of their esteem and affection.

A strong habit of virtue, and great degree of holiness, may cause a moral inability to love wickedness in general,—may render a man unable to take complacence in wicked persons or things, or to choose a wicked life, and prefer it to a virtuous life. And, on the other hand, a great degree of habitual wickedness may lay a man under an inability to love and choose holiness, and render him utterly unable to love any infinitely holy Being, or to choose and cleave to him as his chief good.

Here it may be of use to observe this distinction of moral inability, viz. of that which is *general and habitual*, and that which is *particular and occasional.* By a *general and habitual* moral inability, I mean an inability in the heart to all exercises or acts of will of that nature or kind, through a fixed and habitual inclination, or an habitual and stated defect, or want of a certain kind of inclination. Thus, a very ill-natured man may be unable to exert such acts of benevolence, as another, who is full of good nature, commonly exerts ; and a man, whose heart is habitually void of gratitude, may be unable to exert such and such grateful acts, through that stated defect of a grateful inclination. By *particular and occasional* moral inability, I mean an inability of the will or heart to a particular act, through the strength or defect of present motives, or of inducements presented to the view of the understanding *on this occasion.* If it be so, that the will is always determined by the strongest motive, then it must always have an inability, in this latter sense, to act otherwise than it does ; it not being possible, in any case, that the will should at present go against the motive which has now, all things considered, the greatest strength and advantage to excite and induce it. The former of these kinds of moral inability, consisting in that which is stated, habitual, and general, is most commonly called by the name of inability ; because the word *inability*, in its most proper and original signification, has respect to some stated defect. And this especially obtains the name of *inability* also upon another account. I before observed, that the

word inability, in its original and most common use, is
a relative term, and has respect to will and endeavour,
as supposable in the case, and as insufficient to bring to
pass the thing desired and endeavoured. Now, there
may be more of an appearance and shadow of this, with
respect to the acts which arise from a fixed and strong
habit, than others that arise only from transient occasions and causes. Indeed, will and endeavour against,
or diverse from, *present* acts of the will, are in no case
supposable, whether those acts be occasional or habitual, for that would be to suppose the will at present
to be otherwise than at present it is. But yet there
may be will and endeavour against *future* acts of the
will, or volitions that are likely to take place, as viewed at a distance. It is no contradiction to suppose that
the acts of the will at one time may be against the acts
of the will at another time; and there may be desires
and endeavours to prevent or excite future acts of the
will; but such desires and endeavours are, in many
cases, rendered insufficient and vain, through fixedness
of habit : when the occasion returns, the strength of
habit overcomes and baffles all such opposition. In
this respect, a man may be in miserable slavery and
bondage to a strong habit. But it may be comparative-
ly easy to make an alteration with respect to such
future acts, as are only occasional and transient ; because the occasion or transient cause, if foreseen, may
often easily be prevented or avoided. On this account,
the moral inability that attends fixed habits, especially
obtains the name of *inability*. And then, as the will
may remotely and indirectly resist itself and do it in
vain, in the case of strong habits, so reason may resist
present acts of the will, and its resistance be insufficient ;
and this is more commonly the case also when the
acts arise from strong habit.

But it must be observed, concerning moral inability,
in each kind of it, that the word *inability* is used in a
sense very diverse from its original import. The word
signifies only a natural inability, in the proper use of it;

and is applied to such cases only wherein a present will or inclination to the thing, with respect to which a person is said to be unable, is supposable. It cannot be truly said, according to the ordinary use of language, that a malicious man, let him be ever so malicious, cannot hold his hand from striking, or that he is not able to show his neighbour kindness ; or that a drunkard, let his appetite be ever so strong, cannot keep the cup from his mouth. In the strictest propriety of speech, a man has a thing in his power, if he has it in his choice, or at his election ; and a man cannot be truly said to be unable to do a thing when he can do it if he will. It is improperly said, that a person cannot perform those external actions which are dependent on the act of the will, and which would be easily performed if the act of the will were present. And if it be improperly said, that he cannot perform those external voluntary actions which depend on the will, it is in some respect more improperly said, that he is unable to exert the acts of the will themselves ; because it is more evidently false, with respect to these, that he cannot if he will: for to say so, is a downright contradiction ; it is to say, he *cannot* will, if he *does* will ; and in this case not only is it true that it is easy for a man to do the thing if he will, but the very willing is the doing ; when once he has willed, the thing is performed, and nothing else remains to be done. Therefore, in these things to ascribe a non-performance to the want of power or ability, is not just ; because the thing wanting is not a being *able*, but a being *willing*. There are faculties of the mind, and capacity of nature, and every thing else sufficient, but a disposition: nothing is wanting but a will.

SECTION V.

CONCERNING THE NOTION OF LIBERTY, AND OF MORAL AGENCY.

THE plain and obvious meaning of the words *freedom* and *liberty*, in common speech, is *power, opportunity, or*

advantage, that any one has to do as he pleases. Or in
other words, his being free from hindrance or impediment in the way of doing, or conducting, in any respect,
as he wills.*   And the contrary to liberty, whatever
name we call that by, is a person's being hindered or unable to conduct as he will, or being necessitated to do
otherwise.

If this which I have mentioned be the meaning of the
word liberty, in the ordinary use of language, as I trust
that none that has ever learned to talk, and is unpreju-
diced, will deny; then it will follow that in propriety of
speech, neither liberty, nor its contrary, can properly
be ascribed to any being or thing, but that which has
such a faculty, power, or property, as is called will.
For that which is possessed of no such thing as *will*, cannot have any *power* or *opportunity* of doing *according
to its will*, nor be necessitated to *act contrary to its will*,
nor be restrained from acting agreeably to it.   And
therefore, to talk of liberty, or the contrary, as belonging to the *very will itself*, is not to speak good sense, if
we judge of sense and nonsense by the original and
proper signification of words.   For the *will itself* is not
an agent that *has a will;* the power of choosing itself has
not a power of choosing.   That which has the power of
volition or choice, is the man or the soul, and not the
power of volition itself.   And he that has the liberty of
doing according to his will, is the agent or doer who is
possessed of the will, and not the will which he is possessed of.   We say with propriety, that a bird let loose
has power and liberty to fly ; but not that the bird's
power of flying has a power and liberty of flying.   To
be free, is the property of an agent who is possessed of
powers and faculties, as much as to be cunning, valiant,
bountiful, or zealous.   But these qualities are the properties of men or persons, and not the properties of properties.

* I say, not only *doing,* but *conducting ;* because a voluntary forbearing
to do, sitting still, keeping silence, &c. are instances of persons' *conduct*
about which liberty is exercised; though they are not so properly called
doing.

There are two things that are contrary to this which is called liberty in common speech. One is *constraint;* the same is otherwise called *force, compulsion,* and *coaction,* which is a person's being necessitated to do a thing *contrary* to his will. The other is *restraint;* which is his being hindered, and not having power to do *according* to his will. But that which has no will, cannot be the subject of these things.—I need say the less on this head, Mr Locke having set the same thing forth with so great clearness in his " Essay on the Human Understanding."

But one thing more I would observe concerning what is vulgarly called *liberty ;* namely, that power and opportunity for one to do and conduct as he will, or according to his choice, is all that is meant by it; without taking into the meaning of the word, any thing of the cause or original of that choice, or at all considering how the person came to have such a volition, whether it was caused by some external motive or internal habitual bias ; whether it was determined by some internal antecedent volition, or whether it happened without a cause ; whether it was necessarily connected with something foregoing, or not connected. Let the person come by his volition or choice how he will, yet, if he is able, and there is nothing in the way to hinder his pursuing and executing his will, the man is fully and perfectly free, according to the primary and common notion of freedom.

What has been said may be sufficient to show what is meant by *liberty,* according to the common notions of mankind, and in the usual and primary acceptation of the word: but the word, as used by Arminians, Pelagians, and others, who oppose the Calvinists, has an entirely different signification. These several things belong to their notion of liberty :—1. That it consists in a *self-determining power* in the will, or a certain sovereignty the will has over itself, and its own acts, whereby it determines its own volitions ; so as not to be dependent in its determinations on any cause without itself, nor determined by any thing prior to its own acts. 2. *Indifference* belongs to liberty, in their notion of it,

D

or that the mind, previous to the act of volition, be *in equilibrio.*   3. *Contingence* is another thing that belongs and is essential to it; not in the common acceptation of the word, as that has been already explained, but as opposed to all *necessity,* or any fixed and certain connection with some previous ground or reason of its existence.   They suppose the essence of liberty so much to consist in these things, that unless the will of man be free in this sense, he has no real freedom, how much soever he may be at liberty to act according to his will.

A *moral agent* is a being that is capable of those actions that have a moral quality, and which can properly be denominated good or evil in a moral sense, virtuous or vicious, commendable or faulty.   To moral agency belongs a *moral faculty,* or sense of moral good and evil, or of such a thing as desert or worthiness, of praise or blame, reward or punishment; and a capacity which an agent has of being influenced in his actions by moral inducements or motives, exhibited to the view of understanding and reason, to engage to a conduct agreeable to the moral faculty.

The sun is very excellent and beneficial in its action and influence on the earth, in warming it, and causing it to bring forth its fruits; but it is not a moral agent; its action, though good, is not virtuous or meritorious. Fire that breaks out in a city, and consumes great part of it, is very mischievous in its operation, but is not a moral agent: what it does is not faulty or sinful, or deserving of any punishment.   The brute creatures are not moral agents: the actions of some of them are very profitable and pleasant; others are very hurtful: yet, seeing they have no moral faculty or sense of desert, and do not act from choice guided by understanding, or with a capacity of reasoning and reflecting, but only from instinct, and are not capable of being influenced by moral inducements, their actions are not properly sinful or virtuous; nor are they properly the subjects of any such moral treatment for what they do, as moral agents are for their faults or good deeds.

Here it may be noted, that there is a circumstantial difference between the moral agency of a *ruler* and a *subject*. I call it *circumstantial*, because it lies only in the difference of moral inducements they are capable of being influenced by, arising from the difference of *circumstances*. A *ruler* acting in that capacity only, is not capable of being influenced by a moral law, and its sanctions of threatenings and promises, rewards and punishments, as the *subject* is; though both may be influenced by a knowledge of moral good and evil. And therefore the moral agency of the Supreme Being, who acts only in the capacity of a *ruler* towards his creatures, and never as a *subject*, differs in that respect from the moral agency of created intelligent beings. God's actions, and particularly those which he exerts as a moral governor, have moral qualifications, are morally good in the highest degree. They are most perfectly holy and righteous; and we must conceive of him as influenced in the highest degree by that which, above all others, is properly a moral inducement; viz. the moral good which he sees in such and such things: and therefore he is, in the most proper sense, a moral agent, the source of all moral ability and agency, the fountain and rule of all virtue and moral good; though, by reason of his being supreme over all, it is not possible he should be under the influence of law or command, promises or threatenings, rewards or punishments, counsels or warnings. The essential qualities of a moral agent are in God in the greatest possible perfection; such as understanding, to perceive the difference between moral good and evil; a capacity of discerning that moral worthiness and demerit by which some things are praiseworthy, others deserving of blame and punishment; and also a capacity of choice, and choice guided by understanding, and a power of acting according to his choice or pleasure, and being capable of doing those things which are in the highest sense praiseworthy. And herein does very much consist that image of God wherein he made man (which we read of, Gen. i. 26, 27, and chap. ix. 6), by which God distinguished man from the beasts, viz. in those faculties and principles of nature whereby he is capable of moral agency. Herein very much consists the *natural* image of God; as his *spiritual* and *moral* image, wherein man was made at first, consisted in that moral excellency that he was endowed with.

PART II.

WHEREIN IT IS CONSIDERED, WHETHER THERE IS OR CAN BE ANY SUCH SORT OF FREEDOM OF WILL AS THAT WHEREIN ARMINIANS PLACE THE ESSENCE OF THE LIBERTY OF ALL MORAL AGENTS; AND WHETHER ANY SUCH THING EVER WAS OR CAN BE CONCEIVED OF.

SECTION I.

SHOWING THE MANIFEST INCONSISTENCE OF THE ARMINIAN NOTION OF LIBERTY OF WILL CONSISTING IN THE WILL'S SELF-DETERMINING POWER.

HAVING taken notice of those things which may be necessary to be observed concerning the meaning of the principal terms and phrases made use of in controversies concerning human liberty, and particularly observed what *liberty* is according to the common language and general apprehension of mankind, and what it is as understood and maintained by Arminians; I proceed to consider the Arminian notion of the *freedom of the will*, and the supposed necessity of it in order to moral agency, or in order to any one's being capable of virtue or vice, and properly the subject of command or counsel, praise or blame, promises or threatenings, rewards or punishments; or whether that which has been described as the thing meant by liberty in common speech be not sufficient, and the only liberty which makes, or can make, any one a moral agent ; and so properly the subject of these things.   In *this* Part I shall consider whether any such thing be possible or conceivable, as that freedom of will which Arminians insist on; and shall inquire whether any such sort of liberty be necessary to moral agency, &c. in the *next* Part.

And first of all I shall consider the notion of *a self-determining power* in the will, wherein, according to the Arminians, does most essentially consist the will's freedom ; and shall particularly inquire whether it be not plainly absurd, and a manifest inconsistence, to suppose that *the will itself determines all the free acts of the will.*

Here I shall not insist on the great impropriety of such phrases, and ways of speaking, as *the will's determining itself;* because actions are to be ascribed to agents, and not properly to the powers of agents ; which improper way of speaking leads to many mistakes, and much confusion, as Mr Locke observes.   But I shall suppose that the Arminians, when they speak of the will's determining itself, do by the *will* mean the *soul willing.*   I shall take it for granted, that when they speak of the will, as the determiner, they mean *the soul in the exercise of a power of willing,* or acting voluntarily.   I shall suppose this to be their meaning, because nothing else can be meant, without the grossest and plainest absurdity.   In all cases when we speak of the powers or principles of acting, as doing such things, we mean that the agents which have these powers of acting do them in the exercise of those powers.   So, when we say, valour fights courageously, we mean that the man who is under the influence of valour fights courageously.   When we say, love seeks the object loved, we mean the person loving seeks that object.   When we say, the understanding discerns, we mean the soul in the exercise of that faculty.   So, when it is said, the will decides or determines, the meaning must be, that the person in the exercise of a power of willing and choosing, or the soul acting voluntarily, determines.

Therefore, if the will determines all its own free acts,

the soul determines all the free acts of the will, in the exercise of a power of willing and choosing ; or, which is the same thing, it determines them of choice ; it determines its own acts by choosing its own acts. If the will determines the will, then choice orders and determines the choice; and acts of choice are subject to the decision, and follow the conduct, of other acts of choice. And therefore, if the will determines all its own free acts, then every free act of choice is determined by a preceding act of choice, choosing that act. And if that preceding act of the will or choice be also a free act, then, by these principles, in this act too, the will is self-determined; that is, this, in like manner, is an act that the soul voluntarily chooses ; or, which is the same thing, it is an act determined still by a preceding act of the will choosing that. And the like may again be observed of the last-mentioned act, which brings us directly to a contradiction; for it supposes an act of the will preceding the first act in the whole train, directing and determining the rest ; or a free act of the will, before the first free act of the will. Or else we must come at last to an act of the will, determining the consequent acts, wherein the will is not self-determined, and so is not a free act, in this notion of freedom ; but if the first act in the train, determining and fixing the rest, be not free, none of them all can be free ; as is manifest at first view, but shall be demonstrated presently.

If the will, which we find governs the members of the body, and determines and commands their motions and actions, does also govern itself, and determine its own motions and actions, it doubtless determines them the same way, even by antecedent volitions. The will determines which way the hands and feet shall move, by an act of volition or choice; and there is no other way of the will's determining, directing, or commanding any thing at all. Whatsoever the will commands, it commands by an act of the will. And if it has itself under its command, and determines itself in its own actions, it doubtless does it the same way that it determines

other things which are under its command ; so that if
the freedom of the will consists in this, that it has itself
and its own actions under its command and direction,
and its own volitions are determined by itself, it will follow, that every free volition arises from another antecedent volition, directing and commanding that ; and if
that *directing* volition be also free, in that also the will
is determined ; that is to say, that directing volition is determined by another going before that, and so on, till we
come to the first volition in the whole series : and if that
first volition be free, and the will self-determined in it,
then that is determined by another volition preceding
that, which is a contradiction ; because, by the supposition, it can have none before it to direct or determine it,
being the first in the train.   But if that first volition is
not determined by any preceding act of the will, then
that act is not determined by the will, and so is not free
in the Arminian notion of freedom, which consists in the
will's self-determination.   And if that first act of the will,
which determines and fixes the subsequent acts, be not
free, none of the following acts, which are determined
by it, can be free.   If we suppose there are five acts in
the train, the fifth and last determined by the fourth,
and the fourth by the third, the third by the second, and
the second by the first ; if the first is not determined by
the will, and so not free, then none of them are truly determined by the will : that is, that each of them are as
they are, and not otherwise, is not first owing to the will,
but to the determination of the first in the series, which
is not dependent on the will, and is that which the will
has no hand in the determination of.   And this being
that which decides what the rest shall be, and determines
their existence, therefore the first determination of their
existence is not from the will.   The case is just the same,
if, instead of a chain of five acts of the will, we should
suppose a succession of ten, or a hundred, or ten thousand.   If the first act be not free, being determined by
something out of the will, and this determines the next
to be agreeable to itself, and that the next, and so on ;

they are none of them free, but all originally depend on,
and are determined by, some cause out of the will : and
so all freedom in the case is excluded, and no act of the
will can be free, according to this notion of freedom.   If
we should suppose a long chain of ten thousand links, so
connected that if the first link moves it will move the
next, and that the next ; and so the whole chain must
be determined to motion, and in the direction of its motion, by the motion of the first link ; and that is moved
by something else : in this case, though all the links but
one are moved by other parts of the same chain, yet it
appears that the motion of no one, nor the direction of
its motion, is from any self-moving or self-determining
power in the chain, any more than if every link were
immediately moved by something that did not belong to
the chain.   If the will be not free in the first act, which
causes the next, then neither is it free in the next, which
is caused by that first act : for though, indeed, the will
caused it, yet it did not cause it freely ; because the preceding act, by which it was caused, was not free.   And
again, if the will be not free in the second act, so neither
can it be in the third, which is caused by that ; because,
in like manner, that third was determined by an act of
the will that was not free.   And so we may go on to the
next act, and from that to the next ; and how long soever the succession of acts is, it is all one ; if the first on
which the whole chain depends, and which determines
all the rest, be not a free act, the will is not free in causing or determining any one of those acts ; because the
act by which it determines them all is not a free act, and
therefore the will is no more free in determining them
than if it did not cause them at all.   Thus, this Arminian notion of liberty of the will, consisting in the will's
self-determination, is repugnant to itself, and shuts itself
wholly out of the world.

SECTION II.

SEVERAL SUPPOSED WAYS OF EVADING THE FOREGOING REASONING, CONSIDERED.

IF, to evade the force of what has been observed, it should be said, that when the Arminians speak of the will's determining its own acts, they do not mean that the will determines its acts by any preceding act, or that one act of the will determines another; but only that the faculty or power of will, or the soul in the use of that power, determines its own volitions; and that it does it without any act going before the act determined: such an evasion would be full of the most gross absurdity. I confess it is an evasion of my own inventing; and I do not know but I should wrong the Arminians in supposing that any of them would make use of it. But it being as good a one as I can invent, I would observe upon it a few things.

First, If the faculty or power of the will determines an act of volition, or the soul in the *use* or *exercise of that power* determines it, that is the same thing as for the soul to determine volition *by an act of will*. For an *exercise* of the power of will, and an *act* of that power, are the same thing. Therefore, to say that the power of will, or the soul in the *use* or *exercise* of that power, determines volition, without an *act* of will preceding the volition determined, is a contradiction.

Secondly, If a power of will determines the act of the will, then a power of choosing determines it. For, as was before observed, in every act of will, there is choice; and a power of willing is a power of choosing. But if a power of choosing determines the act of volition, it determines it by choosing it. For it is most absurd to say that a power of choosing determines one thing rather than another, without choosing any thing. But if a power of choosing determines volition by choosing it, then here is an act of volition determined by an antecedent choice, choosing that volition.

Thirdly, to say, the faculty, or the soul, determines its own volition, but not by any act, is a contradiction. Because for the soul to *direct, decide,* or *determine* any thing, is to act; and this is supposed; for the soul is here spoken of as being a cause in this affair, bringing something to pass, or doing something; or, which is the same thing, exerting itself in order to an effect, which effect is the determination of volition, or the particular kind and manner of an act of will. But certainly, this exertion or action is not the same with the effect, in order to the production of which it is exerted; but must be something prior to it.

Again, The advocates for this notion of the freedom of the will speak of a certain sovereignty in the will, whereby it has power to determine its own volitions. And therefore the determination of volition must itself be an act of the will; for, otherwise, it can be no exercise of that supposed power and sovereignty.

Again, If the will determines itself, then either the will is *active* in determining its volitions, or it is not. If it be active in it, then the determination is an *act* of the will; and so there is one act of the will determining another. But if the will is not *active* in the determination, then how does it *exercise* any liberty in it? These gentlemen suppose, that the thing wherein the will *exercises* liberty, is in its determining its own acts. But how can this be, if it be not *active* in determining? Certainly the will, or the soul, cannot *exercise any liberty* in that wherein it doth not *act,* or wherein it doth not *exercise itself.* So that if either part of this dilemma be taken, this scheme of liberty, consisting in self-determining power, is overthrown. If there be an act of the will in determining all its own free acts, then one free act of the will is determined by another; and so we have the absurdity of every free act, even the very first, determined by a foregoing free act. But if there be no act or exercise of the will in determining its own acts, then no liberty is exercised in determining them. From whence it follows, that no liberty consists in the will's power to determine its own acts ; or, which is the same thing, that there is no such thing as liberty consisting in a self-determining power of the will.

If it should be said, that although it be true, if the soul determines its own volitions, it must be active in so doing, and the determination itself must be an act ; yet there is no need of supposing this act to be prior to the volition determined : but the will or soul determines the act of the will *in willing ;* it determines its own volition, *in* the very act of volition ; it directs and limits the act of the will, causing it to be so and not otherwise, *in* exerting the act, without any preceding act to exert that. If any should say after this manner, they must mean one of these three things : either (1) that the determining act, though it be before the act determined in the order of nature, yet is not before it in order of time. Or, (2) that the determining act is not before the act determined, either in the order of time or nature, nor is truly distinct from it ; but that the soul's determining the act of volition is the same thing with its exerting the act of volition : the mind's exerting such a particular act, is its causing and determining the act. Or, (3) that volition has no cause, and is no effect ; but comes into existence, with such a particular determination, without any ground or reason of its existence and determination.—I shall consider these distinctly.

1. If all that is meant be, that the determining act is not before the act determined in order of *time*, it will not help the case at all, though it should be allowed. If it be before the determined act in the order of nature, being the cause or ground of its existence, this as much proves it to be distinct from it and independent on it, as if it were before in the order of time. As the cause of the particular motion of a natural body, in a certain direction, may have no distance as to time, yet cannot be the same with the motion effected by it, but must be as distinct from it as any other cause that is before its effect in the order of time : as the architect is distinct from the house which he builds, or the father distinct

from the son which he begets;—and if the act of the will determining be distinct from the act determined, and before it in the order of nature, then we can go back from one to another, until we come to the first in the series, which has no act of the will before it in the order of nature, determining it; and consequently is an act not determined by the will, and so not a free act, in this notion of freedom. And this being the act which determines all the rest, none of them are free acts. As, when there is a chain of many links, the first of which only is taken hold of and drawn by hand; all the rest may follow and be moved at the same instant, without any distance of time; but yet the motion of one link is before that of another in the order of nature; the last is moved by the next, and that by the next, and so till we come to the first; which not being moved by any other, but by something distinct from the whole chain, this as much proves that no part is moved by any self-moving power in the chain, as if the motion of one link followed that of another in the order of time.

2. If any should say, that the determining act is not before the determined act, either in the order of time or of nature, nor is distinct from it; but that the *exertion* of the act is the *determination* of the act; that for the soul to exert a particular volition, is for it to cause and determine that act of volition: I would on this observe, that the thing in question seems to be forgotten, or kept out of sight, in a darkness and unintelligibleness of speech; unless such an objector would contradict himself. The very act of volition itself is doubtless a determination of mind; *i. e.* it is the mind's drawing up a conclusion, or coming to a choice between two things, or more proposed to it. But determining among external *objects* of choice is not the same with determining the *act* of choice itself, among various possible acts of choice. —The question is, What influences, directs, or determines the mind or will to come to such a conclusion or choice as it does? Or what is the cause, ground, or reason, why it concludes thus, and not otherwise?

Now it must be answered, according to the Arminian notion of freedom, that the will influences, orders, and determines itself thus to act. And if it does, I say it must be by some antecedent act. To say it is caused, influenced, and determined by something, and yet not determined by any thing antecedent, either in order of time or nature, is a contradiction. For that is what is meant by a thing's being prior in the order of nature, that it is some way the cause or reason of the thing with respect to which it is said to be prior.

If the particular act or exertion of will, which comes into existence, be any thing properly determined at all, then it has some cause of its existing, and of its existing in such a particular determinate manner, and not another ; some cause whose influence *decides the matter:* which cause is distinct from the effect, and prior to it. But to say, that the will or mind orders, influences, and determines itself to exert such an act as it does, by the very exertion itself, is to make the exertion both cause and effect; or the exerting such an act, to be a cause of the exertion of such an act. For the question is, What is the cause and reason of the soul's exerting such an act ? To which the answer is : The soul exerts such an act; and that is the cause of it. And so, by this, the exertion must be prior in the order of nature to itself, and distinct from itself.

3. If the meaning be, that the soul's exertion of such a particular act of will is a thing that comes to pass *of itself* without any cause; and that there is absolutely no ground or reason of the soul's being determined to exert such a volition, and make such a choice, rather than another ; I say, if this be the meaning of Arminians, when they contend so earnestly for the will's determining its own acts, and for liberty of will consisting in self-determining power ; they do nothing but confound themselves and others with words without a meaning. In the question, *What determines the will?* and in their answer, that *the will determines itself,* and in all the dispute about it, it seems to be taken for granted, that

something determines the will ; and the controversy on this head is not, whether any thing at all determines it, or whether its determination has any cause or foundation at all ; but where the foundation of it is, whether in the will itself, or somewhere else. But if the thing intended be what is above mentioned, then all comes to this, that nothing at all determines the will; volition having absolutely no cause or foundation of its existence, either within or without. There is a great noise made about self-determining power, as the source of all free acts of the will : but when the matter comes to be explained, the meaning is, that no power at all is the source of these acts, neither self-determining power, nor any other, but they arise from nothing ; no cause, no power, no influence, being at all concerned in the matter.

However, this very thing, even that the free acts of the will are events which come to pass without a cause, is certainly implied in the Arminian notion of liberty of will; though it be very inconsistent with many other things in their scheme, and repugnant to some things implied in their notion of liberty. Their opinion implies, that the particular determination of volition is without any cause ; because they hold the free acts of the will to be *contingent* events ; and contingence is essential to freedom, in their notion of it. But certainly, those things which have a prior ground and reason of their particular existence, a cause which antecedently determines them to be, and determines them to be just as they are, do not happen contingently. If something foregoing, by a casual influence and connexion, determines and fixes precisely their coming to pass, and the manner of it, then it does not remain a contingent thing whether they shall come to pass or no.

And because it is a question in many respects very important, in this controversy about the freedom of will, *whether the free acts of the will are events which come to pass without a cause;* I shall be particular in examining this point in the two following sections.

SECTION III.

WHETHER ANY EVENT WHATSOEVER, AND VOLITION IN PARTICULAR,
CAN COME TO PASS WITHOUT A CAUSE OF ITS EXISTENCE.

BEFORE I enter on any argument on this subject, I
would explain how I would be understood, when I use
the word *cause* in this discourse; since, for want of a
better word, I shall have occasion to use it in a sense
which is more extensive than that in which it is sometimes used. The word is often used in so restrained a
sense as to signify only that which has a *positive efficiency* or influence *to produce* a thing, or bring it to pass.
But there are many things which have no such positive
productive influence, which yet are causes in that respect, that they have truly the nature of a ground or
reason why some things are, rather than others; or
why they are as they are, rather than otherwise. Thus,
the absence of the sun in the night is not the cause
of the falling of the dew at that time, in the same manner as its beams are the cause of the ascending of the
vapours in the day-time; and its withdrawment in the
winter is not in the same manner the cause of the freez-
ing of the waters, as its approach in the spring is the
cause of their thawing. But yet the withdrawment or
absence of the sun is an antecedent, with which these
effects in the night and winter are connected, and on
which they depend; and is one thing that belongs to the
ground and reason why they come to pass at that time
rather than at other times; though the absence of the
sun is nothing positive, nor has any positive influence.

It may be further observed, that when I speak of *connexion of causes and effects,* I have respect to *moral*
causes, as well as those that are called *natural* in distinction from them. Moral causes may be causes in as proper a sense as any causes whatsoever; may have as real
an influence, and may as truly be the ground and reason
of an event's coming to pass.

Therefore I sometimes use the word *cause,* in this inquiry, to signify any *antecedent,* either natural or moral,

positive or negative, on which an event, either a thing, or the manner and circumstance of a thing, so depends, that it is the ground and reason, either in whole or in part, why it is, rather than not ; or why it is as it is, rather than otherwise ; or, in other words, any antecedent with which a consequent event is so connected, that it truly belongs to the reason why the proposition which affirms that event is true, whether it has any positive influence or not.   And in an agreeableness to this I sometimes use the word *effect* for the consequence of another thing, which is, perhaps, rather an occasion than a cause, most properly speaking.

I am the more careful thus to explain my meaning, that I may cut off occasion from any that might seek occasion to cavil and object against some things which I may say concerning the dependence of all things which come to pass on some cause, and their connexion with their cause.

Having thus explained what I mean by *cause,* I assert, that nothing ever comes to pass without a cause. What is self-existent, must be from eternity, and must be unchangeable; but as to all things that *begin to be,* they are not self-existent, and therefore must have some foundation of their existence without themselves.—That whatsoever begins to be, which before was not, must have a cause why it then begins to exist, seems to be the first dictate of the common and natural sense which God hath implanted in the minds of all mankind, and the main foundation of all our reasonings about the existence of things past, present, or to come.

And this dictate of common sense equally respects substances and modes, or things and the manner and circumstances of things.   Thus, if we see a body which has hitherto been at rest, start out of a state of rest, and begin to move, we do as naturally and necessarily suppose there is some cause or reason of this new mode of existence, as of the existence of a body itself which had hitherto not existed. And so, if a body which had hitherto moved in a certain direction, should suddenly change the direction of its motion ; or if it should put off its old figure, and take a new one ; or change its colour : the beginning of these new modes is a new event, and the mind of mankind necessarily supposes that there is some cause or reason of them.

If this grand principle of common sense be taken away, all arguing from effects to causes ceaseth, and so all knowledge of any existence, besides what we have by the most direct and immediate intuition. Particularly all our proof of the being of God ceases ; we argue his being from our own being, and the being of other things, which we are sensible once were not, but have begun to be ; and from the being of the world, with all its constituent parts, and the manner of their existence ; all which we see plainly are not necessary in their own nature, and so not self-existent, and therefore must have a cause. But if things, not in themselves necessary, may begin to be without a cause, all this arguing is vain.

Indeed, I will not affirm, that there is in the nature of things no foundation for the knowledge of the being of God, without any evidence of it from his works. I do suppose there is a great absurdity, in the nature of things simply considered, in supposing that there should be no God, or in denying being in general, and supposing an eternal, absolute, universal nothing : and therefore that here would be foundation of intuitive evidence that it cannot be, and that eternal, infinite, most perfect Being must be ; if we had strength and comprehension of mind sufficient to have a clear idea of general and universal being, or, which is the same thing, of the infinite, eternal, most perfect Divine nature and essence. But then we should not properly come to the knowledge of the being of God by arguing ; but our evidence would be intuitive : we should see it, as we see other things that are necessary in themselves, the contraries of which are in their own nature absurd and contradictory ; as we see that twice two is four ; and as we see that a circle has no angles. If we had as clear an idea of universal, infinite entity, as we have of these other

things, I suppose we should most intuitively see the absurdity of supposing such being not to be; should immediately see there is no room for the question, whether
it is possible that being, in the most general abstracted
notion of it, should not be. But we have not that strength
and extent of mind, to know this certainly in this intuitive independent manner : but the way that mankind
come to the knowledge of the being of God, is that
which the apostle speaks of, Rom. i. 20, " The invisible
things of him, from the creation of the world, are clearly
seen, being understood by the things that are made;
even his eternal power and Godhead." We *first ascend*,
and prove *à posteriori*, or from effects, that there must
be an eternal cause ; and then, *secondly*, prove by argu-
mentation, not intuition, that this being must be necessarily existent ; and then, *thirdly*, from the proved necessity of his existence, we may *descend*, and prove
many of his perfections *à priori*.

But if once this grand principle of common sense be
given up, that *what is not necessary in itself, must have
a cause ;* and we begin to maintain, that things may
come into existence and begin to be, which heretofore
have not been, of themselves, without any cause ; all
our means of ascending in our arguing from the creature
to the Creator, and all our evidence of the being of God,
is cut off at one blow. In this case, we cannot prove
that there is a God, either from the being of the world
and the creatures in it, or from the manner of their
being, their order, beauty, and use. For if things may
come into existence without any cause at all, then they
doubtless may without any cause answerable to the effect. Our minds do alike naturally suppose and determine both these things ; namely, that what begins to be
has a cause, and also that it has a cause proportionable
and agreeable to the effect. The same principle which
leads us to determine, that there cannot be anything coming to pass without a cause, leads us to determine that
there cannot be more in the effect than in the cause.

Yea, if once it should be allowed, that things may

come to pass without a cause, we should not only have no proof of the being of God, but we should be without evidence of the existence of any thing whatsoever, but our own immediately present ideas and consciousness. For we have no way to prove any thing else, but by arguing from effects to causes : from the ideas now immediately in view, we argue other things not immediately in view : from sensations now excited in us, we infer the existence of things without us, as the causes of these sensations : and from the existence of these things, we argue other things, which they depend on, as effects on causes. We infer the past existence of ourselves, or any thing else, by memory ; only as we argue, that the ideas which are now in our minds, are the consequences of past ideas and sensations. We immediately perceive nothing else but the ideas which are at this moment extant in our minds. We perceive or know other things only *by means* of these, as necessarily connected with others, and dependent on them. But if things may be without causes, all this necessary connexion and dependence is dissolved, and so all means of our knowledge is gone. If there be no absurdity or difficulty in supposing one thing to start out of non-existence into being of itself without a cause, then there is no absurdity or difficulty in supposing the same of millions of millions. For nothing, or no difficulty multiplied, still is nothing, or no difficulty : nothing multiplied by nothing, does not increase the sum.

And indeed, according to the hypothesis I am opposing, of the acts of the will coming to pass without a cause, it is the case in fact, that millions of millions of events are continually coming into existence *contingently*, without any cause or reason why they do so, all over the world, every day and hour, through all ages. So it is, in a constant succession, in every moral agent. This contingency, this efficient nothing, this effectual no-cause, is always ready at hand to produce this sort of effects, as long as the agent exists, and as often as he has occasion.

If it were so, that things only of one kind, viz. acts of the will, seemed to come to pass of themselves, but those of this sort in general came into being thus; and it were an event that was continual, and that happened in a course, wherever were capable subjects of such events; this very thing would demonstrate that there was some cause of them, which made such a difference between this event and others, and that they did not really happen contingently. For contingence is blind, and does not pick and choose for a particular sort of events. Nothing has no choice. This no-cause, which causes no existence, cannot cause the existence which comes to pass, to be of one particular sort only, disting- uished from all others. Thus, that only one sort of mat- ter drops out of the heavens, even water, and that this comes so often, so constantly and plentifully, all over the world, in all ages, shews that there is some cause or reason of the falling of water out of the heavens; and that something besides mere contingence has a hand in the matter.

If we should suppose nonentity to be about to bring forth; and things were coming into existence without any cause or antecedent, on which the existence, or kind or manner of existence, depends; or which could at all determine whether the things should be stones, or stars, or beasts, or angels, or human bodies, or souls, or only some new motion or figure in natural bodies, or some new sensations in animals, or new ideas in the human understanding, or new volitions in the will; or any thing else of all the infinite number of possibles; then certainly it would not be expected, although many mil- lions of millions of things are coming into existence in this manner, all over the face of the earth, that they should all be only of one particular kind, and that it should be thus in all ages, and that this sort of exis- tences should never fail to come to pass where there is room for them, or a subject capable of them, and that constantly, whenever there is occasion for them.

If any should imagine, there is something in the sort of event that renders it possible for it to come into existence without a cause, and should say, that the free acts of the will are existences of an exceeding different nature from other things ; by reason of which they may come into existence without any previous ground or reason of it, though other things cannot : if they make this objection in good earnest, it would be an evidence of their strangely forgetting themselves; for they would be giving an account of some ground of the existence of a thing, when at the same time they would maintain there is no ground of its existence. Therefore I would observe, that 'the particular nature of existence, be it never so diverse from others, can lay no foundation for that thing's coming into existence without a cause ; because to suppose this, would be to suppose the particular nature of existence to be a thing prior to the existence ; and so a thing which makes way for existence, with such a circumstance, namely, without a cause or reason of existence. But that which in any respect makes way for a thing's coming into being, or for any manner or circumstance of its first existence, must be prior to the existence. The distinguished nature of the effect, which is something belonging to the effect, cannot have influence backward, to act before it is. The peculiar nature of that thing called volition, can do nothing, can have no influence, while it is not. And afterwards it is too late for its influence ; for then the thing has made sure of existence already, without its help.

So that it is indeed as repugnant to reason to suppose that an act of the will should come into existence without a cause, as to suppose the human soul, or an angel, or the globe of the earth, or the whole universe, should come into existence without a cause. And if once we allow that such a sort of effect as a volition may come to pass without a cause, how do we know but that many other sorts of effects may do so too ? It is not the particular kind of effect that makes the absurdity of supposing it has being without a cause, but something which is common to all things that ever begin to be, viz. that they are not self-existent, or necessary in the nature of things.

SECTION IV.

WHETHER VOLITION CAN ARISE WITHOUT A CAUSE, THROUGH THE
ACTIVITY OF THE NATURE OF THE SOUL.

THE author of the " Essay on the Freedom of the Will
in God and the creatures," in answer to that objection
against his doctrine of a self-determining power in the
will, (p. 68, 69,) *That nothing is, or comes to pass, without a sufficient reason why it is, and why it is in this
manner rather than another,* allows that it is thus in corporeal things, *which are, properly and philosophically
speaking, passive being;* but denies that it is thus in
*spirits, which are beings of an active nature, who have
the spring of action within themselves, and can determine
themselves.* By which it is plainly supposed, that such
an event as an act of the will may come to pass in a
spirit, without a sufficient reason why it comes to pass,
or why it is after this manner rather than another, by
reason of the activity of the nature of a spirit. But certainly this author, in this matter, must be very unwary
and inadvertent. For,

1. The objection or difficulty proposed by this author,
seems to be forgotten in his answer or solution. The
very difficulty, as he himself proposes it, is this: how an
event can *come to pass without a sufficient reason why it
is, or why it is in this manner rather than another ?*
Instead of solving this difficulty, or answering this question with regard to volition, as he proposes, he forgets
himself, and answers another question quite diverse, and
wholly inconsistent with this, viz. What is a sufficient
reason why it is, and why it is in this manner rather
than another? And he assigns the active being's own
determination as the cause, and a cause sufficient for the
effect; and leaves all the difficulty unresolved, and the
question unanswered, which yet returns, even, How the
soul's own determination, which he speaks of, came to
exist, and to be what it was, without a cause? The activity of the soul may enable it to be the cause of effects;
but it does not at all enable or help it to be the subject

of effects which have no cause, which is the thing this author supposes concerning acts of the will. Activity of nature will no more enable a being to produce effects, and determine the manner of their existence, *within* itself, without a cause, than *out of* itself, in some other being. But if an active being should, through its activity, produce and determine an effect in some external object, how absurd would it be to say that the effect was produced without a cause !

2. The question is not so much, How a spirit endowed with activity comes to act, as, Why it exerts such an act and not another ; or why it acts with such a particular determination. If activity of nature be the cause why a spirit (the soul of man, for instance,) acts, and does not lie still, yet that alone is not the cause why its action is thus and thus limited, directed, and determined. Active nature is a *general* thing ; it is an ability or tendency of nature to action, generally taken, which may be a cause why the soul acts as occasion or reason is given ; but this alone cannot be a sufficient cause why the soul exerts such a *particular* act, at such a time, rather than others. In order to this, there must be something besides a *general* tendency to action ; there must also be a *particular* tendency to that individual action. If it should be asked, why the soul of man uses its activity in such a manner as it does ; and it should be answered, that the soul uses its activity thus rather than otherwise, because it has activity, would such an answer satisfy a rational man ? Would it not rather be looked upon as a very impertinent one ?

3. An active being can bring no effects to pass by his activity but what are consequent upon his acting ; he produces nothing by his activity, any other way than by the exercise of his activity, and so nothing but the fruits of its exercise ; he brings nothing to pass by a dormant activity. But the exercise of his activity is action ; and so his action, or exercise of his activity, must be prior to the effects of his activity. If an active being produces an effect in another being, about which his ac-

tivity is conversant, the effect being the fruit of his activity, his activity must be first exercised or exerted, and
the effect of it must follow. So it must be, with equal
reason, if the active being is his own object, and his activity is conversant about himself, to produce and determine some effect in himself; still the exercise of his activity must go before the effect, which he brings to pass
and determines by it. And therefore his activity cannot be the cause of the determination of the first action,
or exercise of activity itself, whence the effects of activity arise; for that would imply a contradiction; it
would be to say, the first exercise of activity is before
the first exercise of activity, and is the cause of it.

4. That the soul, though an active substance, cannot
diversify its own acts, but by first acting ; or be a determining cause of *different* acts, or any different effects,
sometimes of one kind and sometimes of another, any
other way than in consequence of its own diverse acts, is
manifest by this : that if so, then the *same* cause, the
same causal power, force, or influence, *without variation
in any respect*, would produce *different* effects at different times. For the same substance of the soul before it
acts, and the same active nature of the soul before it is
exerted, (*i. e.* before in the order of nature) would be
the cause of different effects, viz. different volitions at
different times. But the substance of the soul before it
acts, and its active nature before it is exerted, are the
same without variation. For it is some act that makes
the first variation in the cause, as to any causal exertion,
force, or influence. But if it be so, that the soul has no
different causality, or diverse causal force or influence in
producing these diverse effects; then it is evident that
the soul has no influence, no hand in the diversity of the
effect, and that the difference of the effect cannot be
owing to any thing in the soul ; or, which is the same
thing, the soul does not determine the diversity of the
effect; which is contrary to the supposition. It is true
the substance of the soul, before it acts, and before there
is any difference in that respect, may be in a different

state and circumstances: but those whom I oppose will
not allow the different circumstances of the soul to be
the determining causes of the acts of the will, as being
contrary to their notion of self-determination and self-
motion.

5. Let us suppose, as these divines do, that there are
no acts of the soul, strictly speaking, but free volitions;
then it will follow, that the soul is an active being in
nothing further than it is a voluntary or elective being;
and whenever it produces effects actively, it produces
effects voluntarily and electively. But to produce effects
thus is the same thing as to produce effects *in consequence of*, and *according to*, its own choice. And if so,
then surely the soul does not by its activity produce all
its own acts of will or choice themselves; for this, by the
supposition, is to produce all its free acts of choice voluntarily and electively, or in consequence of its own free
acts of choice, which brings the matter directly to the
forementioned contradiction, of a free act of choice before the first free act of choice. According to these
gentlemen's own notion of action, if there arises in the
mind a volition, without a free act of the will or choice
to determine and produce it, the mind is not the active
voluntary cause of that volition; because it does not
arise from, nor is regulated by, choice or design. And
therefore it cannot be, that the mind should be the active,
voluntary, determining cause of the first and leading
volition that relates to the affair. The mind's being a *designing* cause, only enables it to produce effects in consequence of its *design;* it will not enable it to be the
designing cause of all its own designs. The mind's being
an *elective* cause will only enable it to produce effects in
consequence of its *elections,* and according to them; but
cannot enable it to be the elective cause of all its own
elections; because that supposes an election before the
first election. So the mind's being an *active* cause enables it to produce effects in consequence of its own *acts,*
but cannot enable it to be the determining cause of all
its own *acts ;* for that is still in the same manner a con-

tradiction, as it supposes a determining act conversant about the first act, and prior to it, having a causal influence on its existence and manner of existence.

I can conceive of nothing else that can be meant by the soul's having power to cause and determine its own volitions, as a being to whom God has given a power of action, but this: that God has given power to the soul sometimes, at least, to excite volitions at its pleasure, or according as it chooses. And this certainly supposes, in all such cases, a choice preceding all volitions which are thus caused, even the first of them; which runs into the fore-mentioned great absurdity.

Therefore the activity of the nature of the soul affords no relief from the difficulties which the notion of a self-determining power in the will is attended with; nor will it help, in the least, its absurdities and inconsistencies.

SECTION V.

SHEWING, THAT IF THE THINGS ASSERTED IN THESE EVASIONS SHOULD BE SUPPOSED TO BE TRUE, THEY ARE ALTOGETHER IMPERTINENT, AND CANNOT HELP THE CAUSE OF ARMINIAN LIBERTY; AND HOW (THIS BEING THE STATE OF THE CASE) ARMINIAN WRITERS ARE OBLIGED TO TALK INCONSISTENTLY.

WHAT was last observed in the preceding section, may shew, not only that the active nature of the soul cannot be a reason why an act of the will is, or why it is in this manner rather than another; but also that if it could be so, and it could be proved that volitions are contingent events, in that sense, that their being and manner of being is not fixed or determined by any cause, or any thing antecedent; it would not at all serve the purpose of Arminians to establish the freedom of the will, according to their notion of its freedom, as consisting in the will's *determination of itself;* which supposes every free act of the will to be determined by some act of the will going before to determine it; inasmuch as for the *will* to determine a thing, is the same as for the soul to determine a thing by *willing;* and there is no other way that the *will* can determine an act of the will, than by willing that act of the will, or, which is the same thing, *choosing* it.   So that here must be two acts of the will in the case, one going before another, one conversant about the other, and the latter the object of the former, and chosen by the former.   If the will does not cause and determine the act by choice, it does not cause or determine it at all; for that which is not determined by choice is not determined voluntarily or *willingly;*—and to say that the will determines something which the soul does not determine willingly, is as much as to say that something is done by the will which the soul doth not with its will.

So that if Arminian liberty of will, consisting in the will's determining its own acts, be maintained, the old absurdity and contradiction must be maintained, that every free act of the will is caused and determined by a foregoing free act of will; which doth not consist with the free acts arising without any cause, and being so contingent as not to be fixed by any thing foregoing. So that this evasion must be given up, as not at all relieving, and as that which, instead of supporting this sort of liberty, directly destroys it.

And if it should be supposed that the soul determines its own acts of will some other way than by a foregoing act of will, still it will not help the cause of their liberty of will.   If it determines them by an act of the understanding, or some other power, then *the will* does not determine *itself;* and so the *self-determining* power of the will is given up.   And what liberty is there exercised, according to their own opinion of liberty, by the soul's being determined by something besides *its own choice?*   The acts of the will, it is true, may be directed and effectually determined and fixed; but it is not done by the soul's own will and pleasure: there is no exercise at all of choice or will in producing the effect; and if *will* and choice are not exercised in it, how is the *liberty of the will* exercised in it?

So that let Arminians turn which way they please with their notion of liberty consisting in the will's determining its own acts, their notion destroys itself. If they hold every free act of will to be determined by the soul's own free choice, or *foregoing* free act of will, *foregoing* either in the order of time or nature, it implies that gross contradiction that the first free act belonging to the affair is determined by a free act which is before it; or if they say that the free acts of the will are determined by some *other act* of the soul, and not an act of will or choice, this also destroys their notion of liberty, consisting in the acts of the will being determined by the *will itself;* or if they hold that the acts of the will are determined by *nothing at all* that is prior to them, but that they are contingent, in that sense, that they are determined and fixed by no cause at all, this also destroys their notion of liberty consisting in the will's determining its own acts.

This being the true state of the Arminian notion of liberty, it hence comes to pass that the writers that defend it are forced into gross inconsistencies in what they say upon this subject. To instance in Dr Whitby : he, in his discourse on the freedom of the will,* opposes the opinion of the Calvinists, who place man's liberty *only in a power of doing what he will,* as that wherein they plainly agree with Mr Hobbes. And yet he himself mentions the very same notion of liberty as the dictate of *the sense and common reason of mankind, and a rule laid down by the light of nature ;* viz. *that liberty is a power of acting from ourselves, or* DOING WHAT WE WILL.† This is indeed, as he says, a thing agreeable to *the sense and common reason of mankind;* and therefore it is not so much to be wondered at, that he unawares acknowledges it against himself : for if liberty does not consist in this, what else can be devised that it should consist in ? If it be said, as Dr. Whitby elsewhere insists, that it does not only consist in liberty of *doing what we will,* but also a liberty of willing without necessity, still the question returns, what does the liberty of willing without necessity consist in, but in a power of willing *as we please,* without being impeded by a contrary necessity; or, in other words, a li-

---

* In his book on the Five Points, second edition, p. 350, 351, 352.
† Ibid. p. 325, 326.

erty for the soul in its willing to act *according to its own choice?* Yea, this very thing the same author seems to allow, and suppose again and again, in the use he makes of sayings of the fathers, whom he quotes as his vouchers. Thus he cites the words of Origen, which he produces as a testimony on his side : * *The soul acts by* HER OWN CHOICE, *and it is free for her to incline to whatever part* SHE WILL. And those words of Justin Martyr : † *The doctrine of the Christians is this, that nothing is done or suffered according to fate, but that every man doth good or evil* ACCORDING TO HIS OWN FREE CHOICE. And from Eusebius these words : ‡ *If fate be established, philosophy and piety are overthrown; all these things depending upon the necessity introduced by the stars, and not upon meditation and exercise* PROCEEDING FROM OUR OWN FREE CHOICE. And again, the words of Maccarius : || *God, to preserve the liberty of man's will, suffered their bodies to die, that it might be* IN THEIR CHOICE *to turn to good or evil. They who are acted by the Holy Spirit are not held under any necessity, but have liberty to turn themselves, and* DO WHAT THEY WILL *in this life.*

Thus, the Doctor, in effect, comes into that very notion of liberty which the Calvinists have ; which he at the same time condemns, as agreeing with the opinion of Mr Hobbes, namely, *the soul's acting by its own choice, men's doing good or evil according to their own free choice, their being in that exercise which proceeds from their own free choice, having it in their choice to turn to good or evil, and doing what they will.* So that if men exercise this liberty in the acts of the will themselves, it must be in exerting acts of will as they will, or *according to their own* free *choice,* or exerting acts of will *that proceed from their choice.* And if it be so, then let every one judge, whether this does not suppose a free choice going before the free act of will, or whether an act of choice does not go before that act of the will which *proceeds from it.* And if it be thus with all free acts of

* Ibid. p. 342.   † Ibid. p. 360.
‡ Ibid. p. 363. || Ibid. p. 369, 370.

the will, then let every one judge, whether it will not
follow, that there is a free choice or will going before
the first free act of the will exerted in the case. And
then let every one judge, whether this be not a contradiction. And finally, let every one judge, whether, in
the scheme of these writers, there be any possibility of
avoiding these absurdities.

If liberty consists, as Dr Whitby himself says, in a
man's *doing what he will;* and a man exercises this
liberty, not only in external actions, but in the acts of
the will themselves ; then, so far as liberty is exercised
in the latter, it consists in *willing what he wills:* and if
any say so, one of these two things must be meant ;
either, 1. That a man has power to will, as he does will ;
because what he wills, he wills; and therefore has power
to will what he has power to will. If this be their meaning, then all this mighty controversy about freedom of
the will and self-determining power, comes wholly to
nothing ; all that is contended for being no more than
this, that the mind of man does what it does, and is the
subject of what it is the subject of, or that what is, is ;
wherein none has any controversy with them. Or, 2.
The meaning must be, that a man has power to will as
he pleases or chooses to will: that is, he has power by
one act of choice, to choose another; by an antecedent
act of will, to choose a consequent act; and therein to
execute his own choice. And if this be their meaning,
it is nothing but reason. For still the question returns,
Wherein lies man's liberty in that antecedent act of will
which chose the consequent act? The answer, according to the same principles, must be, that his liberty in
this also lies in his willing as he would, or as he chose,
or agreeable to another act of choice preceding that. And
so the question returns *in infinitum,* and the like answer must be made *in infinitum:* in order to support
their opinion, there must be no beginning, but free acts
of will must have been chosen by foregoing free acts of
will in the soul of every man, without beginning ; and so
before he had a being, from all eternity.

SECTION VI.

CONCERNING THE WILL'S DETERMINING IN THINGS WHICH ARE PERFECTLY INDIFFERENT IN THE VIEW OF THE MIND.

A GREAT argument for self-determining power is the supposed experience we universally have of an ability to determine our wills, in cases wherein no prevailing motive is presented : the will (as is supposed) has its choice to make between two or more things, that are perfectly equal in the view of the mind : and the will is apparently altogether indifferent; and yet we find no difficulty in coming to a choice; the will can instantly determine itself to one, by a sovereign power which it has over itself, without being moved by any preponderating inducement.

Thus the fore-mentioned author of an "Essay on the Freedom of the Will," &c. pp. 25, 26, 27, supposes, "That there are many instances wherein the will is determined neither by present uneasiness nor by the greatest apparent good, nor by the last dictate of the understanding, nor by any thing else, but merely by itself, as a sovereign self-determining power of the soul; and that the soul does not will this or that action, in some cases, by any other influence but because it will. Thus (says he) I can turn my face to the south, or to the north ; I can point with my finger upward or downward.—And thus, in some cases, the will determines itself in a very sovereign manner, because it will, without a reason borrowed from the understanding ; and hereby it discovers its own perfect power of choice, rising from within itself, and free from all influence or restraint of any kind." And in pages 66, 70, and 73, 74, this author very expressly supposes the will in many cases to be determined by *no motive at all, and acts altogether without motive or ground of preference.*—Here I would observe,

1. The very supposition which is here made, directly contradicts and overthrows itself. For the thing supposed, wherein this grand argument consists, is, that among several things the will actually chooses one before an-

other, at the same time that it is perfectly indifferent;
which is the very same thing as to say the mind has a
preference, at the same time that it has no preference.
What is meant cannot be, that the mind is indifferent
before it comes to have a choice, or until it has a preference; or, which is the same thing, that the mind is
indifferent until it comes to be not indifferent. For
certainly this author did not suppose he had a controversy with any person in supposing this. And then it
is nothing to his purpose, that the mind which chooses
was indifferent once; unless it chooses, remaining indifferent; for otherwise, it does not choose at all in that
case of indifference, concerning which is all the question.
Besides, it appears in fact, that the thing which this
author supposes, is not that the will chooses one thing
before another, concerning which it is indifferent *before
it chooses*, but also is indifferent *when it chooses*, and
that its being otherwise than indifferent is not until afterwards, in consequence of its choice; that the chosen
thing's appearing preferable and more agreeable than another, arises from its choice already made. His words
are, (p. 30), " Where the objects which are proposed
appear equally fit or good, the will is left without a
guide or director; and therefore must take its own
choice by its own determination; it being properly a
self-determining power. And in such cases the will does
as it were make a good to itself by its own choice, *i. e.*
creates its own pleasure or delight in this self-chosen
good. Even as a man, by seizing upon a spot of un-
occupied land in an uninhabited country, makes it his
own possession and property, and as such rejoices in it.
Where things were indifferent before, the will finds nothing to make them more agreeable, considered merely
in themselves; but the pleasure it feels ARISING FROM
ITS OWN CHOICE, and its perseverance therein. We love
many things which we have chosen, AND PURELY BECAUSE
WE CHOSE THEM."

This is as much as to say, that we first begin to prefer many things, now ceasing any longer to be indiffer-

ent with respect to them, purely because we have preferred and chosen them before.—These things must
needs be spoken inconsiderately by this author. Choice
or preference cannot be before itself in the same instance,
either in the order of time or nature. It cannot be the
foundation of itself, or the fruit or consequence of itself.
The very act of choosing one thing *rather than another*,
is *preferring* that thing, and that is setting a higher
value on that thing. But that the mind sets a higher
value on one thing than another, is not, in the first place,
the fruit of its setting a higher value on that thing.

This author says, p. 36, " The will may be perfectly
indifferent, and yet the will may determine itself to
choose one or the other." And again, in the same page,
" I am entirely indifferent to either; and yet my will
may determine itself to choose." And again, " Which
I shall choose must be determined by the mere act of
my will." If the choice is determined by a mere act of
will, then the choice is determined by a mere act of
choice. And concerning this matter, viz. That the act
of the will itself is determined by an act of choice, this
writer is express, in p. 72. Speaking of the case where
there is no superior fitness in objects presented, he has
these words: " There it must act by its own CHOICE, and
determine itself as it PLEASES;"—where it is supposed
that the very *determination*, which is the ground and
spring of the will's act, is an act of *choice* and *pleasure*,
wherein one act is more agreeable, and the mind better
pleased in it, than another; and this *preference* and *superior pleasedness*, is the ground of all it does in the case.
And if so, the mind is not indifferent when it determines
itself, but *had rather* do one thing than another, had rather determine itself one way than another. And therefore the will does not act at all in indifference, not so
much as in the first step it takes, or the first rise and
beginning of its acting. If it be possible for the understanding to act in indifference, yet to be sure the will
never does; because the will's beginning to act is the
very same thing as its beginning to choose or prefer.

And if in the very first act of the will, the mind prefers
something, then the idea of that thing preferred does at
that time preponderate, or prevail in the mind; or, which
is the same thing, the idea of it has a prevailing influence on the will. So that this wholly destroys the thing
supposed, viz. That the mind can by a sovereign power
choose one of two or more things, which in the view of
the mind are, in every respect, perfectly equal, one of
which does not at all preponderate, nor has any prevailing influence on the mind above another.

So that this author, in his grand argument for the
ability of the will to choose one of two or more things,
concerning which it is perfectly indifferent, does at the
same time, in effect, deny the thing he supposes, and allows and asserts the point he endeavours to overthrow;
even that the will, in choosing, is subject to no prevailing influence of the idea, or view of the thing chosen.
And indeed it is impossible to offer this argument without overthrowing it; the thing supposed in it being inconsistent with itself, and that which denies itself.   To
suppose the will to act at all in a state of perfect indifference, either to determine itself, or to do any thing else,
is to assert that the mind chooses without choosing.   To
say that when it is indifferent, it can do as it pleases, is
to say that it can follow its pleasure, when it has no
pleasure to follow.   And therefore, if there be any difficulty in the instances of two cakes, or two eggs, &c.
which are exactly alike, one as good as another; concerning which this author supposes the mind in fact has
a *choice*, and so in effect supposes that it has a *preference*, it as much concerned himself to solve the difficulty, as it does those whom he opposes.   For if these instances prove any thing to his purpose, they prove that
a man chooses without choice.   And yet this is not to
his purpose; because if this is what he asserts, his own
words are as much against him, and do as much contradict him, as the words of those he disputes against can do.

2. There is no great difficulty in showing, in such instances as are alleged, not only *that it must needs be so,*

that the mind must be influenced in its choice by something that has a preponderating influence upon it, but
also *how it is so*. A little attention to our own experience, and a distinct consideration of the acts of our own
minds, in such cases, will be sufficient to clear up the
matter.

Thus, supposing I have a chess-board before me; and
because I am required by a superior, or desired by a
friend, or to make some experiment concerning my own
ability and liberty, or on some other consideration, I am
determined to touch some one of the spots or squares on
the board with my finger; not being limited or directed
in the first proposal, or my own first purpose, which is
general, to any one in particular; and there being nothing in the squares, in themselves considered, that re-
commends any one of all the sixty-four, more than another; in this case my mind determines to give itself up
to what is vulgarly called *accident*,* by determining to
touch that square which happens to be most in view,
which my eye is especially upon at that moment, or
which happens to be most in my mind, or which I shall
be directed to by some other such like accident. Here
are several steps of the mind's proceeding, (though all
may be done as it were in a moment): the *first* step is
its *general* determination that it will touch one of the
squares. The *next* step is another *general* determination
to give itself up to accident, in some certain way; as to
touch that which shall be most in the eye or mind at
that time, or to some other such like accident. The
third and last step is a *particular* determination to touch
a certain individual spot, even that square which, by
that sort of accident the mind has pitched upon, has
actually offered itself beyond others. Now it is apparent, that in none of these several steps does the mind
proceed in absolute indifference, but in each of them is

---

* I have elsewhere observed what that is which is vulgarly called *accident;* that it is nothing akin to the Arminian metaphysical notion of *contingence,* something not connected with any thing foregoing; but that it is
something that comes to pass in the course of things, in some affair that men
are concerned in, unforeseen, and not owing to their design.

influenced by a preponderating inducement. So it is in the *first* step; the mind's general determination to touch one of the sixty-four spots: the mind is not absolutely indifferent whether it does so or no; it is induced to it, for the sake of making some experiment, or by the desire of a friend, or some other motive that prevails. So it is in the *second* step; the mind's determining to give itself up to accident, by touching that which shall be most in the eye, or the idea of which shall be most prevalent in the mind, &c. The mind is not absolutely indifferent whether it proceeds by this rule or no; but chooses it because it appears at that time a convenient and requisite expedient in order to fulfil the general purpose aforesaid. And so it is in the *third* and last step; it is determining to touch that individual spot which actually does prevail in the mind's view. The mind is not indifferent concerning this; but is influenced by a prevailing inducement and reason; which is, that this is a prosecution of the preceding determination, which appeared requisite, and was fixed before in the second step.

Accident will ever serve a man, without hindering him a moment in such a case. It will always be so among a number of objects in view; one will prevail in the eye, or in idea, beyond others. When we have our eyes open in the clear sunshine, many objects strike the eye at once, and innumerable images may be at once painted in it by the rays of light; but the attention of the mind is not equal to several of them at once; or if it be, it does not continue so for any time. And so it is with respect to the ideas of the mind in general; several ideas are not in equal strength in the mind's view and notice at once; or at least, do not remain so for any sensible continuance. There is nothing in the world more constantly varying, than the ideas of the mind: they do not remain precisely in the same state for the least perceivable space of time; as is evident by this: That all perceivable time is judged and perceived by the mind only by the succession or the successive changes of its own ideas. Therefore, while the views or perceptions of the mind remain precisely in the same state, there is no perceivable space or length of time, because no sensible succession at all.

As the acts of the will, in each step of the fore-mentioned procedure, do not come to pass without a particular cause, every act is owing to a prevailing inducement : so the accident, as I have called it, or that which happens in the unsearchable course of things, to which the mind yields itself, and by which it is guided, is not any thing that comes to pass without a cause; and the mind, in determining to be guided by it, is not determined by something that has no cause, any more than if it determined to be guided by a lot, or the casting of a die. For though the die's falling in such a manner be accidental to him that casts it, yet none will suppose that there is no cause why it falls as it does. The involuntary changes in the succession of our ideas, though the cause may not be observed, have as much a cause, as the changeable motions of the motes that float in the air, or the continual, infinitely various, successive changes of the unevennesses on the surface of the water.

There are two things especially, which are probably the occasions of confusion in the minds of them who insist upon it, that the will acts in a proper indifference, and without being moved by any inducement, in its determinations in such cases as have been mentioned.

1. They seem to mistake the point in question, or at least not to keep it distinctly in view. The question they dispute about, is, Whether the mind be indifferent about the *objects* presented, one of which is to be taken, touched, pointed to, &c., as two eggs, two cakes, which appear equally good. Whereas the question to be considered is, Whether the person be indifferent with respect to his own *actions;* whether he does not, on some consideration or other, prefer one act with respect to these objects before another. The mind in its determination and choice, in these cases, is not most immediately and directly conversant about the *objects presented;* but *the acts to be done* concerning these objects. The objects

may appear equal, and the mind may never properly make any choice between them: but the next act of the will being about the external actions to be performed, taking, touching, &c., these may not appear equal, and one action may properly be chosen before another. In each step of the mind's progress, the determination is not about the objects, unless indirectly and improperly, but about the actions, which it chooses for other reasons than any preference of the objects, and for reasons not taken at all from the object.

There is no necessity of supposing that the mind does ever at all properly choose one of the objects before another; either before it has taken, or afterwards. Indeed, the man chooses to *take* or *touch* one rather than another; but not because it chooses the *thing taken*, or *touched*, but from foreign considerations. The case may be so, that of two things offered, a man may, for certain reasons, choose and prefer the taking of that which he *undervalues*, and choose to neglect to take that which his mind *prefers*. In such a case, choosing the thing taken, and choosing to take, are diverse; and that they are in a case where the things presented are equal in the mind's esteem, and neither of them preferred. All that fact and experience make evident is, that the mind chooses one action rather than another; and therefore the arguments which they bring, in order to be to their purpose, ought to be to prove that the mind chooses the action in perfect indifference with respect to *that action;* and not to prove that the mind chooses the action in perfect indifference with respect to the *object;* which is very possible, and yet the will not act at all without prevalent inducement, and proper preponderation.

2. Another reason of confusion and difficulty in this matter seems to be, not distinguishing between a *general* indifference, or an indifference with respect to what is to be done in a more distant and general view of it, and a *particular* indifference, or an indifference with respect to the next immediate act, viewed with its par-

ticular and present circumstances.   A man may be perfectly indifferent with respect to his own *actions,* in the
former respect, and yet not in the latter.   Thus, in the
foregoing instance of touching one of the squares of a
chess-board; when it is first proposed that I should
touch one of them, I may be perfectly indifferent which
I touch; because as yet I view the matter remotely and
generally, being but in the first step of the mind's progress in the affair.   But yet, when I am actually come
to the last step, and the very next thing to be determined
is which is to be touched, having already determined that
I will touch that which happens to be most in my eye
or mind, and my mind being now fixed on a particular
one, the act of touching that, considered thus immediately, and in these particular present circumstances,
is not what my mind is absolutely indifferent about.

SECTION VII.

CONCERNING THE NOTION OF LIBERTY OF WILL, CONSISTING IN INDIFFERENCE.

WHAT has been said in the foregoing section has a
tendency, in some measure, to evince the absurdity of
the opinion of such as place liberty in indifference, or in
that equilibrium whereby the will is without all antecedent determination, or bias, and left hitherto free
from any prepossessing inclination to one side or the
other; that the determination of the will to either side
may be entirely from itself, and that it may be owing
only to its own power, and that sovereignty which it
has over itself, that it goes this way rather than that.*

* Dr Whitby, and some other Arminians, make a distinction of different kinds of freedom; one of God, and perfect spirits above; another of
persons in a state of trial.   The former, Dr Whitby allows to consist with
necessity; the latter he holds to be without necessity; and this latter he
supposes to be requisite to our being the subjects of praise or dispraise, rewards or punishments, precepts and prohibitions, promises and threats,
exhortations and dehortations, and a covenant treaty.   And to this freedom
he supposes *indifference* to be requisite.   In his discourse on the Five Points
pp. 299, 300, he says.—" It is freedom (speaking of a freedom not only from
co-action, but from necessity) requisite, as we conceive, to render us capable of trial or probation, and to render our actions worthy of praise or dispraise, and our persons of rewards or punishments."   And in next page,
speaking of the same matter, he says, " Excellent to this purpose are the
words of Mr Thorndike : *We say not that indifference is requisite to all
freedom, but to the freedom of man alone in this state of travail and profi-*

But inasmuch as this has been of such long standing, and has been so generally received, and so much insisted on by Pelagians, Jesuits, Socinians, Arminians, and others, it may deserve a more full consideration. And therefore I shall now proceed to a more particular and thorough inquiry into this notion.

Now, lest some should suppose that I do not understand those that place liberty in indifference, or should charge me with misrepresenting their opinion, I would signify, that I am sensible there are some, who, when they talk of the liberty of the will as consisting in indifference, express themselves as though they would not be understood of the indifference of the inclination or tendency of the will, but of, I know not what, indifference of the soul's power of willing; or that the will, with respect to its power or ability to choose, is indifferent, can go either way indifferently, either to the right hand or left, either act or forbear to act, one as well as the other. Though this seems to be a refining only of some particular writers, and newly invented, and which will by no means consist with the manner of expression used by the defenders of liberty of indifference in general. And I wish such refiners would thoroughly consider whether they distinctly know their own meaning, when they make a distinction between indifference of the soul as to its *power* or *ability* of willing or choosing, and the soul's indifference as to the preference or choice itself: and whether they do not deceive themselves in imagining that they have any distinct meaning at all. The indifference of the soul as to its ability or power to will, must be the same thing as the indifference of the state of the power or faculty of the will, or the indifference of the state which the soul itself, which has that power or faculty, hitherto remains in, as to the exercise of that power, in the choice it shall by and by make.

cience: *the ground of which is God's tender of a treaty and conditions of peace and reconcilement to fallen man, together with those precepts and prohibitions, those promises and threats, those exhortations and dehortations it is enforced with."*

But not to insist any longer on the abstruseness and inexplicableness of this distinction, let what will be supposed concerning the meaning of them that make use of it, thus much must at least be intended by Arminians when they talk of indifference as essential to liberty of will, if they intend any thing in any respect to their purpose; viz. that it is such an indifference as leaves the will not determined already; but free from actual possession, and vacant of predetermination, so far, that there may be room for the exercise of the *self-determining power* of the will; and that the will's freedom consists in, or depends upon, this vacancy and opportunity that is left for the will itself to be the determiner of the act that is to be the free act.

And here I would observe in the *first* place, that to make out this scheme of liberty, the indifference must be *perfect* and *absolute;* there must be a perfect freedom from all antecedent preponderation, or inclination. Because, if the will be already inclined, before it exerts its own sovereign power on itself, then its inclination is not wholly owing to itself: if when two opposites are proposed to the soul for its choice, the proposal does not find the soul wholly in a state of indifference, then it is not found in a state of liberty for mere self-determination. The least degree of an antecedent bias must be inconsistent with their notion of liberty. For so long as prior inclination possesses the will, and is not removed, it binds the will, so that it is utterly impossible that the will should act otherwise than agreeably to it. Surely the will cannot act or choose contrary to a remaining prevailing inclination of the will. To suppose otherwise would be the same thing as to suppose that the will is *inclined* contrary to its present prevailing *inclination,* or contrary to what it is *inclined* to. That which the will chooses and prefers, that, all things considered, it preponderates and inclines to. It is equally impossible for the will to choose contrary to its own remaining and present preponderating inclination, as it is to *prefer* contrary to its own present *preference,* or *choose* contrary to its own present *choice*. The will, therefore, so long as it is under the influence of an old preponderating inclination, is not at liberty for a new free act, or any act that shall now be an act of self-determination. The act which is a self-determined free act, must be an act which the will determines in the possession and use of such a liberty as consists in a freedom from every thing, which, if it were there, would make it impossible that the will at that time, should be otherwise than that way to which it tends.

If any one should say there is no need that the indifference should be perfect; but although a former inclination and preference still remains, yet, if it be not very strong and violent, possibly the strength of the will may oppose and overcome it: this is grossly absurd; for the strength of the will, let it be never so great, does not at all enable it to act one way, and the contrary way, both at the same time. It gives it no such sovereignty and command, as to cause itself to prefer and not to prefer at the same time, or to choose contrary to its own present choice.

Therefore, if there be the least degree of antecedent preponderation of the will, it must be perfectly abolished before the will can be at liberty to determine itself the contrary way. And if the will determines itself the same way, it was not a *free determination*, because the will is not wholly at liberty in so doing, its determination is not altogether *from itself*, but it was partly determined before, in its prior inclination; and all the freedom the will exercises in the case is in an increase of inclination, which it gives itself, over and above what it had by foregoing bias; so much is from itself, and so much is from perfect indifference. For though the will had a previous tendency that way, yet as to that additional degree of inclination, it had no tendency; therefore the previous tendency is of no consideration, with respect to the act wherein the will is free. So that it comes to the same thing which was said at first, that as to the act of the will, wherein the will is free, there must be *perfect indifference* or *equilibrium*.

To illustrate this: if we should suppose a sovereign self-moving power in a natural body, but that the body is in motion already, by an antecedent bias; for instance, gravitation towards the centre of the earth; and has one degree of motion already, by virtue of that previous tendency; but by its self-moving power it adds one degree more to its motion, and moves so much more swiftly towards the centre of the earth than it would do by its gravity only: it is evident, that all that is owing to a self-moving power in this case, is the additional degree of motion; and that the other degree of motion which it had from gravity, is of no consideration in the case, does not help the effect of the free self-moving power in the least; the effect is just the same as if the body had received from itself one degree of motion from a state of perfect rest. So, if we should suppose a self-moving power given to the scale of a balance, which has a weight of one degree beyond the opposite scale; and we ascribe to it an ability to add to itself another degree of force the same way, by its self-moving power; this is just the same thing as to ascribe to it a power to give itself one degree of preponderation from a perfect equilibrium; and so much power as the scale has to give itself an overbalance from a perfect equipoise, so much self-moving, self-preponderating power it has, and no more. So that its free power this way is always to be measured from perfect equilibrium.

I need say no more to prove, that if indifference be essential to liberty, it must be perfect indifference; and that so far as the will is destitute of this, so far it is destitute of that freedom by which it is its own master, and in a capacity of being its own determiner, without being at all passive, or subject to the power and sway of something else, in its motions and determinations.

Having observed these things, let us now try whether this notion of the liberty of the will consisting in indif-

ference and equilibrium, and the will's self-determination in such a state, be not absurd and inconsistent.

And here I would lay down this as an axiom of undoubted truth,—*that every free act is done in a state of
freedom, and not only after such a state.* If an act of
the will be an act wherein the soul is free, it must be
exerted in a *state of freedom*, and in the *time of freedom*.
It will not suffice, that the act immediately follows a
state of liberty; but liberty must yet continue, and co-
exist with the act; the soul remaining in possession of
liberty. Because that is the notion of a free act of the
soul, even an act wherein the soul *uses* or *exercises liberty*. But if the soul is not, in the very time of the
act, in the *possession* of liberty, it cannot at that time
be in the *use* of it.

Now, the question is, whether ever the soul of man
puts forth an act of will, while it yet remains in a
state of liberty, in that notion of a state of liberty, viz.
as implying a state of indifference; or whether the soul
ever exerts an act of choice or preference, while at that
very time the will is in a perfect equilibrium, not inclining one way more than another. The very putting
of the question is sufficient to show the absurdity of the
affirmative answer; for how ridiculous would it be for
any body to insist, that the soul chooses one thing before another, when at the very same instant it is perfectly indifferent with respect to each! This is the
same thing as to say, the soul prefers one thing to another, at the very same time that it has no preference.
Choice and preference can no more be in a state of indifference, than motion can be in a state of rest, or than the
preponderation of the scale of a balance can be in a state
of equilibrium. Motion may be the next moment after
rest; but cannot co-exist with it in *any*, even the *least*
part of it. So, choice may be immediately after a state
of indifference, but has no co-existence with it: even
the very beginning of it is not in a state of indifference.
And therefore, if this be liberty, no act of the will, in
any degree, is ever performed in a state of liberty, or in

the time of liberty. Volition and liberty are so far from agreeing together, and being essential one to another, that they are contrary one to another, and one excludes and destroys the other, as much as motion and rest, light and darkness, or life and death. So that the will acts not at all, does not so much as begin to act, in the time of such liberty : freedom is perfectly at an end, and has ceased to be, at the first moment of action ; and therefore liberty cannot reach the action, to affect or qualify it, or give it a denomination, or any part of it, any more than if it had ceased to be, twenty years before the action began. The moment that liberty ceases to be, it ceases to be a qualification of any thing. If light and darkness succeed one another instantaneously, light qualifies nothing after it is gone out, to make any thing lightsome or bright, any more at the first moment of perfect darkness, than months or years after it. Life denominates nothing *vital* at the first moment of perfect death. So freedom, if it consists in, or implies indifference, can denominate nothing free, at the first moment of preference or preponderation. Therefore it is manifest, that no liberty which the soul is possessed of, or ever uses, in any of its acts of volition, consists in indifference ; and that the opinion of such as suppose that indifference belongs to the very essence of liberty, is to the highest degree absurd and contradictory.

If any one should imagine that this manner of arguing is nothing but a trick and delusion ; and, to evade the reasoning, should say, that the thing wherein the will exercises its liberty, is not in the act of choice or preponderation itself, but in *determining* itself to a certain choice or preference ; that the act of the will wherein it is free, and uses its own sovereignty, consists in its *causing* or *determining* the *change* or *transition* from a state of indifference to a certain preference, or determining to give a certain turn to the balance, which has hitherto been even ; and that this act the will exerts in a state of liberty, or while the will yet remains in equilibrium, and perfect master of itself :—I say, if any one chooses to express his notion of liberty after this, or some such manner, let us see if he can make out his matters any better than before.

What is asserted is, that the will, while it yet remains in perfect equilibrium, without preference, determines to change itself from that state, and excite in itself a certain choice or preference. Now, let us see whether this does not come to the same absurdity we had before. If it be so, that the will, while it yet remains perfectly indifferent, determines to put itself out of that state, and give itself a certain preponderation; then I would inquire, whether the soul does not determine this of choice; or whether the will's coming to a determination to do so, be not the same thing as the soul's coming to a choice to do so. If the soul does not determine this of choice, or in the exercise of choice, then it does not determine it voluntarily; and if the soul does not determine it voluntarily, or of its own *will*, then in what sense does its *will* determine it? And if the will does not determine it, then how is the *liberty of the will* exercised in the determination? What sort of liberty is exercised by the soul in those determinations, wherein there is no exercise of choice, which are not voluntary, and wherein the will is not concerned? But if it be allowed that this determination is an act of choice, and it be insisted on, that the soul, while it yet remains in a state of perfect indifference, chooses to put itself out of that state, and to turn itself one way; then the soul is already come to a choice, and chooses that way. And so we have the very same absurdity which we had before. Here is the soul in a state of choice, and in a state of equilibrium, both at the same time: the soul already choosing one way, while it remains in a state of perfect indifference and has no choice of one way more than the other. And indeed this manner of talking, though it may a little hide the absurdity in the obscurity of expression, is more nonsensical, and increases the inconsistency. To say, the free act of the will, or the act which the will exerts in a state of freedom and indifference, does not

imply preference in it, but is what the will does in order
to causing or producing a preference, is as much as to
say, the soul chooses (for to will and to choose are the
same thing) without choice, and prefers without preference, in order to cause or produce the beginning of a
preference, or the first choice. And that is, that the
first choice is exerted without choice, in order to produce itself.

If any, to evade these things, should own, that a state
of liberty and a state of indifference are not the same,
and that the former may be without the latter; but
should say, that indifference is still *essential* to the freedom of an act of will, in some sort, namely, as it is
necessary to go immediately *before* it; it being essential
to the freedom of an act of will that it should directly and immediately *arise out* of a state of indifference:
still this will not help the cause of Arminian liberty, or
make it consistent with itself. For if the act springs
immediately out of a state of indifference, then it does
not arise from *antecedent* choice or preference. But if
the act arises directly out of a state of indifference, without any intervening choice to choose and determine it,
then the act not being determined by choice, is not determined by the will; the mind exercises no free choice
in the affair, and free choice and free will have no hand
in the determination of the act,—which is entirely inconsistent with their notion of the freedom of volition.

If any should suppose that these difficulties and absurdities may be avoided by saying, that the liberty of
the mind consists in a power to *suspend* the act of the
will, and so to keep it in a state of *indifference* until
there has been opportunity for consideration ; and so
shall say, that however indifference is not essential to
liberty in such a manner that the mind must make its
choice in a state of indifference, which is an inconsistency, or that the act of will must spring immediately
out of indifference, yet indifference may be essential to
the liberty of acts of the will in this respect, viz. That
liberty consists in a power of the mind to forbear or sus-

pend the act of volition, and keep the mind in a state of indifference for the present, until there has been opportunity for proper deliberation: I say, if any one imagines that this helps the matter, it is a great mistake; it reconciles no inconsistency, and relieves no difficulty, which the affair is attended with. For here the following things must be observed:

1. That this *suspending* of volition, if there be properly any such thing, is itself an act of volition. If the mind determines to suspend its act, it determines it voluntarily; it chooses, on some consideration, to suspend it. And this choice or determination is an act of the will: and indeed it is supposed to be so in the very hypothesis; for it is supposed that the liberty *of the will* consists in its power to do this, and that its doing it is the very thing wherein *the will exercises its liberty.* But how can the will exercise liberty in it, if it be not an act of the will? The liberty of the will is not exercised in any thing but what the will does.

2. This determining to suspend acting is not only an act of the will, but it is supposed to be the only free act of the will; because it is said, that *this is the thing wherein the liberty of the will consists.* Now, if this be so, then this is all the act of will that we have to consider in this controversy, about the liberty of will, and in our inquiries, wherein the liberty of man consists. And now the fore-mentioned difficulties remain: the former question returns upon us, viz. Wherein consists the freedom of the will *in those acts* wherein it is free? And if this act of determining a suspension be the only act in which the will is free, then wherein consists the will's freedom with respect to this act of suspension? And how is indifference essential to this act? The answer must be, according to what is supposed in the evasion under consideration, That the liberty of the will, in this act of suspension, consists in a power to suspend even this act, until there has been opportunity for thorough deliberation. But this will be to plunge directly into the grossest nonsense: for it is the act of sus-

pension itself that we are speaking of; and there is no
room for a space of deliberation and suspension in order
to determine whether we will suspend or no. For that
supposes that even suspension itself may be deferred;
which is absurd : for the very deferring the determination of suspension, to consider whether we will suspend
or no, will be actually suspending. For during the space
of suspension, to consider whether to suspend, the act is
ipso facto suspended. There is no medium between suspending to act, and immediately acting; and therefore
no possibility of avoiding either the one or the other
one moment.

And besides, this is attended with ridiculous absurdity
another way: for now it is come to that, that liberty
consists wholly in the mind's having power to suspend
its determination whether to suspend or no; that there
may be time for consideration, whether it be best to suspend. And if liberty consists in this only, then this is
the liberty under consideration; we have to inquire
now, how liberty with respect to this act of suspending
a determination of suspension, consists in indifference,
or how indifference is essential to it. The answer, according to the hypothesis we are upon, must be, that it
consists in a power of suspending even this last-mentioned act, to have time to consider whether to suspend
that. And then the same difficulties and inquiries return
over again with respect to that; and so on for ever,
—which, if it would show any thing, would show only
that there is no such thing as a free act. It drives the
exercise of freedom back *in infinitum;* and that is to
drive it out of the world.

And besides all this, there is a delusion, and a latent
gross contradiction, in the affair another way; inasmuch
as, in explaining how, or in what respect, the will is
free with regard to a particular act of volition, it is said,
that its liberty consists in a power to determine to suspend that act, which places liberty not in that act of
volition which the inquiry is about, but altogether in
another antecedent act,—which contradicts the thing

F

supposed in both the question and answer. The question is, wherein consists the mind's liberty in any particular act of volition? And the answer, in pretending to show wherein lies the mind's liberty in that act, in effect says, it does not lie in that act at all, but in another, viz. a volition to suspend that act. And therefore the answer is both contradictory, and altogether impertinent and beside the purpose. For it does not show wherein the liberty of the will consists in the act in question; instead of that, it supposes it does not consist in that act at all, but in another distinct from it, even a volition to suspend that act, and take time to consider of it. And no account is pretended to be given wherein the mind is free with respect to that act, wherein this answer supposes the liberty of the mind indeed consists, viz. the act of suspension, or of determining the suspension.

On the whole, it is exceeding manifest, that the liberty of the mind does not consist in indifference, and that indifference is not essential or necessary to it, or at all belonging to it, as the Arminians suppose; that opinion being full of nothing but absurdity and self-contradiction.

SECTION VIII.

CONCERNING THE SUPPOSED LIBERTY OF THE WILL, AS OPPOSITE TO ALL NECESSITY.

It is a thing chiefly insisted on by Arminians, in this controversy, as a thing most important and essential in human liberty, that volitions, or the acts of the will, are *contingent* events; understanding contingence as opposite, not only to constraint, but to all necessity. Therefore I would particularly consider this matter. And,

1. I would inquire, whether there is, or can be, any such thing as a volition which is contingent in such a sense, as not only to come to pass without any necessity of constraint or co-action, but also without a *necessity of consequence*, or an infallible connexion with anything foregoing.

2. Whether, if it were so, this would at all help the cause of liberty.

I would consider whether volition is a thing that ever does, or can, come to pass, in this manner, contingently.

And here it must be remembered, that it has been already shown, that nothing can ever come to pass without a cause, or reason why it exists in this manner rather than another; and the evidence of this has been particularly applied to the acts of the will. Now, if this be so, it will demonstrably follow, that the acts of the will are never contingent, or without necessity, in the sense spoken of; inasmuch as those things which have a cause or reason of their existence, must be connected with their cause. This appears by the following considerations:—

1. For an event to have a cause and ground of its existence, and yet not to be connected with its cause, is an inconsistency. For if the event be not connected with the cause, it is not dependent on the cause; its existence is, as it were, loose from its influence, and may attend it, or may not; it being a mere contingence, whether it follows or attends the influence of the cause or not: and that is the same thing as not to be dependent on it. And to say the event is not dependent on its cause, is absurd: it is the same thing as to say, it is not its cause, nor the event the effect of it; for dependence on the influence of a cause is the very notion of an effect. If there be no such relation between one thing and another, consisting in the connexion and dependence of one thing on the influence of another, then it is certain there is no such relation between them as is signified by the terms *cause* and *effect*. So far as an event is dependent on a cause, and connected with it, so much causality is there in the case, and no more. The cause does, or brings to pass, no more in any event, than is dependent on it. If we say, the connexion and dependence is not total, but partial, and that the effect, though it has some connexion and dependence, yet is not entirely dependent on it; that is the same thing as to say, that not all that is in the event is an effect of that cause, but that only part of it arises from thence, and part some other way.

2. If there are some events which are not necessarily connected with their causes, then it will follow, that there are some things which come to pass without any cause, contrary to the supposition. For if there be any event which was not necessarily connected with the influence of the cause under such circumstances, then it was contingent whether it would attend or follow the influence of the cause, or no; it might have followed and it might not, when the cause was the same, its influence the same, and under the same circumstances. And if so, why did it follow, rather than not follow? There is no cause or reason of this. Therefore, here is something without any cause or reason why it is, viz. the following of the effect on the influence of the cause, with which it was not necessarily connected. If there be a necessary connexion of the effect on any thing antecedent, then we may suppose that sometimes the event will follow the cause, and sometimes not, when the cause is the same, and in every respect in the same state and circumstances. And what can be the cause and reason of this strange phenomenon, even this diversity, that in one instance the effect should follow, in another not? It is evident by the supposition, that this is wholly without any cause or ground. Here is something in the present manner of the existence of things, and state of the world, that is absolutely without a cause,—which is contrary to the supposition, and contrary to what has been before demonstrated.

3. To suppose there are some events which have a cause and ground of their existence, that yet are not necessarily connected with their cause, is to suppose that they have a cause which is not their cause. Thus, if the effect be not necessarily connected with the cause, with its influence, and influential circumstances; then, as I observed before, it is a thing possible and supposable, that the cause may sometimes exert the same influence, under the same circumstances, and yet the effect not follow. And if this actually happens in any instance, this instance is a proof, in fact, that the influ-

ence of the cause is not sufficient to produce the effect. For if it had been sufficient, it would have done it. And yet, by the supposition, in another instance, the same cause, with perfectly the same influence, and when all circumstances which have any influence are the same, it *was followed* with the effect,—by which it is manifest, that the effect in this last instance was not owing to the influence of the cause, but must come to pass some other way. For it was proved before, that the influence of the cause was not sufficient to produce the effect. And if it was not sufficient to produce it, then the production of it could not be owing to that influence, but must be owing to something else, or owing to nothing. And if the effect be not owing to the influence of the cause, then it is not the cause,—which brings us to the contradiction of a cause, and no cause; that which is the ground and reason of the existence of a thing, and at the same time is not the ground and reason of its existence, nor is sufficient to be so.

If the matter be not already so plain as to render any further reasoning upon it impertinent, I would say, that that which seems to be the cause in the supposed case, can be no cause; its power and influence having, on a full trial, proved insufficient to produce such an effect: and if it be not sufficient to produce it, then it does not produce it. To say otherwise, is to say, there is power to do that which there is not power to do. If there be in a cause sufficient power exerted, and in circumstances sufficient to produce an effect, and so the effect be actually produced at *one time;* these things all concurring, will produce the effect at *all times.* And so we may turn it the other way; that which proves not sufficient at one time, cannot be sufficient at another, with precisely the same influential circumstances. And therefore if the effect follows, it is not owing to that cause: unless the different time be a circumstance which has influence; but that is contrary to the supposition; for it is supposed that all circumstances that have influence are the same. And besides, this would be to suppose the time to be the cause; which is contrary to the supposition of other things being the cause. But if merely diversity of time has no influence, then it is evident that it is as much of an absurdity to say, the cause was sufficient to produce the effect at one time, and not at another; as to say, that it is sufficient to produce the effect at a certain time, and yet not sufficient to produce the same effect at the same time.

On the whole, it is clearly manifest, that every effect has a necessary connexion with its cause, or with that which is the true ground and reason of its existence. And therefore, if there be no event without a cause, as was proved before, then no event whatsoever is contingent in the manner that Arminians suppose the free acts of the will to be contingent.

SECTION IX.

OF THE CONNEXION OF THE ACTS OF THE WILL WITH THE DICTATES OF THE UNDERSTANDING.

IT is manifest, that the acts of the will are none of them contingent in such a sense as to be without all necessity, or so as not to be necessary with a necessity of consequence and connexion; because every act of the will is some way connected with the understanding, and is as the greatest apparent good is, in the manner which has already been explained; namely, that the soul always wills or chooses that which, in the present view of the mind, considered in the whole of that view, and all that belongs to it, appears most agreeable. Because, as was observed before, nothing is more evident than that, when men act voluntarily, and do what they please, then they do what appears most agreeable to them; and to say otherwise, would be as much as to affirm, that men do not choose what appears to suit them best, or what seems most pleasing to them: or that they do not choose what they prefer,—which brings the matter to a contradiction.

And it is evident in itself, that the acts of the will

have some connexion with the dictates or views of the understanding; so this is allowed by some of the chief of the Arminian writers, particularly by Dr Whitby and Dr Samuel Clarke. Dr Turnbull, though a great enemy to the doctrine of necessity, allows the same thing. In his " Christian Philosophy," (p. 196) he with much approbation cites another philosopher, as of the same mind, in these words: " No man (says an excellent philosopher) sets himself about anything but upon some view or other, which serves him for a reason for what he does: and whatsoever faculties he employs, the understanding, with such light as it has, well or ill formed, constantly leads; and by that light, true or false, all her operative powers are directed. The will itself, how absolute and incontrollable soever it may be thought, never fails in its obedience to the dictates of the understanding. Temples have their sacred images; and we see what influence they have always had over a great part of mankind; but in truth the ideas and images in men's minds are the invisible powers that constantly govern them; and to these they all pay universally a ready submission.

But whether this be in a just consistence with themselves, and their own notions of liberty, I desire may now be impartially considered.

Dr Whitby plainly supposes, that the acts and determinations of the will always follow the understanding's apprehension or view of the greatest good to be obtained, or evil to be avoided; or, in other words, that the determinations of the will constantly and infallibly follow these two things in the understanding: 1. The *degree of good* to be obtained and evil to be avoided, proposed to the understanding, and apprehended, viewed, and taken notice of by it. 2. The *degree of the understanding's view*, notice, or apprehension of that good or evil; which is increased by attention and consideration. That this is an opinion he is exceeding peremptory in, (as he is in every opinion which he maintains in his controversy with the Calvinists) with disdain of the contrary opinion, as absurd and self-contradictory, will appear by the following words of his, in his discourse on the Five Points.*

"Now it is certain, that what naturally makes the understanding to perceive, is evidence proposed and apprehended, considered or adverted to: for nothing else can be requisite to make us come to the knowledge of the truth. Again, what makes the will choose, is something approved by the understanding; and consequently appearing to the soul as good. And whatsoever it refuseth, is something represented by the understanding, and so appearing to the will as evil. Whence all that God requires of us is and can be only this—to refuse the evil, and choose the good. Wherefore, to say that evidence proposed, apprehended, and considered, is not sufficient to make the understanding approve; or that the greatest good proposed, the greatest evil threatened, when equally believed and reflected on, is not sufficient to engage the will to choose the good and refuse the evil, is in effect to say, *that which alone doth move the will to choose or to refuse,* is not sufficient to engage us so to do,—which being contradictory to itself, must of necessity be false. Be it then so, that we naturally have an aversion to the truths proposed to us in the Gospel; that only can make us indisposed to attend to them, but cannot hinder our conviction, when we do apprehend them, and attend to them. Be it, that there is in us also a renitency to the good we are to choose; that only can indispose us to believe it is, and to approve it as our chiefest good. Be it, that we are prone to the evil that we should decline; that only can render it the more difficult for us to believe it is the worst of evils. But yet, what we do really believe to be our chiefest good, will still be chosen; and what we apprehend to be the worst of evils, will, whilst we do continue under that conviction, be refused by us. It therefore can be only requisite, in order to these ends, that the good Spirit should so illuminate our understandings, that we, attending to, and consider-

* Second edit. pp. 211—213.

ing what lies before us, should apprehend, and be convinced of our duty; and that the blessings of the Gospel should be so propounded to us, as that we may discern them to be our chiefest good; and the miseries it threateneth, so as we may be convinced that they are the worst of evils; that we may choose the one, and refuse the other."

Here let it be observed, how plainly and peremptorily it is asserted, that the greatest good proposed, and the greatest evil threatened, when equally believed and reflected on, is sufficient to engage the will to choose the good, and refuse the evil, and is that alone which doth move the will to choose or to refuse; and that it is contradictory to itself, to suppose otherwise; and, therefore, must of necessity be false; and then what we do really believe to be our chiefest good will still be chosen; and what we apprehend to be the worst of evils, will, whilst we continue under that conviction, be refused by us. Nothing could have been said more to the purpose, fully to signify and declare, that the determinations of the will must evermore follow the illumination, conviction, and notice of the understanding, with regard to the greatest good and evil proposed, reckoning both the degree of good and evil understood, and the degree of understanding, notice, and conviction, of that proposed good and evil; and that it is thus necessarily, and can be otherwise in no instance; because it is asserted, that it implies a contradiction, to suppose it ever to be otherwise.

I am sensible the Doctor's aim in these assertions is against the Calvinists; to show, in opposition to them, that there is no need of any physical operation of the Spirit of God on the will, to change and determine that to a good choice, but that God's operation and assistance is only moral, suggesting ideas to the understanding; which he supposes to be enough, if those ideas are attended to, infallibly to obtain the end. But whatever his design was, nothing can more directly and fully prove that every determination of the will in choosing and refusing, is *necessary*, directly contrary to his own

notion of the liberty of the will. For if the determination of the will evermore in this manner follows the
light, conviction, and view of the understanding, concerning the greatest good and evil, and this be that alone
which moves the will, and it be a contradiction to suppose otherwise; then it is *necessarily* so,—the will necessarily follows this light or view of the understanding
not only in some of its acts, but in every act of choosing
and refusing. So that the will does not determine itself
in any one of its own acts; but all its acts, every act of
choice and refusal, depends on, and is necessarily connected with, some antecedent cause, which cause is not
the will itself, nor any act of its own, nor any thing
pertaining to that faculty, but something belonging to
another faculty, whose acts go before the will, in all its
acts, and govern and determine them every one.

Here, if it should be replied, that although it be true,
that, according to the Doctor, the final determination of
the will always depends upon, and is infallibly connected
with, the understanding's conviction and notice of the
greatest good; yet the acts of the will are not necessary,
because that conviction and notice of the understanding
is first dependent on a preceding act of the will, in determining to attend to, and take notice of the evidence
exhibited; by which means the mind obtains that degree of conviction, which is sufficient and effectual to
determine the consequent and ultimate choice of the
will; and that the will with regard to that preceding
act, whereby it determines whether to attend or no, is
not necessary; and that in this the liberty of the will
consists, that when God holds forth sufficient objective
light, the will is at liberty whether to command the attention of the mind to it.

Nothing can be more weak and inconsiderate than
such a reply as this. For that preceding act of the will,
in determining to attend and consider, still is an act of the
will, (it is so to be sure, if the liberty of the will consists in it, as is supposed,) and if it be an act of the will,
it is an act of choice or refusal. And therefore, if what

the Doctor asserts be true, it is determined by some antecedent light in the understanding, concerning the greatest apparent good or evil. For he asserts, it is that light which alone doth move the will to choose or refuse. And therefore the will must be moved by that in choosing to attend to the objective light offered, in order to another consequent act of choice: so that this act is no less necessary than the other. And if we suppose another act of the will, still preceding both these mentioned, to determine both, still that also must be an act of the will, and an act of choice; and so must, by the same principles, be infallibly determined by some certain degree of light in the understanding concerning the greatest good. And let us suppose as many acts of the will, one preceding another, as we please, yet they are every one of them necessarily determined by a certain degree of light in the understanding, concerning the greatest and most eligible good in that case; and so, not one of them free, according to Dr Whitby's notion of freedom. And if it be said, the reason, why men do not attend to light held forth, is because of ill habits contracted by evil acts committed before, whereby their minds are indisposed to attend to, and consider of the truth held forth to them by God; the difficulty is not at all avoided: still the question returns, What determined the will in those preceding evil acts? It must, by Dr Whitby's principles, still be the view of the understanding concerning the greatest good and evil. If this view of the understanding be that alone which doth move the will to choose or refuse, as the Doctor asserts, then every act of choice or refusal, from a man's first existence, is moved and determined by this view, and this view of the understanding exciting and governing the act, must be before the act: and therefore the will is necessarily determined in every one of its acts, from a man's first existence, by a cause beside the will, and a cause that does not proceed from, or depend on, any act of the will at all,—which at once utterly abolishes the Doctor's whole scheme of liberty of will; and he, at one stroke, has cut the sinews of all his arguments from the goodness, righteousness, faithfulness, and sincerity of God, in his commands, promises, threatenings, calls, invitations, expostulations; which he makes use of, under the heads of reprobation, election, universal redemption, sufficient and effectual grace, and the freedom of the will of man; and has enervated and made vain all those exclamations against the doctrine of the Calvinists, as charging God with manifest unrighteousness, unfaithfulnes, hypocrisy, fallaciousness, and cruelty; which he has over, and over, and over again, numberless times in his book.

Dr Samuel Clarke, in his " Demonstration of the Being and Attributes of God,"* to evade the argument to prove the necessity of volition, from its necessary connexion with the last dictate of the understanding, supposes the latter not to be diverse from the act of the will itself. But if it be so, it will not alter the case as to the evidence of the necessity of the act of the will. If the dictate of the understanding be the very same with the determination of the will or choice, as Dr Clarke supposes, then this determination is no *fruit* or *effect of choice:* and if so, no liberty of choice has any hand in it: as to volition or choice, it is necessary, that is, choice cannot prevent it. If the last dictate of the understanding be the same with the determination of volition itself, then the existence of that determination must be necessary as to volition; inasmuch as volition can have no opportunity to determine whether it shall exist or no, it having existence already before volition has opportunity to determine any thing. It is itself the very rise and existence of volition. But a thing, after it exists, has no opportunity to determine as to its own existence; it is too late for that.

If liberty consists in that which Arminians suppose, viz. in the will's determining its own acts, having free opportunity, and being without all necessity; this is the same as to say, that liberty consists in the soul's having power and opportunity to have what determinations of

* Sixth edit. p. 93.

the will it pleases or chooses. And if the determinations of the will, and the last dictates of the understanding, be the same thing, then liberty consists in the mind's having power to have what dictates of the understanding it pleases, having opportunity to choose its own dictates of understanding. But this is absurd: for it is to make the determination of choice prior to the dictate of the understanding, and the ground of it, which cannot consist with the dictate of understanding's being the determination of choice itself.

Here is no way to do in this case, but only to recur to the old absurdity of one determination before another, and the cause of it; and another before that, determining that; and so on *in infinitum.* If the last dictate of the understanding be the determination of the will itself, and the soul be free with regard to that dictate, in the Arminian notion of freedom; then the soul, before that dictate of its understanding exists, voluntarily and according to its own choice determines, in every case, what that dictate of the understanding shall be; otherwise, that dictate, as to the will, is necessary, and the acts determined by it must also be necessary. So that here is a determination of the mind prior to that dictate of the understanding; an act of choice going before it, choosing and determining what that dictate of the understanding shall be: and this preceding act of choice, being a free act of will, must also be the same with another last dictate of the understanding: and if the mind also be free in that dictate of understanding, that must be determined still by another; and so on for ever.

Besides, if the dictate of the understanding, and determination of the will, be the same, this confounds the understanding and will, and makes them the same. Whether they be the same or no, I will not now dispute; but only would observe, that if it be so, and the Arminian notion of liberty consists in a self-determining power in the understanding, free of all necessity; being independent, undetermined by any thing prior to its own acts and determinations; and the more the understanding is thus independent, and sovereign over its own determinations, the more free. By this therefore the freedom of the soul, as a moral agent, must consist in the independence of the understanding on any evidence or appearance of things, or any thing whatsoever, that stands forth to the view of the mind, prior to the understanding's determination. And what a sort of liberty is this! consisting in an ability, freedom, and easiness of judging, either according to evidence, or against it; having a sovereign command over itself at all times, to judge, either agreeably or disagreeably to what is plainly exhibited to its own view. Certainly, it is no liberty that renders persons the proper subjects of persuasive reasoning, arguments, expostulations, and such like moral means and inducements,—the use of which with mankind is a main argument of the Arminians, to defend their notion of liberty without all necessity; for according to this, the more free men are, the less they are under the government of such means, less subject to the power of evidence and reason, and more independent on their influence in their determinations.

And whether the understanding and will are the same or no, as Dr Clarke seems to suppose, yet, in order to maintain the Arminian notion of liberty without necessity, the free will is not determined by the understanding, nor necessarily connected with the understanding; and the further from such connexion, the greater the freedom. And when the liberty is full and complete, the determinations of the will have no connexion at all with the dictates of the understanding. And if so, in vain are all the applications to the understanding, in order to induce to any free virtuous act; and so in vain are all instructions, counsels, invitations, expostulations, and all arguments and persuasives whatsoever; for these are but applications to the understanding, and a clear and lively exhibition of the objects of choice to the mind's view. But if, after all, the will must be self-determined, and independent on the understanding, to

what purpose are things thus represented to the understanding, in order to determine the choice?

SECTION X.

VOLITION NECESSARILY CONNECTED WITH THE INFLUENCE OF MOTIVES:
WITH PARTICULAR OBSERVATIONS ON THE GREAT INCONSISTENCE OF
MR CHUBB'S ASSERTIONS AND REASONINGS ABOUT THE FREEDOM OF
THE WILL.

THAT every act of the will has some cause, and consequently (by what has been already proved) has a necessary connexion with its cause, and so is necessary by a
necessity of connexion and consequence, is evident by
this, that every act of the will whatsoever is excited by
some motive: which is manifest, because, if the will or
mind, in willing and choosing after the manner that it
does, is excited so to do by no motive or inducement,
then it has no end which it proposes to itself, or pursues
in so doing; it aims at nothing, and seeks nothing.
And if it seeks nothing, then it does not go after any
thing, or exert any inclination or preference towards
any thing,—which brings the matter to a contradiction; because, for the mind to will something, and for it
to go after something by an act of preference and inclination, are the same thing.

But if every act of the will is excited by a motive,
then that motive is the cause of the act of the will. If
the acts of the will are excited by motives, then motives
are the causes of their being excited; or, which is the
same thing, the cause of their being put forth into act and
existence. And if so, the existence of the acts of the will
is properly the effect of their motives. Motives do nothing as motives or inducements, but by their influence;
and so much as is done by their influence is the effect
of them. For that is the notion of an effect, something
that is brought to pass by the influence of another thing.

And if volitions are properly the effects of their motives, then they are necessarily connected with their
motives; every effort and event being, as was proved
before, necessarily connected with that which is the pro-

per ground and reason of its existence. Thus it is manifest that volition is necessary, and is not from any self-
determining power in the will; the volition, which is
caused by previous motive and inducement, is not caused
by the will exercising a sovereign power over itself, to
determine, cause, and excite volitions in itself. This is
not consistent with the will's acting in a state of indifference and equilibrium to determine itself to a preference; for the way in which motives operate, is by biassing the will, and giving it a certain inclination or preponderation one way.

Here it may be proper to observe, that Mr Chubb, in
his Collection of Tracts on various subjects, has advanced
a scheme of liberty which is greatly divided against itself, and thoroughly subversive of itself; and that many
ways.

1. He is abundant in asserting, that the will, in all its
acts, is influenced by motive and excitement; and that
this is the previous ground and reason of all its acts, and
that it is never otherwise in any instance. He says, p.
262: "No action can take place without some motive to
excite it." And in p. 263: "Volition cannot take place
without some previous reason or motive to induce it."
And in p. 310: "Action would not take place without
some reason or motive to induce it; it being absurd to
suppose, that the active faculty would be exerted without some *previous* reason to dispose the mind to action."
So also p. 257. And he speaks of these things, as what
we may be absolutely certain of, and which are the
foundation, the only foundation we have, of a certainty
of the moral perfections of God. Pages 252—255, 261
—264.

And yet, at the same time, by his scheme the influence of motives upon us, to excite to action, and to be
actually a ground of volition, is *consequent* on the volition or choice of the mind. For he very greatly insists
upon it that in all free actions, before the mind is the
subject of those volitions which motives excite, it chooses
to be so. It chooses, whether it will comply with the

motive which presents itself in view, or not; and when various motives are presented, it chooses which it will yield to, and which it will reject. So p. 256: "Every man has power to act, or to refrain from acting, agreeably with, or contrary to, any motive that presents." P. 257: "Every man is at liberty to act, or refrain from acting, agreeably with, or contrary to, what each of these motives, considered singly, would excite him to.—Man has power, and is as much at liberty, to reject the motive that does prevail, as he has power, and is at liberty, to reject those motives that do not." And so pp. 310, 311: "In order to constitute a moral agent, it is necessary that he should have power to act, or to refrain from acting, upon such moral motives as he pleases." And to the like purpose in many other places. According to these things, the will acts first, and chooses or refuses to comply with the motive that is presented, before it falls under its prevailing influence: and it is first determined by the mind's pleasure or choice, what motives it will be induced by, before it is induced by them.

Now, how can these things hang together? How can the mind first act, and by its act of *volition* and *choice* determine what motives shall be the ground and reason of its *volition* and *choice?* For this supposes the choice is already made before the motive has its effect; and that the volition is already exerted before the motive prevails, so as actually to be the ground of the volition; and makes the prevailing of the motive the consequence of the volition, which yet it is the ground of. If the mind has already chosen to comply with a motive, and to yield to its excitement, it does not need to yield to it after this: for the thing is effected already that the motive would excite to, and the will is beforehand with the excitement; and the excitement comes in too late, and is needless and in vain afterwards. If the mind has already chosen to yield to a motive which *invites* to a thing, that implies, and in fact is, a choosing the thing *invited to;* and the very act of choice is before the influence of the motive which induces, and is the ground

G

of the choice: the son is beforehand with the father that begets him; the choice is supposed to be the ground of that influence of the motive, which very influence is supposed to be the ground of the choice. And so, *vice versâ*, the choice is supposed to be the consequence of the influence of the motive, which influence of the motive is the consequence of that very choice.

And besides, if the will acts first towards the motive before it falls under its influence, and the prevailing of the motive upon it to induce it to act and choose, be the fruit and consequence of its act and choice, then how is the motive " a *previous* ground and reason of the act and choice," so that, " in the nature of the things, volition cannot take place without some *previous* reason and motive to induce it;" and that this act is consequent upon, and follows the motive?—which things Mr Chubb often asserts, as of certain and undoubted truth. So that the very same motive is both *previous* and *consequent*, both before and after, both the ground and fruit of the very same thing!

II. Agreeable to the forementioned inconsistent notion of the will's first acting towards the motive, choosing whether it will comply with it, in order to its becoming a ground of the will's acting, before any act of volition can take place, Mr Chubb frequently calls motives and excitements to the action of the will, "the passive ground or reason of that action,"—which is a remarkable phrase, than which I presume there is none more unintelligible, and void of distinct and consistent meaning, in all the writings of Duns Scotus or Thomas Aquinas. When he represents the motive to action or volition as passive, he must mean—passive in that affair, or passive with respect to that action, which he speaks of; otherwise it is nothing to his purpose, or relating to the design of his argument: he must mean, (if that be called a meaning,) that the motive to volition is first acted *upon* or *towards* by the volition choosing to yield to it, making it a ground of action, or determining to fetch its influence from thence; and so to make it a previous ground of its

own excitation and existence,—which is the same absurdity, as if one should say, that the soul of man, or
any other thing, should, previous to its existing, choose
what cause it would come into existence by, and should
act upon its cause to fetch influence from thence to bring
it into being; and so its cause should be a passive ground
of its existence!

Mr Chubb does very plainly suppose motive or excitement to be the *ground of the being* of volition.¹ He
speaks of it as the ground or reason of the EXERTION of
an act of the will, pp. 391, 392, and expressly says, that
volition cannot *take place* without some previous ground
or motive to induce it, p. 363. And he speaks of the act
as "*from* the motive," and "*from the influence* of the
motive," p. 352; and from the influence that the motive
has on the man for the *production* of an action, p. 317.
Certainly there is no need of multiplying words about
this; it is easily judged, whether motive can be the
ground of volition's being exerted and taking place, so
that the very production of it is from the influence of
the motive, and yet the motive, before it becomes the
ground of the volition, is passive, or acted upon by the
volition.   But this I will say, that a man who insists so
much on clearness of meaning in others, and is so much
in blaming their confusion and inconsistence, ought, if
he was able, to have explained his meaning in this phrase
of *passive ground of action*, so as to show it not to be
confused and inconsistent.

If any should suppose that Mr Chubb, when he speaks
of motive as a *passive ground of action*, does not mean passive with regard to that volition which it is the ground of,
but some other antecedent volition, (though his purpose,
and argument, and whole discourse, will by no means allow of such a supposition,) yet it would not help the matter in the least. For, (1.) If we suppose there be an act of
volition or choice, by which the soul chooses to yield to
the invitation of a motive to another volition, by which
the soul chooses something else; both these supposed volitions are in effect the very same. A volition, or choosing
to yield to the force of a motive inviting to choose some-

thing, comes to just the same thing as choosing the thing
which the motive invites to, as I observed before. So
that here can be no room to help the matter, by a distinction of two volitions. (2.) If the motive be passive
with respect, not to the same volition that the motive
excites to, but one truly distinct and prior; yet, by
Mr Chubb, that prior volition cannot take place, without a motive or excitement, as a *previous ground* of its
existence. For he insists, that it is absurd to suppose
any volition should take place without some previous
motive to induce it. So that at last it comes to just the
same absurdity; for if *every* volition must have a previous motive, then the very *first* in the whole series must
be excited by a previous motive; and yet the motive to
that first volition is passive; but cannot be passive with
regard to another antecedent volition, because, by the
supposition, it is the very first: therefore, if it be passive
with respect to any volition, it must be so with regard
to that very volition that it is the ground of, and that is
excited by it.

III. Though Mr Chubb asserts, as above, that every
volition has some motive, and that in the nature of the
thing, no volition can take place without some motive
to induce it; yet he asserts, that volition does not always
follow the strongest motive; or, in other words, is not
governed by any superior strength of the motive that is
followed, beyond motives to the contrary, previous to
the volition itself. His own words, p. 258, are as follow:
" Though with regard to physical causes, that which is
strongest always prevails, yet it is otherwise with regard
to moral causes. Of these, sometimes the stronger, sometimes the weaker, prevails. And the ground of this difference is evident, namely, that what we call moral
causes, strictly speaking, are no causes at all, but barely
passive reasons of, or excitements to, the action, or to
the refraining from acting: which excitements we have
power, or are at liberty, to comply with or reject, as I
have showed above." And so, throughout the para-
graph, he, in a variety of phrases, insists, that the will
is not always determined by the strongest motive, unless

by strongest we preposterously mean actually prevailing
in the event; which is not in the motive, but in the will;
but that the will is not always determined by the motive,
which is strongest, by any strength previous to the volition itself. And he elsewhere does abundantly assert,
that the will is determined by no superior strength or
advantage that motives have from any constitution or
state of things, or any circumstances whatsoever, previous to the actual determination of the will. And indeed his whole discourse on human liberty implies it,
his whole scheme is founded upon it.

But these things cannot stand together.—There is such
a thing as a diversity of strength in motives to choice,
previous to the choice itself. Mr Chubb himself supposes, that they do previously invite, induce, excite, and
dispose the mind to action. This implies that they have
something in themselves that is *inviting*, some tendency
to *induce* and *dispose* to volition, previous to volition itself. And if they have in themselves this nature and
tendency, doubtless they have in it certain limited degrees, which are capable of diversity; and some have it
in greater degrees, others in less; and they that have
most of this tendency, considered with all their nature
and circumstances, previous to volition, they are the
strongest motives; and those that have least are the
weakest motives.

Now, if volition sometimes does not follow the motive
which is strongest, or has most previous tendency or advantage, all things considered, to induce or excite it, but
follows the weakest, or that which, as it stands previously
in the mind's view, has least tendency to induce it; herein
the will apparently acts wholly without motive, without
any previous reason to dispose the mind to it, contrary
to what the same author supposes. The act, wherein the
will must proceed without a previous motive to induce
it, is the act of preferring the weakest motive. For how
absurd is it to say, the mind sees previous reason in the
motive to prefer that motive before the other; and at the
same time to suppose, that there is nothing in the mo-

tive, in its nature, state, or any circumstance of it whatsoever, as it stands in the previous view of the mind,
that gives it any preference; but, on the contrary, the
other motive that stands in competition with it, in all
these respects, has most belonging to it that is inviting
and moving, and has most of a tendency to choice and
preference! This is certainly as much as to say, there
is previous ground and reason in the motive for the act
of preference, and yet no previous reason for it. By the
supposition, as to all that is in the two rival motives,
which tends to preference, previous to the act of preference, it is not in that which is preferred, but wholly in
the other: because appearing superior strength, and all
appearing preferableness, is in that; and yet Mr Chubb
supposes, that the act of preference is from previous
ground and reason in the motive which is preferred.
But are these things consistent? Can there be previous
ground in a thing for an event that takes place, and yet no
previous tendency in it to that event? If one thing follows
another, without any previous tendency to its following,
then I should think it very plain that it follows it without
any manner of previous reason why it should follow.

Yea, in this case, Mr Chubb supposes that the event
follows an antecedent or a previous thing, as the ground
of its existence, not only that has no tendency to it, but
a contrary tendency. The event is, the preference
which the mind gives to that motive which is weaker,
as it stands in the previous view of the mind; the immediate antecedent is, the view the mind has of the two
rival motives conjunctly; in which previous view of the
mind, all the preferableness, or previous tendency to
preference, is supposed to be on the other side, or in the
contrary motive; and all the unworthiness of preference,
and so previous tendency to comparative neglect, rejection, or undervaluing, is on that side which is preferred:
and yet in this view of the mind is supposed to be the
previous ground or reason of this act of preference, exciting it and disposing the mind to it,—which I leave
the reader to judge, whether it be absurd or not. If it

be not, then it is not absurd to say, that the previous
tendency of an antecedent to a consequent, is a ground
and reason why that consequent does not follow; and
the want of a previous tendency to an event, yea, a tendency to the contrary, is the true ground and reason
why that event does follow.

An act of choice or preference is a comparative act,
wherein the mind acts with reference to two or more
things that are compared, and stand in competition in
the mind's view. If the mind, in this comparative act,
prefers that which appears inferior in the comparison,
then the mind herein acts absolutely without motive,
or inducement, or any temptation whatsoever. Then, if
a hungry man has the offer of two sorts of food, both
which he finds an appetite to, but has a stronger appetite to one than the other, and there be no circumstances or excitements whatsoever in the case to induce him
to take either the one or the other, but merely his appetite; if in the choice he makes between them, he chooses
that which he has least appetite to, and refuses that to
which he has the strongest appetite, this is a choice made
absolutely without previous motive, excitement, reason,
or temptation, as much as if he were perfectly without
all appetite to either: because his volition in this case is
a comparative act, attending and following a comparative view of the food which he chooses, viewing it as re-
lated to, and compared with, the other sort of food, in
which view his preference has absolutely no previous
ground, yea, is against all previous ground and motive.
And if there be any principle in man, from whence an
act of choice may arise after this manner, from the same
principle volition may arise wholly without motive on
either side. If the mind in its volition can go beyond
motive, then it can go without motive; for when it
is beyond the motive, it is out of the reach of the motive,
out of the limits of its influence, and so without motive.
If volition goes beyond the strength and tendency of
motive, and especially if it goes against its tendency, this
demonstrates the independence of volition or motive.

And if so, no reason can be given for what Mr Chubb so often asserts, even that "in the nature of things volition cannot take place without a motive to induce it."

If the Most High should endow a balance with agency or activity of nature, in such a manner, that when unequal weights are put into the scales, its agency could enable it to cause that scale to descend which has the least weight, and so to raise the greater weight; this would clearly demonstrate, that the motion of the balance does not depend on weights in the scales, at least as much as if the balance should move itself, when there is no weight in either scale. And the activity of the balance, which is sufficient to move itself against the greater weight, must certainly be more than sufficient to move it when there is no weight at all.

Mr Chubb supposes, that the will cannot stir at all without some motive, and also supposes, that if there be a motive to one thing, and none to the contrary, volition will infallibly follow that motive. This is virtually to suppose an entire dependence of the will on motives: if it were not wholly dependent on them, it could surely help itself a little without them, or help itself a little against a motive, without help from the strength and weight of a contrary motive. And yet his supposing that the will, when it has before it various opposite motives, can use them as it pleases, and choose its own influence from them, and neglect the strongest, 'and follow the weakest, supposes it to be wholly independent on motives.

It further appears, on Mr Chubb's supposition, that volition must be without any previous ground in any motive, thus: if it be as he supposes, that the will is not determined by any previous superior strength of the motive, but determines and chooses its own motive, then, when the rival motives are exactly equal in strength and tendency to induce in all respects, it may follow either; and may in such a case sometimes follow one, sometimes the other. And if so, this diversity which appears between the acts of the will, is plainly without previous ground in either of the motives; for all that is previously in the motives, is supposed precisely and perfectly the same, without any diversity whatsoever. Now, perfect identity, as to all that is previous in the antecedent, cannot be the ground and reason of diversity in the consequent. Perfect identity in the ground cannot be a reason why it is not followed with the same consequence. And therefore the source of this diversity of consequence must be sought for elsewhere.

And lastly, it may be observed, that however Mr Chubb does much insist that no volition can take place without some motive to induce it, which previously disposes the mind to it; yet, as he also insists that the mind, without reference to any superior strength of motives, picks and chooses for its motive to follow; he himself herein plainly supposes, that with regard to the mind's preference of one motive before another, it is not the motive that disposes the will, but the will disposes itself to follow the motive.

IV. Mr Chubb supposes necessity to be utterly inconsistent with agency; and that to suppose a being to be an agent in that which is necessary, is a plain contradiction. At p. 311, and throughout his discourses on the subject of liberty, he supposes, that necessity cannot consist with agency, or freedom; and that to suppose otherwise, is to make liberty and necessity, action, and passion, the same thing. And so he seems to suppose, that there is no action, strictly speaking, but volition; and that as to the effects of volition in body or mind, in themselves considered, being necessary, they are said to be free, only as they are the effects of an act that is not necessary.

And yet, according to him, volition itself is the effect of volition; yea, every act of free volition: and therefore every act of free volition must, by what has now been observed from him, be necessary. That every act of free volition is itself the effect of volition, is abundantly supposed by him. In p. 341, he says, " If a man is such a creature as I have proved him to be, that is, if he has in him a power or liberty of doing either good or evil,

and either of these is the subject of his own free choice
so that he might, *if he had pleased,* have chosen and
done the contrary." Here he supposes, all that is good
or evil in man is the effect of his choice; and so that his
good or evil choice itself is the effect of his pleasure or
choice, in these words, he might, "if he had *pleased,* have
chosen the contrary." So in p. 356, "Though it be
highly reasonable, that a man should always choose the
greater good,—yet he may, if he *please, choose* otherwise,"—which is the same thing as if he had said, *he
may, if he chooses, choose otherwise.* And then he goes
on,—" that is, he may, *if he pleases, choose* what is good
for himself," &c. And again, in the same page, "The
will is not confined by the understanding to any particular sort of good, whether greater or less; but is at
liberty *to choose* what kind of good *it pleases.*" If there
be any meaning in the last words, the meaning must be
this, that *the will is at liberty to choose what kind of good
it chooses to choose;* supposing the act of choice itself
determined by an antecedent choice. The liberty Mr
Chubb speaks of, is not only a man's having power
to move his body agreeably to an antecedent act of
choice, but to use or exert the faculties of his soul.
Thus, in p. 379, speaking of the faculties of his mind,
he says, "Man has power, and is at liberty, to neglect
these faculties, to use them aright, or to abuse them, *as
he pleases.* And that he supposes an act of choice, or
exercise of pleasure, properly distinct *from,* and antecedent *to,* those acts thus chosen, directing, commanding,
and producing the chosen acts, and even the acts of
choice themselves, is very plain in p. 283. " He can
command his actions, and herein consists his liberty;
he can give or deny himself that pleasure, *as he pleases.*"
And p. 377. " If the actions of men are not the produce of a free choice, or election, but spring from a necessity of nature,—he cannot in reason be the object of
reward or punishment on their account. Whereas, if
action in man, whether good or evil, is the produce of
will or free choice, so that a man, in either case, had it

in his power, and was at liberty, to have *chosen* the contrary; he is the proper object of reward or punishment, according as he *chooses* to behave himself." Here, in these last words, he speaks of liberty of *choosing*, according as he *chooses*. So that the behaviour which he speaks of, as subject to his choice, is his choosing itself, as well as his external conduct consequent upon it. And therefore it is evident, he means not only external actions, but the acts of choice themselves, when he speaks of all free actions as the *produce* of free choice. And this is abundantly evident in what he says in pp. 372, 373.

Now these things imply a twofold great absurdity and inconsistence.

1. To suppose, as Mr Chubb plainly does, that every free act of choice is *commanded by*, and is the *produce of, free choice*, is to suppose the first free act of choice belonging to the case, yea, the first free act of choice that ever man exerted, to be the produce of an antecedent act of choice. But I hope I need not labour at all to convince my readers, that it is an absurdity to say, the very *first* act is the produce of another act that went *before* it.

2. If it were both possible and real, as Mr Chubb insists, that every free act of choice were the produce or the effect of a free act of choice; yet even then, according to his principles, no one act of choice would be free, but every one necessary; because, every act of choice being the effect of a foregoing act, every act would be necessarily connected with that foregoing cause. For Mr Chubb himself says, p. 389, "When the self-moving power is exerted, it becomes the necessary cause of its effects."—So that his notion of a free act, that is rewardable or punishable, is a heap of contradictions. It is a free act, and yet, by his own notion of freedom, is necessary; and therefore by him it is a contradiction to suppose it to be free. According to him, every free act is the produce of a free act; so that there must be an infinite number of free acts in succession, without any beginning in an agent that has a beginning. And therefore here is an infinite number of free acts, every

one of them free; and yet not any one of them free, but every act in the whole infinite chain a necessary effect. All the acts are rewardable or punishable, and yet the agent cannot, in reason, be the object of reward or punishment on account of any one of these actions. He is active in them all, and passive in none; yet active in none, but passive in all, &c.

V. Mr Chubb does most strenuously deny that motives are causes of the acts of the will; or that the moving principle in man is moved, or caused to be exerted, by motives. His words, pp. 280, 388, are, " If the moving principle in man is *moved, or caused to be exerted*, by something external to man, which all motives are, then it would not be a self-moving principle, seeing it would be moved by a principle external to itself. And to say, that a self-moving principle is *moved*, or *caused to be exerted*, by a cause external to itself, is absurd and a contradiction," &c.—And in the next page it is particularly and largely insisted, that motives are causes in no case, that they are merely passive in the production of action, and have no causality in the production of it —no causality to be the cause of the exertion of the will.

Now I desire it may be considered, how this can possibly consist with what he says in other places. Let it be noted here,

1. Mr Chubb abundantly speaks of motives as excitements of the acts of the will; and says, that motives do excite volition, and induce it, and that they are necessary to this end; that in the reason and nature of things, volition cannot take place without motives to excite it. But now, if motives excite the will, they *move* it; and yet he says, it is absurd to say the will is moved by motives. And again, (if language is of any significancy at all,) if motives excite volition, then they are the *cause* of its being excited; and to cause volition to be excited, is to cause it to be put forth or *exerted*. Yea, Mr Chubb says himself, p. 317, motive is necessary to the *exertion* of the active faculty. To excite, is positively to *do* something; and certainly that which does something, is the cause of the thing *done* by it. To create, is

to cause to be created; to make, is to cause to be made: to kill, is to cause to be killed; to quicken, is to cause to be quickened; and *to excite* is to *cause to be excited.* To excite, is to be a cause, in the most proper sense; not merely a negative occasion, but a ground of existence by positive influence. The notion of *exciting,* is exerting influence to cause the effect to arise or come forth into existence.

2. Mr Chubb himself, p. 317, speaks of motives as the ground and reason of action *by influence,* and *by prevailing influence.* Now, what can be meant by a cause, but something that is the ground and reason of a thing by its influence, an influence that is *prevalent,* and so effectual?

3. This author not only speaks of motives as the ground and reason of action, by prevailing influence; but expressly of their influence as prevailing *for the production* of an action, in the same page (317): which makes the inconsistency still more palpable and notorious. The production of an effect is certainly the *causing* of an effect; and *productive influence* is *causal influence,* if any thing is; and that which has this influence prevalently, so as thereby to become the ground of another thing, is a cause of that thing, if there be any such thing as a cause. This influence Mr Chubb says motives have to produce an action; and yet he says it is absurd and a contradiction to say they are causes.

4. In the same page, he once and again speaks of motives as disposing the agent to action, by their influence. His words are these: "As motive, which takes place in the understanding, and is the product of intelligence, is *necessary* to action, that is, to the *exertion* of the active faculty, because that faculty would not be exerted without some *previous reason* to *dispose* the mind to action; so from hence it plainly appears, that when a man is said to be *disposed* to one action rather than another, this properly signifies the *prevailing influence* that one motive has upon a man *for the production* of an action, or for the being at rest, before all other motives for the *production* of the contrary. For as motive is the ground

and reason of any action, so the motive that prevails, *disposes* the agent to the performance of that action.

Now, if motives dispose the mind to action, then they cause the mind to be disposed; and to cause the mind to be disposed, is to cause it to be willing; and to cause it to be willing, is to cause it to will; and that is the same thing as to be the cause of an act of the will. And yet this same Mr Chubb holds it to be absurd to suppose motive to be a cause of the act of the will.

And if we compare these things together, we have here again a whole heap of inconsistencies. Motives are the previous ground and reason of the acts of the will; yea, the necessary ground and reason of their exertion, without which they will not be exerted, and cannot, in the nature of things, take place; and they do excite these acts of the will, and do this by a prevailing influence; yea, an influence which prevails for the production of the act of the will, and for the disposing of the mind to it; and yet it is absurd to suppose motive to be a cause of an act of the will, or that a principle of will is moved or caused to be exerted by it, or that it has any causality in the production of it, or any causality to be the cause of the exertion of the will.

A due consideration of these things which Mr Chubb has advanced, the strange inconsistencies which the notion of liberty, consisting in the will's power of self-determination void of all necessity, united with that dictate of common sense, that there can be no volition without a motive, drove him into, may be sufficient to convince us, that it is utterly impossible ever to make that notion of liberty consistent with the influence of motives in volition. And as it is in a manner self-evident, that there can be no act of will, choice, or preference of the mind, without some motive or inducement, something in the mind's view, which it aims at, seeks, inclines to, and goes after; so it is most manifest, there is no such liberty in the universe as Arminians insist on; nor any such thing possible or conceivable.

SECTION XI.

THE EVIDENCE OF GOD'S CERTAIN FOREKNOWLEDGE OF THE VOLITIONS
OF MORAL AGENTS.

THAT the acts of the wills of moral agents are not contingent events, in that sense as to be without all necessity, appears by God's certain foreknowledge of such events.

In handling this argument, I would, in the *first* place, prove that God has a certain foreknowledge of the voluntary acts of moral agents; and, *secondly,* show the consequence, or how it follows from hence, that the volitions of moral agents are not contingent, so as to be without necessity of connexion and consequence.

First, I am to prove, that God has an absolute and certain foreknowledge of the free actions of moral agents.

One would think it should be wholly needless to enter on such an argument with any that profess themselves Christians: but so it is; God's certain foreknowledge of the free acts of moral agents, is denied by some that pretend to believe the Scriptures to be the word of God; and especially of late. I therefore shall consider the evidence of such a prescience in the Most High, as fully as the designed limits of this essay will admit of; supposing myself herein to have to do with such as own the truth of the Bible.

Arg. I. My *first* argument shall be taken from God's *prediction* of such events. Here I would, in the first place, lay down these two things as axioms.

1. If God does not foreknow, he cannot foretell such events; that is, he cannot peremptorily and certainly foretell them. If God has no more than an uncertain guess concerning events of this kind, then he can declare no more than an uncertain guess. Positively to foretell, is to profess to foreknow, or declare positive foreknowledge.

2. If God does not certainly foreknow the future volitions of moral agents, then neither can he certainly fore-

know those events which are consequent and dependent on these volitions. The existence of the one depending on the existence of the other, the knowledge of the existence of the one depends on the knowledge of the existence of the other; and the one cannot be more certain than the other.

Therefore, how many, how great, and how extensive soever the consequences of the volitions of moral agents may be; though they should extend to an alteration of the state of things through the universe, and should be continued in a series of successive events to all eternity, and should, in the progress of things, branch forth into an infinite number of series, each of them going on in an endless line or chain of events; God must be as ignorant of all these consequences, as he is of the volition whence they first take their rise: all these events, and the whole state of things depending on them, how important, extensive, and vast soever, must be hid from him.

These positions being such as, I suppose, none will deny, I now proceed to observe the following things.

1. Men's moral conduct and qualities, their virtues and vices, their wickedness and good practice, things rewardable and punishable, have often been foretold by God.—Pharaoh's moral conduct, in refusing to obey God's command, in letting his people go, was foretold. God says to Moses, Exod. iii. 19, " I am sure that the king of Egypt will not let you go." Here God professes not only to guess at, but to know, Pharaoh's future disobedience. In chap. vii. 4, God says, " but Pharaoh shall not hearken unto you; that I may lay mine hand upon Egypt," &c. And chap. ix. 30, Moses says to Pharaoh, " as for thee, and thy servants, I know that ye will not fear the Lord." See also chap. xi. 9.—The moral conduct of Josiah, by name, in his zealously exerting himself in opposition to idolatry, in particular acts of his, was foretold above three hundred years before he was born, and the prophecy sealed by a miracle, and renewed and confirmed by the words of a second prophet, as what surely would not fail, 1 Kings xiii. 1—6, 32.

This prophecy was also in effect a prediction of the moral conduct of the people, in upholding their schismatical and idolatrous worship until that time, and the idolatry of those priests of the high places which it is foretold Josiah should offer upon that altar of Bethel. —Micaiah foretold the foolish and sinful conduct of Ahab in refusing to hearken to the word of the Lord by him, and choosing rather to hearken to the false prophets, in going to Ramoth-Gilead to his ruin, 1 Kings xxi. 20—22. The moral conduct of Hazael was foretold, in that cruelty he should be guilty of; on which Hazael says, "What! is thy servant a dog that he should do this thing?" The prophet speaks of the event as what he knew, and not what he conjectured, 2 Kings viii. 12, "I know the evil thou wilt do unto the children of Israel: thou wilt dash their children, and rip up their women with child." The moral conduct of Cyrus is foretold long before he had a being, in his mercy to God's people, and regard to the true God, in turning the captivity of the Jews, and promoting the building of the temple, Isa. xliv. 28, and lxv. 13. Compare 2 Chron. xxxvi. 22, 23. and Ezra i. 1—4. How many instances of the moral conduct of the kings of the north and south, particular instances of the wicked behaviour of the kings of Syria and Egypt, are foretold in the 11th chapter of Daniel! their corruption, violence, robbery, treachery, and lies. And particularly, how much is foretold of the horrid wickedness of Antiochus Epiphanes, called there a *vile person*, instead of Epiphanes, or *illustrious!* In that chapter, and also in chap. viii. ver. 9, 14, 23, to the end, are foretold his flattery, deceit, and lies, his having his heart set to do mischief, and set against the holy covenant, his destroying and treading under foot the holy people, in a marvellous manner, his having indignation against the holy covenant, setting his heart against it, and conspiring against it, his polluting the sanctuary of strength, treading it under foot, taking away the daily sacrifice, and placing the abomination that maketh desolate; his great pride, mag-

H

nifying himself against God, and uttering marvellous blasphemies against him, until God in indignation should destroy him. Withal, the moral conduct of the Jews, on occasion of his persecution, is predicted. It is foretold that " he should corrupt many by flatteries," chap. xi. 32—34. But that others should behave with a glorious constancy and fortitude, in opposition to him, ver. 32. And that some good men should fall and repent, ver. 35. Christ foretold Peter's sin in denying his Lord, with its circumstances, in a peremptory manner. And so that great sin of Judas in betraying his Master, and its dreadful and eternal punishment in hell, was foretold in the like positive manner, Matt. xxvi. 21—25, and parallel places in the other evangelists.

2. Many events have been foretold by God, which are consequent and dependent on the moral conduct of particular persons, and were accomplished either by their virtuous or vicious actions. Thus, the children of Israel's going down into Egypt to dwell there, was foretold to Abraham, Gen. xv., which was brought about by the wickedness of Joseph's brethren in selling him, and the wickedness of Joseph's mistress, and his own signal virtue in resisting her temptation. The accomplishment of the thing prefigured in Joseph's dream depended on the same moral conduct. Jotham's parable and prophecy, Judges ix. 15—20, was accomplished by the wicked conduct of Abimelech and the men of Shechem. The prophecies against the house of Eli, 1 Sam. chap. ii. and iii. were accomplished by the wickedness of Doeg the Edomite, in accusing the priests, and the great impiety and extreme cruelty of Saul in destroying the priests at Nob, 1 Sam. xxii. Nathan's prophecy against David, 2 Sam. xii. 11, 12, was fulfilled by the horrible wickedness of Absalom, in rebelling against his father, seeking his life, and lying with his concubines in the sight of the sun. The prophecy against Solomon, 1 Kings xi. 11—13, was fulfilled by Jeroboam's rebellion and usurpation, which are spoken of as his wickedness, 2 Chron. xiii. 5, 6, compare ver. 18. The prophecy

against Jeroboam's family, 1 Kings xiv., was fulfilled
by the conspiracy, treason, and cruel murders of Baasha,
2 Kings xv. 27, &c. The predictions of the prophet
Jehu against the house of Baasha, 1 Kings xvi., at the
beginning, were fulfilled by the treason and parricide of
Zimri, 1 Kings xvi. 9—13, 20.

3. How often has God foretold the future moral conduct of nations and people, of numbers, bodies, and suc-
cessions of men; with God's judicial proceedings, and
many other events consequent and dependent on their
virtues and vices; which could not be foreknown, if the
volitions of men, wherein they acted as moral agents,
had not been foreseen? The future cruelty of the Egyp-
tians in oppressing Israel, and God's judging and punishing them for it, was foretold long before it came to pass,
Gen. xv. 13, 14. The continuance of the iniquity of
the Amorites, and the increase of it until it should be
full, and they ripe for destruction, was foretold above
four hundred years beforehand, Gen. xv. 16; Acts vii. 6,
7. The prophecies of the destruction of Jerusalem and
the land of Judah, were absolute; 2 Kings xx. 17—19;
chap. xxii. 15, to the end. It was foretold in Hezekiah's
time, and was abundantly insisted on in the book of the
prophet Isaiah, who wrote nothing after Hezekiah's
days. It was foretold in Josiah's time, in the beginning
of a great reformation, 2 Kings xxii. And it is manifest by innumerable things in the prediction of the prophets, relating to this event, its time, its circumstances,
its continuance and end; the return from the captivity,
the restoration of the temple, city, and land, and many
circumstances and consequences of *that;* I say, these
show plainly that the prophecies of this great event
were *absolute.* And yet this event was connected with
and dependent on, two things in men's moral conduct:
first, the injurious rapine and violence of the king of
Babylon and his people, as the efficient cause; which
God often speaks of as what he highly resented, and
would severely punish: and, secondly, the final obstinacy of the Jews. That great event is often spoken of

as suspended on this, Jer. iv. 1, and v. 1; vii. 1—7; xi. 1—6; xvii. 24, to the end; xxv. 1—7; xxvi. 1—8, 13; and xxxviii. 17, 18. Therefore, this destruction and captivity could not be foreknown, unless such a moral conduct of the Chaldeans and Jews had been foreknown. And then it was foretold, that the people should be finally obstinate, to the destruction and utter desolation of the city and land. Isaiah vi. 9—11; Jer. i. 18, 19; vii. 27, 29; Ezek. iii. 7; and xxiv. 13, 14.

The final obstinacy of those Jews who were left in the land of Israel, in their idolatry and rejection of the true God, was foretold by God, and the prediction confirmed with an oath, Jer. xliv. 26, 27. And God tells the people, Isa. xlviii. 3, 4—8, that he had predicted those things which should be consequent on their treachery and obstinacy, because he knew they would be obstinate; and that he had declared these things beforehand, for their conviction of his being the only true God, &c.

The destruction of Babylon, with many of the circumstances of it, was foretold, as the judgment of God for the exceeding pride and haughtiness of the heads of that monarchy, Nebuchadnezzar, and his successors, and their wickedly destroying other nations, and particularly for their exalting themselves against the true God and his people, before any of these monarchs had a being; Isa. chap. xiii. xiv. xlvii.: compare Habakkuk ii. 5, to the end, and Jer. chap. l. and li. That Babylon's destruction was to be a " recompence, according to the works of their own hands," appears by Jer. xxv. 14. The immorality which the people of Babylon, and particularly her princes and great men, were guilty of, that very night that the city was destroyed, their revelling and drunkenness at Belshazzar's idolatrous feast, was foretold, Jer. li. 39, 57.

The return of the Jews from the Babylonish captivity is often very particularly foretold, with many circumstances, and the promises of it are very peremptory; Jer. xxxi. 35—40, and xxxii. 6—15, 41—44, and xxxiii. 24—26. And the very time of their return was pre-

fixed; Jer. xxv. 11, 12; xxix. 10, 11; 2 Chron. xxxvi.
21; Ezek. iv. 6, and Dan. ix. 2.   And yet the prophecies represent their return as consequent on their
repentance.   And their repentance itself is very expressly and particularly foretold, Jer. xxix. 12, 13, 14;
xxxi. 8, 9, 18—31; xxxiii. 8; l. 4, 5; Ezek. vi. 8, 9,
10; vii. 16; xiv. 22, 23; and xx. 43, 44.

It was foretold, under the Old Testament, that the
Messiah should suffer greatly through the malice and
cruelty of men; as is largely and fully set forth, Ps.
xxii., applied to Christ in the New Testament, Matt.
xxvii. 35, 43; Luke xxiii. 34; John xix. 24; Heb.
ii. 12.   And likewise in Ps. lxix., which, it is also evident by the New Testament, is spoken of Christ; John
xv. 25; vii. 5, &c.; and ii. 17; Rom. xv. 3; Matt.
xxvii. 34, 48; Mark xv. 23; John xix. 29.   The
same thing is also foretold, Isa. liii. and l. 6; and Micah
v. 1.   This cruelty of men was their sin, and what they
acted as moral agents.   It was foretold that there should
be an union of heathen and Jewish rulers against Christ,
Ps. ii. 1, 2, compared with Acts iv. 25—28.   It was foretold that the Jews should generally reject and despise
the Messiah, Isa. xlix. 5, 6, 7, and liii. 1—3; Ps. xxii.
6, 7, and lxix. 4, 8, 19, 20.   And it was foretold that
the body of that nation should be rejected in the Messiah's days from being God's people, for their obstinacy
in sin; Isa. xlix. 4—7, and viii. 14, 15, 16, compared
with Rom. x. 19. and Isa. lxv. at the beginning, compared with Rom. x. 20, 21.   It was foretold that Christ
should be rejected by the chief priests and rulers among
the Jews, Ps. cxviii. 22, compared with Matt. xxi. 42;
Acts iv. 11; 1 Pet. ii. 4, 7.

Christ himself foretold his being delivered into the
hands of the elders, chief priests, and scribes, and his
being cruelly treated by them, and condemned to death;
and that he by them should be delivered to the Gentiles; and that he should be mocked and scourged and
crucified, (Matt. xvi. 21, and xx. 17—19; Luke ix.
22 ; John viii. 28 ;) and that the people should be con-

cerned in and consenting to his death, (Luke xx. 13—
18,) especially the inhabitants of Jerusalem; Luke xiii.
33—35. He foretold that the disciples should all be offended because of him that night that he was betrayed,
and should forsake him; Matt. xxvi. 31; John xvi. 32.
He foretold that he should be rejected of that generation, even the body of the people, and that they should
continue obstinate to their ruin; Matt. xii. 45; xxi. 33
—42, and xxii. 1—7; Luke xiii. 16, 21, 24; xvii. 25;
xix. 14, 27, 41—44; xx. 13—18, and xxiii. 34—39.

As it was foretold in both Old Testament and New,
that the Jews should reject the Messiah, so it was foretold that the Gentiles should receive him, and so be admitted to the privileges of God's people, in places too
many to be now particularly mentioned. It was foretold in the Old Testament, that the Jews should envy
the Gentiles on this account; Deut. xxxii. 21, compared with Rom. x. 19. Christ himself often foretold that the
Gentiles would embrace the true religion, and become
his followers and people; Matt. viii. 10, 11, 12; xxi. 41
—43, and xxii. 8—10; Luke xiii. 28; xiv. 16—24, and
xx. 16; John x. 16. He also foretold the Jews' envy
of the Gentiles on this occasion; Matt. xx. 12—16;
Luke xv. 26, to the end. He foretold that they should
continue in this opposition and envy, and should manifest it in the cruel persecutions of his followers, to their
utter destruction; Matt. xxi. 33—42; xxii. 6, and xxiii.
34—39; Luke xi. 49—51. The Jews' obstinacy is also
foretold, Acts xxii. 18. Christ often foretold the great
persecutions his followers should meet with, both from
Jews and Gentiles; Matt. x. 16—18, 21, 22, 34—36,
and xxiv. 9; Mark xiii. 9; Luke x. 3; xii. 11, 49—
53, and xxi. 12, 16, 17; John xv. 18—21, and xvi. 1—
4, 20—22, 23. He foretold the martyrdom of particular persons; Matt. xx. 23; John xiii. 36, and xxi. 18,
19, 22. He foretold the great success of the gospel in
the city of Samaria, as near approaching; which afterwards was fulfilled by the preaching of Philip; John iv.
35—38. He foretold the rising of many deceivers after

his departure, Matt. xxiv. 4, 5, 11, and the apostacy of many of his professed followers, Matt. xxiv. 10—22.

The persecutions which the apostle Paul was to meet with in the world, were foretold; Acts ix. 16 ; xx. 23, and xxi. 11. The apostle says to the Christian Ephesians, Acts xx. 29, 30: " I know, that after my departure shall grievous wolves enter in among you, not sparing the flock : also of your own selves shall men arise, speaking perverse things, to draw away disciples after them." The apostle says, he knew this: but he did not know it, if God did not know the future actions of moral agents.

4. Unless God foreknows the future acts of moral agents, all the prophecies we have in Scripture concerning the great antichristian apostacy, the rise, reign, wicked qualities, and deeds of the Man of sin, and his instruments and adherents, the extent and long continuance of his dominion, his influence on the minds of princes and others, to corrupt them, and draw them away to idolatry and other foul vices; his great and cruel persecutions; the behaviour of the saints under these great temptations, &c. &c.; I say, unless the volitions of moral agents are foreseen, all these prophecies are uttered without knowing the things foretold.

The predictions relating to this great apostacy are all of a moral nature, relating to men's virtues and vices, and their exercises, fruits, and consequences, and events depending on them; and are very particular; and most of them often repeated, with many precise characteristics, descriptions, and limitations of qualities, conduct, influence, effects, extent, duration, periods, circumstances, final issue, &c., which it would be very long to mention particularly. And to suppose all these are predicted by God without any certain knowledge of the future moral behaviour of free agents, would be to the utmost degree absurd.

5. Unless God foreknows the future acts of men's wills, and their behaviour as moral agents, all those great things which are foretold in both Old Testament

and New concerning the erection, establishment, and universal extent of the kingdom of the Messiah, were predicted and promised, while God was in ignorance whether any of these things would come to pass or no, and did but guess at them. For that kingdom is not of this world; it does not consist in things external, but is within men, and consists in the dominion of virtue in their hearts, in righteousness, and peace, and joy in the Holy Ghost; and in these things made manifest in practice, to the praise and glory of God. The Messiah came to save men from their sins, and deliver them from their spiritual enemies, that they might serve him in righteousness and holiness before him; he gave himself for us, that he might redeem us from all iniquity, and purify unto himself a peculiar people, zealous of good works. And therefore his success consists in gaining men's hearts to virtue, in their being made God's willing people in the day of his power. His conquest of his enemies consists in his victory over men's corruption and vices. And such success, such victory, and such a reign and dominion, is often expressly foretold:—that his kingdom shall fill the earth; that all people, nations, and languages, should serve and obey him: and so that all nations should go up to the mountain of the house of the Lord, that he might teach them his ways, and that they might walk in his paths; and that all men should be drawn to Christ, and the earth be full of the knowledge of the Lord, (by which, in the style of Scripture, is meant true virtue and religion,) as the waters cover the seas; that God's law should be put into men's inward parts, and written in their hearts; and that God's people should be all righteous, &c. &c.

A very great part of the prophecies of the Old Testament is taken up in such predictions as these.—And here I would observe, that the prophecies of the universal prevalence of the kingdom of the Messiah, and true religion of Jesus Christ, are delivered in the most peremptory manner, and confirmed by the oath of God, Isa. xlv. 22, to the end, " Look unto me, and be ye saved, all the ends of the earth; for I am God, and there is none else. I have sworn by myself, the word is gone out of my mouth in righteousness, and shall not return, That unto me every knee shall bow, and every tongue shall swear. Surely, shall one say, In the Lord have I righteousness and strength: even to him shall men come," &c. But here this peremptory declaration, and great oath of the Most High, are delivered with such mighty solemnity to things God did not know, if he did not certainly foresee the volitions of moral agents.

And all the predictions of Christ and his apostles, to the like purpose, must be without knowledge; as those of our Saviour comparing the kingdom of God to a grain of mustard-seed, growing exceeding great, from a small beginning; and to leaven, hid in three measures of meal, until the whole was leavened, &c.—And the prophecies in the epistles concerning the restoration of the nation of the Jews to the true church of God, and the bringing in the fulness of the Gentiles; and the prophecies in all the Revelation concerning the glorious change in the moral state of the world of mankind, attending the destruction of antichrist, the kingdoms of the world becoming the kingdoms of our Lord and of his Christ; and its being granted to the church to be arrayed in that fine linen, white and clean, which is the righteousness of saints, &c.

Corol. 1. Hence that great promise and oath of God to Abraham, Isaac, and Jacob, so much celebrated in Scripture, both in the Old Testament and New, namely, " That in their seed all the nations and families of the earth should be blessed," must be made on uncertainties, if God does not certainly foreknow the volitions of moral agents. For the fulfilment of this promise consists in that success of Christ in the work of redemption, and that setting up of his spiritual kingdom over the nations of the world, which has been spoken of. Men are blessed in Christ no otherwise than as they are brought to acknowledge him, trust in him, love and serve him, as is represented and predicted in Psal. lxxii.

11, " All kings shall fall down before him ; all nations shall serve him." With ver. 17, " Men shall be blessed in him; all nations shall call him blessed." This oath to Jacob and Abraham is fulfilled in subduing men's iniquities; as is implied in that of the prophet Micah, chap. vii. 19, 20.

Corol. 2. Hence also it appears, that first gospel promise that ever was made to mankind, that great prediction of the salvation of the Messiah, and his victory over Satan, made to our first parents, Gen. iii. 15, if there be no certain prescience of the volitions of moral agents, must have no better foundation than conjecture. For Christ's victory over Satan consists in men's being saved from sin, and in the victory of virtue and holiness, over that vice and wickedness, which Satan by his temptation has introduced, and wherein his kingdom consists.

6. If it be so, that God has not a prescience of the future actions of moral agents, it will follow, that the prophecies of Scripture in general are without foreknowledge. For Scripture prophecies, almost all of them, if not universally, without any exception, are either predictions of the actings and behaviours of moral agents, or of events depending on them, or some way connected with them ; judicial dispensations, judgments on men for their wickedness, or rewards of virtue and righteousness, remarkable manifestations of favour to the righteous, or manifestations of sovereign mercy to sinners, forgiving their iniquities, and magnifying the riches of Divine grace; or dispensations of providence, in some respect or other, relating to the conduct of the subjects of God's moral government, wisely adapted thereto; either providing for what should be in a future state of things, through the volitions and voluntary actions of moral agents, or consequent upon them, and regulated and ordered according to them. So that all events that are foretold, are either moral events, or other events which are connected with, and accommodated to, moral events.

That the predictions of Scripture in general must be without knowledge, if God does not foresee the volitions

of men, will further appear, if it be considered, that almost all events belonging to the future state of the
world of mankind, the changes and revolutions which
come to pass in empires, kingdoms, and nations, and all
societies, depend in innumerable ways on the acts of men's
wills; yea, on an innumerable multitude of millions of
millions of volitions of mankind. Such is the state and
course of things in the world of mankind, that one
single event, which appears in itself exceeding inconsiderable, may, in the progress and series of things, occasion a succession of the greatest and most important
and extensive events; causing the state of mankind to
be vastly different from what it would otherwise have
been, for all succeeding generations.

For instance, the coming into existence of those particular men, who have been the great conquerors of the
world, who, under God, have had the main hand in all
the consequent state of the world in all after ages; such
as Nebuchadnezzar, Cyrus, Alexander, Pompey, Julius
Cæsar, &c. undoubtedly depended on many millions of
acts of the will, which followed and were occasioned one
by another, in their parents. And perhaps most of
these volitions depended on millions of volitions of hundreds and thousands of others, their contemporaries of
the same generation; and most of these on millions of
millions of volitions of others in preceding generations.
—As we go back, still the number of volitions, which
were some way the occasion of the event, multiply as
the branches of a river, until they come at last, as it
were, to an infinite number. This will not seem strange
to any one who well considers the matter; if we recol-
lect what philosophers tell us of the innumerable multitudes of those things which are, as it were, the *princi-
pia*, or *stamina vitæ*, concerned in generation; the *ani-
malcula* in *semen masculo*, and the *ova* in the womb of
the female; the impregnation, or animating of one of
these in distinction from all the rest, must depend on
things infinitely minute, relating to the time and circumstances of the act of the parents, the state of their

bodies, &c. which must depend on innumerable foregoing circumstances and occurrences; which must depend,
infinite ways, on foregoing acts of their wills; which are
occasioned by innumerable things that happen in the
course of their lives, in which their own, and their
neighbours' behaviour, must have a hand an infinite
number of ways. And as the volitions of others must
be so many ways concerned in the conception and birth
of such men; so, no less in their preservation, and circumstances of life, their particular determinations and
actions, on which the great revolutions they were the
occasions of, depended. As, for instance, when the con-
spirators in Persia against the Magi, were consulting
about the succession to the empire, it came into the
mind of one of them to propose, that he whose horse
neighed first, when they came together the next morning, should be king. Now such a thing's coming into
his mind, might depend on innumerable incidents,
wherein the volitions of mankind had been concerned.
But, in consequence of this accident, Darius the son of
Hystaspes, was king. And if this had not been, probably his successor would not have been the same, and
all the circumstances of the Persian empire might have
been far otherwise. And then perhaps Alexander might
never have conquered that empire. And then probably
the circumstances of the world, in all succeeding ages,
might have been vastly otherwise. I might further instance in many other occurrences; such as those on
which depended Alexander's preservation in the many
critical junctures of his life, wherein a small trifle would
have turned the scale against him; and the preservation
and success of the Roman people in the infancy of their
kingdom and commonwealth, and afterwards; which all
the succeeding changes in their state, and the mighty
revolutions that afterwards came to pass in the habit-
able world, depended upon. But these hints may be
sufficient for every discerning considerate person, to
convince him, that the whole state of the world of mankind, in all ages, and the very being of every person who

has ever lived in it, in every age, since the times of the ancient prophets, has depended on more volitions, or acts of the wills of men, than there are sands on the sea-shore.

And therefore, unless God does most exactly and perfectly foresee the future acts of men's wills, all the predictions which he ever uttered concerning David, Hezekiah, Josiah, Nebuchadnezzar, Cyrus, Alexander; concerning the four monarchies, and the revolutions in them; and concerning all the wars, commotions, victories, prosperities, and calamities, of any of the kingdoms, nations, or communities of the world, have all been without knowledge.

So that, according to this notion of God's not foreseeing the volitions and free actions of men, God could foresee nothing appertaining to the state of the world of mankind in future ages; not so much as the being of one person that should live in it; and could foreknow no events, but only such as he would bring to pass himself by the extraordinary interposition of his immediate power; or things which should come to pass in the natural material world, by the laws of motion, and course of nature, wherein that is independent on the actions or works of mankind: that is, as he might, like a very able mathematician and astronomer, with great exactness calculate the revolutions of the heavenly bodies, and the greater wheels of the machine of the external creation.

And if we closely consider the matter, there will appear reason to convince us, that he could not, with any absolute certainty, foresee even these. As to the *first*, namely, things done by the immediate and extraordinary interposition of God's power, these cannot be foreseen, unless it can be foreseen when there shall be occasion for such extraordinary interposition; and that cannot be foreseen, unless the state of the moral world can be foreseen. For whenever God thus interposes, it is with regard to the state of the moral world requiring such divine interposition. Thus, God could not certainly foresee the universal deluge, the calling of Abraham, the destruction of Sodom and Gomorrah, the plagues on Egypt, and

Israel's redemption out of it, the expelling the seven nations of Canaan, and the bringing Israel into that land;
for these all are represented as connected with things
belonging to the state of the moral world. Nor can
God foreknow the most proper and convenient time of
the day of judgment and general conflagration; for that
chiefly depends on the course and state of things in the
moral world.

Nor, *secondly*, can we on this supposition reasonably
think, that God can certainly foresee what things shall
come to pass in the course of things, in the natural and
material world, even those which in an ordinary state
of things might be calculated by a good astronomer.
For the moral world is the end of the natural world;
and the course of things in the former is undoubtedly
subordinate to God's designs with respect to the latter.
Therefore he has seen cause, from regard to the state of
things in the moral world, extraordinarily to interpose,
to interrupt and lay an arrest on the course of things in
the natural world; and even in the greater wheels of its
motion, even so as to stop the sun in its course. And
unless he can foresee the volitions of men, and so know
something of the future state of the moral world, he
cannot know but that he may still have as great occasion to interpose in this manner, as ever he had: nor
can he foresee how, or when, he shall have occasion
thus to interpose.

Corol. 1. It appears from the things which have been
observed, that unless God foresees the volitions of moral
agents, that cannot be true which is observed by the
apostle James, Acts xv. 18; "Known unto God are all
his works from the beginning of the world."

Corol. 2. It appears from what has been observed, that
unless God foreknows the volitions of moral agents, all
the prophecies of Scripture have no better foundation
than mere conjecture; and *that*, in most instances, a
conjecture which must have the utmost uncertainty;
depending on an innumerable, and, as it were, infinite
multitude of volitions, which are all, even to God, uncer-

tain events: however, these prophecies are delivered as
absolute predictions, and very many of them in the most
positive manner, with asseverations; and some of them
with the most solemn oaths.

Corol. 3. It also follows, from what has been observed,
that if this notion of God's ignorance of future volitions
be true, in vain did Christ say (after uttering many
great and important predictions concerning God's moral
kingdom, and things depending on men's moral actions,)
Matt. xxiv. 35: " Heaven and earth shall pass away; but
my words shall not pass away."

Corol. 4. From the same notion of God's ignorance, it
would follow, that in vain has God himself often spoken
of the predictions of his word as evidence of foreknowledge ; and so as evidences of that which is his prerogative as God, and his peculiar glory, greatly distinguishing him from all other beings ; as in Isa. xli. 22—26 ;
xliii. 9, 10 ; xliv. 8 ; xlv. 21 ; xlvi. 10 ; xlviii. 14.

Arg. II. If God does not foreknow the volitions of
moral agents, then he did not foreknow the fall of man,
nor of angels, and so could not foreknow the great things
which are consequent on these events; such as his sending his Son into the world to die for sinners, and all things
pertaining to the great work of redemption ; all the things
which were done for four thousand years before Christ
came, to prepare the way for it; and the incarnation,
life, death, resurrection, and ascension, of Christ ; and
the setting him at the head of the universe, as King
of heaven and earth, angels and men ; and the setting
up his church and kingdom in this world, and appointing
him the Judge of the world ; and all that Satan should
do in the world in opposition to the kingdom of Christ ;
and the great transactions of the day of judgment, that
men and devils shall be the subjects of, and angels concerned in ;—they are all what God was ignorant of before the fall. And if so, the following Scriptures, and
others like them, must be without any meaning, or contrary to truth. Eph. i. 4, " According as he hath chosen us in him before the foundation of the world." 1 Pet.

i. 20, " Who verily was fore-ordained before the foundation of the world." 2 Tim. i. 9, " Who hath saved us,
and called us with a holy calling ; not according to our
works, but according to his purpose and grace, which
was given us in Christ Jesus before the world began."
So, Eph. iii. 11, (speaking of the wisdom of God in the
work of redemption,) " According to the eternal purpose
which he purposed in Christ Jesus." Tit. i. 2, " In hope
of eternal life, which God, that cannot lie, promised before the world began." Rom. viii. 29, " Whom he did
foreknow, them he also did predestinate," &c. 1 Pet. i.
2, " Elect, according to the foreknowledge of God the
Father."

If God did not foreknow the fall of man, nor the redemption by Jesus Christ, nor the volitions of man since
the fall ; then he did not foreknow the saints in any
sense ; neither as particular persons, nor as societies or
nations ; either by election, or mere foresight of their
virtue or good works ; or any foresight of any thing
about them relating to their salvation; or any benefit
they have by Christ, or any manner of concern of their's
with a Redeemer.

Arg. III. On the supposition of God's ignorance of the
future volitions of free agents, it will follow, that God
must in many cases truly repent what he has done, so as
properly to wish he had done otherwise : by reason that
the event of things, in those affairs which are most important, viz. the affairs of his moral kingdom, being uncertain and contingent, often happens quite otherwise
than he was aware beforehand. And there would be
reason to understand that in the most literal sense in
Gen. vi. 6, " It repented the Lord that he had made
man on the earth, and it grieved him at his heart." And
that 1 Sam. xv. 11. contrary to that, Num. xxiii. 19,
" God is not the son of man, that he should repent."
And 1 Sam. xv. 19, 25, " Also the Strength of Israel
will not lie, nor repent; for he is not a man, that he
should repent." Yea, from this notion it would follow,
that God is liable to repent and be grieved at his heart,

in a literal sense, continually ; and is always exposed to
an infinite number of real disappointments in his governing the world, and to manifold, constant, great perplex-
ity and vexation: but this is not very consistent with
his title of " God over all, blessed for evermore," which
represents him as possessed of perfect, constant, and un-
interrupted tranquillity and felicity, as God over the
universe, and in his management of the affairs of the
world as supreme and universal ruler.   See Rom. i. 25;
ix. 5; 2 Cor. xi. 31; 1 Tim. vi. 15.

Arg. IV. It will also follow, from this notion, that as
God is liable to be continually repenting what he has
done, so he must be exposed to be constantly changing
his mind and intentions as to his future conduct; alter-
ing his measures, relinquishing his old designs, and forming new schemes and projections.   For his purposes,
even as to the main parts of his scheme, namely, such
as belong to the state of his moral kingdom, must
be always liable to be broken, through want of foresight; and he must be continually putting his system to
rights, as it gets out of order, through the contingence
of the actions of moral agents: he must be a being, who,
instead of being absolutely immutable, must necessarily
be the subject of infinitely the most numerous acts of
repentance and changes of intention, of any being whatsoever; for this plain reason, that his vastly extensive charge
comprehends an infinitely greater number of those things
which are to him contingent and uncertain.   In such a
situation, he must have little else to do but to mend
broken links as well as he can, and be rectifying his dis-
jointed frame, and disordered movements, in the best
manner the case will allow.   The supreme Lord of all
things must needs be under great and miserable disadvantages, in governing the world which he has made,
and has the care of, through his being utterly unable to
find out things of chief importance which hereafter shall
befall his system, which, if he did but know, he might
make seasonable provision for.   In many cases there
may be very great necessity that he should make pro-

I

vision, in the manner of his ordering and disposing things, for some great events which are to happen, of vast and extensive influence, and endless consequence to the universe, which he may see afterwards, when it is too late, and may wish in vain that he had known beforehand, that he might have ordered his affairs accordingly. And it is in the power of man, on these principles, by his devices, purposes, and actions, thus to disappoint God, break his measures, make him continually to change his mind, subject him to vexation, and bring him into confusion.

But how do these things consist with reason, or with the word of God? which represents that all God's works, all that he has ever to do, the whole scheme and series of his operations, are from the beginning perfectly in his view; and declares that, whatever devices and designs are in the hearts of men, " the counsel of the Lord is that which shall stand, and the thoughts of his heart to all generations," Prov. xix. 21; Ps. xxxiii. 10, 11. " And that which the Lord of Hosts hath purposed none shall disannul," Isa. xiv. 27. And that he cannot be frustrated in one design or thought, Job xlii. 2. And " that which God doth, it shall be for ever, that nothing can be put to it or taken from it," Eccl. iii. 14. The stability and perpetuity of God's counsels are expressly spoken of as connected with the foreknowledge of God, Isa. xlvi. 10, " Declaring the end from the beginning, and from ancient times the things that are not yet done; saying, My counsel shall stand, and I will do all my pleasure." And how are these things consistent with what the Scripture says of God's immutability, which represents him as " without variableness or shadow of turning," and speaks of him most particularly as unchangeable with regard to his purposes, Mal. iii. 6, " I am the Lord; I change not; therefore ye sons of Jacob are not consumed." Exod. iii. 14, " I AM THAT I AM." Job. xxiii. 13, 14. " He is in one mind; and who can turn him? And what his soul desireth, even that he doth: for he performeth the thing that is appointed for me."

Arg. V. If this notion of God's ignorance of future volitions of moral agents be thoroughly considered in its consequences, it will appear to follow from it, that God, after he had made the world, was liable to be wholly frustrated of his end in the creation of it; and so has been, in like manner, liable to be frustrated of his end in all the great works he hath wrought. It is manifest, the moral world is the end of the natural: the rest of the creation is but an house which God hath built, with furniture, for moral agents: and the good or bad state of the moral world depends on the improvement they make of their natural agency, and so depends on their volitions. And therefore, if these cannot be foreseen by God, because they are contingent, and subject to no kind of necessity, then the affairs of the moral world are liable to go wrong, to any assignable degree; yea, liable to be utterly ruined. As, on this scheme, it may well be supposed to be literally said, when mankind, by the abuse of their moral agency, became very corrupt before the flood, "that the Lord repented that he had made man on the earth, and it grieved him at his heart;" so, when he made the universe, he did not know but that he might be so disappointed in it, that it might grieve him at his heart that he had made it. It actually proved, that all mankind became sinful, and a very great part of the angels apostatised: and how could God know beforehand that all of them would not? And how could God know but that all mankind, notwithstanding means used to reclaim them, being still left to the freedom of their own will, would continue in their apostacy, and grow worse and worse, as they of the old world before the flood did?

According to the scheme I am endeavouring to confute, neither the fall of men nor angels could be foreseen, and God must be greatly disappointed in these events; and so the grand scheme and contrivance for our redemption, and destroying the works of the devil, by the Messiah, and all the great things God has done in the prosecution of these designs, must be only the fruits of his own disappointment, and contrivances of his to mend and patch up, as well as he could, his system, which originally was all very good, and perfectly beautiful, but was marred, broken, and confounded by the free will of angels and men. And still he must be liable to be totally disappointed a second time. He could not know that he should have his desired success in the incarnation, life, death, resurrection, and exaltation of his only-begotten Son, and other great works accomplished to restore the state of things: he could not know, after all, whether there would actually be any tolerable measure of restoration; for this depended on the free will of man. There has been a general great apostacy of almost all the Christian world, to that which was worse than heathenism, which continued for many ages. And how could God, without foreseeing men's volitions, know whether ever Christendom would return from this apostacy? And which way could he tell beforehand how soon it would begin? The apostle says it began to work in his time; and how could it be known how far it would proceed in that age? Yea, how could it be known that the gospel, which was not effectual for the reformation of the Jews, would ever be effectual for the turning of the heathen nations from their heathen apostacy, which they had been confirmed in for so many ages?

It is represented often in Scripture, that God, who made the world for himself, and created it for his pleasure, would infallibly obtain his end in the creation, and in all his works; that as all things are *of* him, so they would all be *to* him; and that in the final issue of things, it would appear that he is "the first and the last." Rev. xxi. 6, "And he said unto me, It is done. I am Alpha and Omega, the beginning and the end, the first and the last." But these things are not consistent with God's being so liable to be disappointed in all his works, nor indeed with his failing of his end in any thing that he has undertaken or done.

SECTION XII.

GOD'S CERTAIN FOREKNOWLEDGE OF THE FUTURE VOLITIONS OF MORAL
AGENTS, INCONSISTENT WITH SUCH A CONTINGENCE OF THOSE VOLI-
TIONS AS IS WITHOUT ALL NECESSITY.

Having proved that God has a certain and infallible prescience of the act of the will of moral agents, I come now, in the *second* place, to show the consequence; to show how it follows from hence, that these events are *necessary*, with a necessity of connexion or consequence.

The chief Arminian divines, so far as I have had opportunity to observe, deny this consequence; and affirm, that if such foreknowledge be allowed, it is no evidence of any necessity of the event foreknown. Now, I desire that this matter may be particularly and thoroughly inquired into. I cannot but think that, on particular and full consideration, it may be perfectly determined, whether it be indeed so or not.

In order to a proper consideration of this matter, I would observe the following things.

I. It is very evident, with regard to a thing whose existence is infallibly and indissolubly connected with something which already hath, or has had, existence, the existence of that thing is necessary. Here may be noted:

1. I observed before, in explaining the nature of necessity, that in things which are past, their past existence is now necessary: having already made sure of existence, it is too late for any possibility of alteration in that respect: it is now impossible that it should be otherwise than true that that thing has existed.

2. If there be any such thing as a divine foreknowledge of the volitions of free agents, that foreknowledge, by the supposition, is a thing which already has, and long ago had, existence; and so, now its existence is necessary; it is now utterly impossible to be otherwise than that this foreknowledge should be, or should have been.

3. It is also very manifest, that those things which are indissolubly connected with other things that are necessary, are themselves necessary. As that proposition whose truth is necessarily connected with another proposition, which is necessarily true, is itself necessarily true. To say otherwise, would be a contradiction: it would be in effect to say, that the connexion was indissoluble, and yet was not so, but might be broken. If that, whose existence is indissolubly connected with something whose existence is now necessary, is itself not necessary, then it may possibly not exist, notwithstanding that indissoluble connexion of its existence.—Whether the absurdity be not glaring, let the reader judge.

4. It is no less evident, that if there be a full, certain, and infallible foreknowledge of the future existence of the volitions of moral agents, then there is a certain infallible and indissoluble connexion between those events and that foreknowledge; and that therefore, by the preceding observations, those events are necessary events; being infallibly and indissolubly connected with that, whose existence already is, and so is now necessary, and cannot but have been.

To say the foreknowledge is certain and infallible, and yet the connexion of the event with that foreknowledge is not indissoluble, but dissoluble and fallible, is very absurd. To affirm it, would be the same thing as to affirm that there is no necessary connexion between a proposition's being infallibly known to be true, and its being true indeed. So that it is perfectly demonstrable, that if there be any infallible knowledge of future volitions the event is *necessary;* or, in other words, that it is *impossible* but the event should come to pass. For if it be not impossible but that it may be otherwise, then it is not impossible but that the proposition which affirms its future coming to pass, may not now be true. But how absurd is that, on the supposition that there is now an infallible knowledge (*i. e.* knowledge which it is impossible should fail) that it is true. There is this absurdity in it, that it is not impossible but that there now should be no truth in that proposition which is now infallibly known to be true.

II. That no future event can be certainly foreknown, whose existence is contingent, and without all necessity, may be proved thus: it is impossible for a thing to be certainly known to any intellect without evidence. To suppose otherwise, implies a contradiction: because, for a thing to be certainly known to any understanding, is for it to be evident to that understanding: and for a thing to be evident to any understanding, is the same thing as for that understanding to see evidence of it: but no understanding, created or increated, can see evidence where there is none: for that is the same thing as to see that to be which is not. And therefore, if there be any truth which is absolutely without evidence, that truth is absolutely unknowable, insomuch that it implies a contradiction to suppose that it is known.

But if there be any future event, whose existence is contingent, without all necessity, the future existence of the event is absolutely without evidence. If there be any evidence of it, it must be one of these two sorts, either self-evidence or proof; for there can be no other sort of evidence but one of these two; an evident thing must be either evident in itself, or evident in something else; that is, evident by connexion with something else. But a future thing, whose existence is without all necessity, can have neither of these sorts of evidence. It cannot be self-evident; for if it be, it may be now known, by what is now to be seen in the thing itself; either its present existence, or the necessity of its nature: but both these are contrary to the supposition. It is supposed, both that the thing has no present existence to be seen, and also that it is not of such a nature as to be necessarily existent for the future: so that its future existence is not self-evident. And, *secondly,* neither is there any proof, or evidence in any thing else, or evidence of connexion with something else that is evident; for this is also contrary to the supposition. It is supposed, that there is now nothing existent, with which the future existence of the contingent event is connected. For such a connexion destroys its contingence, and supposes necessity. Thus it is demonstrated, that there is in the nature of things absolutely no evidence at all of the future existence of that event, which is contingent, without all necessity (if any such event there be,) neither self-evidence nor proof. And therefore the thing in reality is not evident; and so cannot be seen to be evident, or, which is the same thing, cannot be known.

Let us consider this in an example. Suppose that five thousand seven hundred and sixty years ago there was no other being but the Divine Being; and then this world, or some particular body or spirit, all at once starts out of nothing into being, and takes on itself a particular nature and form; all in *absolute contingence*, without any concern of God, or any other cause, in the matter; without any manner of ground or reason of its existence; or any dependence upon, or connexion at all with, any thing foregoing: I say, that if this be supposed, there was no evidence of that event beforehand. There was no evidence of it to be seen *in the thing itself;* for the thing itself as yet was not. And there was no evidence of it to be seen *in any thing else;* for *evidence in* something else, is *connexion with* something else: but such connexion is contrary to the supposition. There was no evidence before, that this thing would happen; for, by the supposition, there was no reason why it should happen, rather than something else, or rather than nothing. And if so, then all things before were exactly equal and the same, with respect to that and other possible things: there was no preponderation, no superior weight or value; and therefore nothing that could be of any weight or value to determine any understanding. The thing was absolutely without evidence, and absolutely unknowable. An increase of understanding, or of the capacity of discerning, has no tendency, and makes no advance, to a discerning any signs or evidences of it, let it be increased never so much; yea, if it be increased infinitely. The increase of the strength of sight may have a tendency to enable to discern the evidence which is far off, and very much hid, and deeply involved in clouds and darkness; but it has no tendency to enable to discern evidence where there is none. If the sight be infinitely strong, and the capacity of discerning infinitely great, it will enable to see all that there is, and to see it perfectly and with ease: yet it has no tendency at all to enable a being to discern that evidence which is not; but, on the contrary, it has a tendency to enable to discern with great certainty that there is none.

III. To suppose the future volitions of moral agents not to be necessary events; or, which is the same thing, events which it is not impossible but that they may not come to pass; and yet to suppose that God certainly foreknows them, and knows all things, is to suppose God's knowledge to be inconsistent with itself. For to say, that God certainly, and without all conjecture, knows that a thing will infallibly be, which at the same time he knows to be so contingent that it may possibly not be, is to suppose his knowledge inconsistent with itself; or that one thing that he knows, is utterly inconsistent with another thing that he knows. It is the same thing as to say, he now knows a proposition to be of certain infallible truth, which he knows to be of contingent uncertain truth. If a future volition is so without all necessity, that there is nothing hinders but that it may not be, then the proposition which asserts its future existence is so uncertain, that there is nothing hinders but that the truth of it may entirely fail. And if God knows all things, he knows this proposition to be thus uncertain. And that is inconsistent with his knowing that it is infallibly true, and so inconsistent with his infallibly knowing that it is true. If the thing be indeed contingent, God views it so, and judges it to be contingent, if he views things as they are. If the event be not necessary, then it is possible it may never

be : and if it be possible it may never be, God knows it
may possibly not be true, and that is to know that the
truth of it is uncertain; which surely is inconsistent
with his knowing it as a certain truth. If volitions are
in themselves contingent events, without all necessity,
then it is no argument of perfection of knowledge in
any being to determine peremptorily that they will be;
but, on the contrary, an argument of ignorance and mistake; because it would argue, that he supposes that
proposition to be certain, which, in its own nature, and
all things considered, is uncertain and contingent. To
say, in such a case, that God may have ways of knowing contingent events which we cannot conceive of, is
ridiculous; as much so, as to say that God may know
contradictions to be true, for aught we know, or that he
may know a thing to be certain, and at the same time
know it not to be certain, though we cannot conceive
how; because he has ways of knowing which we cannot
comprehend.

Corol. 1. From what has been observed, it is evident
that the absolute *decrees* of God are no more inconsistent
with human liberty, on account of any necessity of the
event which follows from such decrees, than the absolute *foreknowledge* of God. Because the connexion between the event and certain foreknowledge, is as infallible and indissoluble as between the event and an absolute decree. That is, it is no more impossible, that the
event and decree should not agree together, than that the
event and absolute knowledge should disagree. The
connexion between the event and foreknowledge is absolutely perfect, by the supposition ; because it is supposed, that the certainty and infallibility of the knowledge is absolutely perfect. And it being so, the certainty cannot be increased ; and therefore the connexion
between the knowledge and thing known cannot be increased; so that if a decree be added to the foreknowledge, it does not at all increase the connexion, or make
it more infallible and indissoluble. If it were not so,
the certainty of knowledge might be increased by the

addition of a decree; which is contrary to the supposition, which is, that the knowledge is absolutely perfect, or perfect to the highest possible degree.

There is as much of an impossibility but that the things which are infallibly foreknown, should be, or (which is the same thing) as great a necessity of their future existence, as if the event were already written down, and was known and read by all mankind, through all preceding ages, and there was the most indissoluble and perfect connexion possible between the writing and the thing written. In such a case, it would be as impossible the event should fail of existence, as if it had existed already ; and a decree cannot make an event surer or more necessary than this.

And therefore, if there be any such foreknowledge, as it has been proved there is, then necessity of connexion and consequence is not at all inconsistent with any liberty which man or any other creature enjoys. And from hence it may be inferred, that absolute decrees of God, which do not at all increase the necessity, are not at all inconsistent with the liberty which man enjoys, on any such account, as that they make the event decreed necessary, and render it utterly impossible but that it should come to pass. Therefore, if absolute decrees are inconsistent with man's liberty as a moral agent, or his liberty in a state of probation, or any liberty whatsoever that he enjoys, it is not on account of any necessity which absolute decrees infer.

Dr Whitby supposes there is a great difference between God's foreknowledge, and his decrees, with regard to necessity of future events. In his " Discourse on the Five Points," p. 474, &c., he says, " God's prescience has no influence at all on our actions.—Should God, by immediate revelation, give me the knowledge of the event of any man's state or actions, would my knowledge of them have any influence upon his actions? Surely none at all—our knowledge doth not affect the things we know, to make them more certain, or more future, than they would be without it. Now, foreknowledge in God is knowledge. As therefore knowledge has no influence on things that are, so neither has foreknowledge on things that shall be. And, consequently, the foreknowledge of any action that would be otherwise free, cannot alter or diminish that freedom. Whereas God's decree of election is powerful and active, and comprehends the preparation and exhibition of such means as shall unfrustrably produce the end. Hence God's prescience renders no actions necessary." And to this purpose, p. 473, he cites Origen, where he says, "God's prescience is not the cause of things future, but their being future is the cause of God's prescience that they will be;" and Le Blanc, where he says, "This is the truest resolution of this difficulty, that prescience is not the cause that things are future; but their being future is the cause they are foreseen." In like manner, Dr Clarke, in his "Demonstration of the Being and Attributes of God," pp. 95—99. And the author of the "Freedom of Will in God and the Creature," speaking to the like purpose with Dr Whitby, represents "foreknowledge as having no more influence on things known, to make them necessary, than after-knowledge," or to that purpose.

To all which I would say, that what is said about knowledge, its not having influence on the thing known to make it necessary, is nothing to the purpose, nor does it in the least affect the foregoing reasoning. Whether prescience be the thing that *makes* the event necessary or no, it alters not the case. Infallible foreknowledge may *prove* the necessity of the event foreknown, and yet not be the thing which *causes* the necessity. If the foreknowledge be absolute, this *proves* the event known to be necessary, or proves that it is impossible but that the event should be, by some means or other, either by a decree, or some other way, if there be any other way: because, as was said before, it is absurd to say, that a proposition is known to be certainly and infallibly true, which yet may possibly prove not true.

The whole of the seeming force of this evasion lies in

this : that, inasmuch as certain foreknowledge does no *cause* an event to be necessary, as a decree does : therefore it does not *prove* it to be necessary, as a decree does. But there is no force in this arguing : for it is built wholly on this supposition, that nothing can *prove*, or *be an evidence* of a thing's being necessary, but that which has *a causal influence to make it so*. But this can never be maintained. If certain foreknowledge of the future existing of an event, be not the thing which first *makes* it impossible that it should fail of existence : yet it may, and certainly does, *demonstrate* that it is impossible it should fail of it, however that impossibility comes. If foreknowledge be not the cause, but the effect, of this impossibility, it may prove that there is such an impossibility, as much as if it were the cause. It is as strong arguing from the effect to the cause, as from the cause to the effect. It is enough that an existence, which is infallibly foreknown, cannot fail whether that impossibility arises from the foreknowledge, or is prior to it. It is as evident, as it is possible any thing should be, that it is impossible a thing which is infallibly known to be true, should prove not to be true : therefore there is a necessity that it should be otherwise ; whether the knowledge be the cause of this necessity, or the necessity the cause of the knowledge.

All certain knowledge, whether it be foreknowledge or after-knowledge, or concomitant knowledge, proves the thing known now to be necessary, by some means or other ; or proves that it is impossible it should now be otherwise than true. I freely allow, that foreknowledge does not prove a thing to be necessary, any more than after-knowledge ; but then after-knowledge, which is certain and infallible, proves that it is now become impossible but that the proposition known should be true. Certain after-knowledge proves that it is now, in the time of the knowledge, by some means or other, become impossible but that the proposition which predicates *past* existence on the event, should be true. And so does certain foreknowledge prove, that now, in the time of the knowledge, it is, by some means or other, become impossible but that the proposition which predicates *future* existence on the event, should be true. The necessity of the truth of the propositions, consisting in the present impossibility of the non-existence of the event affirmed, in both cases is the immediate ground of the certainty of the knowledge; there can be no certainty of knowledge without it.

There must be a certainty in things themselves, before they are certainly known, or (which is the same thing) known to be certain. For certainty of knowledge is nothing else but knowing or discerning the certainty there is in the things themselves, which are known. Therefore there must be a certainty in things to be a ground of certainty of knowledge, and to render things capable of being known to be certain. And this is nothing but the necessity of the truth known, or its being impossible but that it should be true; or, in other words, the firm and infallible connexion between the subject and predicate of the proposition that contains that truth. All certainty of knowledge consists in the view of the firmness of that connexion. So God's certain foreknowledge of the future existence of any event, is his view of the firm and indissoluble connexion of the subject and predicate of the proposition that affirms its future existence. The subject is that possible event; the predicate is its future existing: but if future existence be firmly and indissolubly connected with that event, then the future existence of that event is necessary. If God certainly knows the future existence of an event which is wholly contingent, and may possibly never be, then he sees a firm connexion between a subject and predicate that are not firmly connected; which is a contradiction.

I allow what Dr Whitby says to be true, "that mere knowledge does not affect the thing known, to make it more certain or more future." But yet, I say, it supposes and proves the thing to be already both future and certain; *i. e.* necessarily future. Knowledge of futurity supposes futurity; and a certain knowledge of

futurity supposes certain futurity, antecedent to that
certain knowledge. But there is no other certain futurity of a thing, antecedent to certainty of knowledge,
than a prior impossibility but that the thing should
prove true; or (which is the same thing) the necessity
of the event.

I would observe one thing further concerning this
matter; it is this: that if it be as those forementioned
writers suppose, that God's foreknowledge is not the
cause, but the effect, of the existence of the event foreknown; this is so far from showing that this foreknowledge doth not infer the necessity of the existence of
that event, that it rather shows the contrary the more
plainly. Because it shows the existence of the event to
be so settled and firm, that it is as if it had already been;
inasmuch as in effect it actually exists already; its future existence has already had actual influence and efficiency, and has produced an effect, viz. prescience: the
effect exists already; and as the effect supposes, the cause
is connected with the cause, and depends entirely upon
it, therefore it is as if the future event, which is the
cause, had existed already. The effect is firm as possible, it having already the possession of existence, and
has made sure of it. But the effect cannot be more firm
and stable than its cause, ground, and reason. The building cannot be firmer than the foundation.

To illustrate this matter, let us suppose the appearances and images of things in a glass; for instance, a reflecting telescope, to be the real effects of heavenly bodies
(at a distance, and out of sight) which they resemble:
if it be so, then, as these images in the telescope have
had a past actual existence, and it is become utterly
impossible now that it should be otherwise than that
they have existed; so they being the true effects of the
heavenly bodies they resemble, this proves the existing
of those heavenly bodies to be as real, infallible, firm,
and necessary, as the existing of these effects; the one
being connected with, and wholly depending on, the
other.—Now let us suppose future existences some way

or other to have influence back, to produce effects beforehand, and cause exact and perfect images of themselves
in a glass, a thousand years before they exist, yea, in all
preceding ages; but yet that these images are real effects
of these future existences, perfectly dependent on, and,
connected with, their cause; these effects and images
having already had actual existence, rendering that matter of their existing perfectly firm and stable, and utterly impossible to be otherwise: this proves in like manner, as in the other instance, that the existence of the
things, which are their causes, is also equally sure, firm,
and necessary; and that it is alike impossible but that
they should be, as if they had been already, as their
effects have. And if, instead of images in a glass, we
suppose the antecedent effects to be perfect ideas of them
in the Divine Mind, which have existed there from all
eternity, which are as properly effects, as truly and properly connected with their cause, the case is not altered.

Another thing which has been said by some Arminians to take off the force of what is urged from God's
prescience, against the contingence of the volitions of
moral agents, is to this purpose:—" That when we talk
of foreknowledge in God, there is no strict propriety in
our so speaking; and that although it be true, that there
is in God the most perfect knowledge of all events, from
eternity to eternity, yet there is no such thing as *before*
and *after* in God, but he sees all things by one perfect,
unchangeable view, without any succession." To this I
answer:

1. It has been already shown, that all certain knowledge proves the necessity of the truth known; whether
it be before, after, or at the same time. Though it be
true, that there is no succession in God's knowledge,
and the manner of his knowledge is to us inconceivable,
yet thus much we know concerning it, that there is no
event, past, present, or to come, that God is ever uncertain of; he never is, never was, and never will be, without infallible knowledge of it; he always sees the existence of it to be certain and infallible. And as he always

sees things just as they are in truth, hence there never
is in reality any thing contingent in such a sense, as
that possibly it may happen never to exist. If, strictly
speaking, there is no foreknowledge in God, it is because
those things which are future to us, are as present to God
as if they already had existence; and that is as much as
to say, that future events are always in God's view as
evident, clear, sure, and necessary, as if they already
were. If there never is a time wherein the existence
of the event is not present with God, then there never is
a time wherein it is not as much impossible for it to fail
of existence, as if its existence were present, and were
already come to pass.

God's viewing things so perfectly and unchangeably
as that there is no succession in his ideas or judgment,
does not hinder but that there is properly now, in the
mind of God, a certain and perfect knowledge of moral
actions of men, which to us are an hundred years hence:
yea, the objection supposes this; and therefore it certainly does not hinder but that, by the foregoing arguments, it is now impossible these moral actions should
not come to pass.

We know that God knows the future voluntary actions of men in such a sense beforehand, as that he is
able particularly to declare, and foretell them, and write
them, or cause them to be written down in a book, as
he often has done; and that therefore the necessary connexion which there is between God's knowledge and
the event known, does as much prove the event to be
necessary beforehand, as if the Divine knowledge were
in the same sense before the event, as the prediction or
writing is. If the knowledge be infallible, then the expression of it in the written prediction is infallible; that
is, there is an infallible connexion between that written
prediction and the event. And if so, then it is impossible it should ever be otherwise, than that that prediction and the event should agree; and this is the same
thing as to say, it is impossible but that the event
should come to pass; and this is the same as to say, that

its coming to pass is necessary. So that it is manifest, that there being no proper succession in God's mind, makes no alteration as to the necessity of the existence of the events which God knows. Yea,

2. This is so far from weakening the proof which has been given of the impossibility of the not coming to pass of future events known, as that it establishes that wherein the strength of the foregoing arguments consists, and shows the clearness of the evidence. For,

(1.) The very reason why God's knowledge is without succession, is, because it is absolutely perfect, to the highest possible degree of clearness and certainty: all things, whether past, present, or to come, being viewed with equal evidence and fulness; future things being seen with as much clearness as if they were present; the view is always in absolute perfection; and absolute constant perfection admits of no alteration, and so no succession; the actual existence of the thing known, does not at all increase or add to the clearness or certainty of the thing known: God calls the things that are not as though they were; they are all one to him as if they had already existed. But herein consists the strength of the demonstration before given, of the impossibility of the not existing of those things, whose existence God knows; that it is as impossible they should fail of existence, as if they existed already. This objection, instead of weakening this argument, sets it in the clearest and strongest light; for it supposes it to be so indeed, that the existence of future events is in God's view so much as if it already had been, that when they come actually to exist, it makes not the least alteration or variation in his view or knowledge of them.

(2.) The objection is founded on the immutability of God's knowledge: for it is the immutability of knowledge makes his knowledge to be without succession. But this most directly and plainly demonstrates the thing I insist on, viz. that it is utterly impossible the known events should fail of existence. For if that were possible, then it would be possible for there to be a change in God's knowledge and view of things. For if the known event should fail of existence, and not come into being, as God expected, then God would see it, and so would change his mind, and see his former mistake; and thus there would be change and succession in his knowledge. But as God is immutable, and so it is utterly infinitely impossible that his view should be changed; so it is, for the same reason, just so impossible that the foreknown event should not exist; and that is to be impossible in the highest degree: and therefore the contrary is necessary. Nothing is more impossible than that the immutable God should be changed by the succession of time; who comprehends all things, from eternity to eternity, in one most perfect and unalterable view; so that his whole eternal duration is *vita interminabilis, tota, simul, et perfecta possessio.*

On the whole, I need not fear to say, that there is no geometrical theorem or proposition whatsoever more capable of strict demonstration, than that God's certain prescience of the volitions of moral agents is inconsistent with such a contingence of these events, as it is without all necessity; and so is inconsistent with the Arminian notion of liberty.

Corol. 2. Hence the doctrine of the Calvinists, concerning the absolute decrees of God, does not at all infer any more fatality in things, than will demonstrably follow from the doctrine of most Arminian divines, who acknowledge God's omniscience and universal prescience. Therefore all objections they make against the doctrine of the Calvinists, as implying Hobbes's doctrine of necessity, or the Stoical doctrine of fate, lie no more against the doctrine of Calvinists than their own doctrine; and therefore it doth not become those divines to raise such an outcry against the Calvinists on this account.

Corol. 3. Hence all arguing, from necessity, against the doctrine of the inability of unregenerate men to perform the conditions of salvation, and the commands of God requiring spiritual duties, and against the Calvinistic doctrine of efficacious grace; I say, all arguings of Arminians (such of them as own God's omniscience) against these things, on this ground, that these doctrines, though they do not suppose men to be under any constraint or coaction, yet suppose them under necessity with respect to their moral actions, and those things which are required of them in order to their acceptance with God; and their arguing against the necessity of men's volitions, taken from the reasonableness of God's commands, promises, and threatenings, and the sincerity of his counsels and invitations; and all objections against any doctrines of the Calvinists, as being inconsistent with human liberty, because they infer necessity; I say, all these arguments and objections must fall to the ground, and be justly esteemed vain and frivolous, as coming from them; being maintained in an inconsistence with themselves, and in like manner levelled against their own doctrine, as against the doctrine of the Calvinists.

SECTION XIII.

WHETHER WE SUPPOSE THE VOLITIONS OF MORAL AGENTS TO BE CONNECTED WITH ANY THING ANTECEDENT, OR NOT, YET THEY MUST BE NECESSARY IN SUCH A SENSE AS TO OVERTHROW ARMINIAN LIBERTY.

EVERY act of the will has a cause, or it has not. If it has a cause, then, according to what has already been demonstrated, it is not contingent, but necessary; the effect being necessarily dependent and consequent on its cause; and that, let the cause be what it will. If the cause is the will itself, by antecedent acts choosing and determining, still the determined and caused act must be a necessary effect. The act, that is the determined effect of the foregoing act which is its cause, cannot prevent the efficiency of its cause, but must be wholly subject to its determination and command, as much as the motions of the hands and feet. The consequent commanded acts of the will are as passive and as necessary, with respect to the antecedent determining acts, as the

parts of the body are to the volitions which determine
and command them. And therefore, if all the free acts
of the will are thus, if they are all determined effects,
determined by the will itself, that is, determined by antecedent choice, then they are all necessary ; they are
all subject to, and decisively fixed by the foregoing act,
which is their cause: yea, even the determining act itself; for that must be determined and fixed by another
act, preceding that, if it be a free and voluntary act;
and so must be necessary. So that by this all the free
acts of the will are necessary, and cannot be free unless
they are necessary: because they cannot be free, according to the Arminian notion of freedom, unless they are
determined by the will, which is to be determined by
antecedent choice; which being their cause, proves them
necessary. And yet they say, necessity is utterly inconsistent with liberty. So that, by their scheme, the
acts of the will cannot be free, unless they are necessary,
and yet cannot be free if they be not necessary!

But if the other part of the dilemma be taken, and it
be affirmed that the free acts of the will have no cause,
and are connected with nothing whatsoever that goes
before them and determines them, in order to maintain
their proper and absolute contingence, and this should
be allowed to be possible; still it will not serve their
turn. For if the volition come to pass by perfect contingence, and without any cause at all, then it is certain,
no act of the will, no prior act of the soul, was the
cause; no determination or choice of the soul had any
hand in it. The will, or the soul, was indeed the subject of what happened to it accidentally, but was not
the cause. The will is not active in causing or determining, but purely the passive subject; at least according to their notion of action and passion. In this case,
contingence does as much prevent the determination of
the will, as a proper cause; and as to the will, it was necessary, and could be no otherwise. For to suppose
that it could have been otherwise, if the will or soul had
pleased, is to suppose that the act is dependent on some
prior act of choice or pleasure; contrary to what now is

supposed: it is to suppose that it might have been otherwise, if its cause had made it or ordered it otherwise.
But this does not agree to its having no cause or orderer
at all. That must be necessary as to the soul, which is
dependent on no free act of the soul: but that which is
without a cause, is dependent on no free act of the soul;
because, by the supposition, it is dependent on nothing,
and is connected with nothing. In such a case, the soul
is necessarily subjected to what accident brings to pass,
from time to time, as much as the earth, that is inactive, is necessarily subjected to what falls upon it. But
this does not consist with the Arminian notion of liberty, which is the will's power of determining itself in its
own acts, and being wholly active in it, without passiveness, and without being subject to necessity. Thus,
contingence belongs to the Arminian notion of liberty,
and yet is inconsistent with it.

I would here observe, that the author of the "Essay
on the Freedom of Will in God and the Creature,"
pages 76, 77, says as follows: "The word *chance* always
means something done without design. Chance and design stand in direct opposition to each other; and chance
can never be properly applied to acts of the will, which
is the spring of all design, and which designs to choose
whatsoever it doth choose, whether there be any superi-
or fitness in the thing which it chooses, or no; and it
designs to determine itself to one thing, where two
things, perfectly equal, are proposed, merely because it
will." But herein appears a very great inadvertence in
this author. For if "the will be the spring of all design," as he says, then certainly it is not always the effect of design; and the acts of the will themselves must
sometimes come to pass, when they do not spring from
design; and consequently come to pass by chance, according to his own definition of chance. And if "the
will designs to choose whatsoever it does choose," and
"designs to determine itself," as he says, then it designs
to determine all its designs: which carries us back from
one design to a foregoing design determining that, and
to another determining that; and so on *in infinitum*.

The very first design must be the effect of foregoing design, or else it must be by chance, in his notion of it.

Here another alternative may be proposed, relating to the connexion of the acts of the will with something foregoing, that is their cause, not much unlike to the other; which is this: either human liberty is such, that it may well stand with volitions being necessarily connected with the views of the understanding, and so is consistent with necessity; or it is inconsistent with, and contrary to, such a connexion and necessity. The former is directly subversive of the Arminian notion of liberty, consisting in freedom from all necessity. And if the latter be chosen, and it be said that liberty is inconsistent with any such necessary connexion of volition with foregoing views of the understanding, it consisting in freedom from any such necessity of the will as that would imply; then the liberty of the soul consists (in part at least) in the freedom from restraint, limitation, and government, in its actings by the understanding, and in liberty and liableness to act contrary to the understanding's views and dictates; and consequently, the more the soul has of this disengagedness in its acting, the more liberty. Now let it be considered what this brings the noble principle of human liberty to, particularly when it is possessed and enjoyed in its perfection, viz. a full and perfect freedom and liableness to act altogether at random, without the least connexion with, or restraint or government by, any dictate of reason, or any thing whatsoever apprehended, considered, or viewed by the understanding; as being inconsistent with the full and perfect sovereignty of the will over its own determinations. The notion mankind have conceived of liberty, is some dignity or privilege, something worth claiming. But what dignity or privilege is there, in being given up to such a wild contingence as this, to be perfectly and constantly liable to act unintelligently and unreasonably, and as much without the guidance of understanding, as if we had none, or were as destitute of perception as the smoke that is driven by the wind!

PART III.

SECTION I.

GOD'S MORAL EXCELLENCY NECESSARY, YET VIRTUOUS AND PRAISEWORTHY.

HAVING considered the *first* thing that was proposed to be inquired into, relating to that freedom of will which Arminians maintain; namely, whether any such thing does, ever did, or ever can exist, or be conceived of; I come now to the *second* thing proposed to be the subject of inquiry, *viz.* Whether any such kind of liberty be requisite to moral agency, virtue and vice, praise and blame, reward and punishment, &c.

I shall begin with some consideration of the virtue and agency of the supreme moral Agent, and Fountain of all agency and virtue.

Dr Whitby, in his discourse on the " Five Points," p. 14, says, " If all human actions are necessary, virtue and vice must be empty names; we being capable of nothing that is blame-worthy, or deserveth praise; for who can blame a person for doing only what he could not help, or judge that he deserveth praise only for what he could not avoid?" To the like purpose he speaks in places innumerable; especially in his discourse on the " Freedom of the Will;" constantly maintaining, that a freedom not only from coaction, but necessity, is absolutely requisite, in order to actions being either worthy of blame, or deserving of praise. And to this agrees, as is well known, the current doctrine of Arminian writers, who, in general, hold, that there is no virtue or vice, reward or punishment, nothing to be commended or blamed, without this freedom. And yet Dr Whitby, p.

300, allows, that God is without this freedom; and
Arminians, so far as I have had opportunity to observe,
generally acknowledge that God is necessarily holy, and
his will necessarily determined to that which is good.

So that, putting these things together, the infinitely
holy God, who always used to be esteemed by God's
people not only virtuous, but a Being in whom is all
possible virtue, and every virtue in the most absolute
purity and perfection, and in infinitely greater brightness and amiableness than in any creature: the most
perfect pattern of virtue, and the fountain from whom
all others' virtue is but as beams from the sun; and who
has been supposed to be, on the account of his virtue
and holiness, infinitely more worthy to be esteemed, loved,
honoured, admired, commended, extolled, and praised,
than any creature: and he who is thus every where represented in Scripture; I say, this Being, according to
this notion of Dr Whitby, and other Arminians, has no
virtue at all: virtue, when ascribed to him, is but an
empty name; and he is deserving of no commendation
or praise; because he is under necessity, he cannot avoid
being holy and good as he is; therefore no thanks to
him for it. It seems, the holiness, justice, faithfulness,
&c. of the Most High, must not be accounted to be of
the nature of that which is virtuous, and praiseworthy.
They will not deny, that these things in God are good; but
then we must understand them, that they are no more
virtuous, or of the nature of any thing commendable,
than the good that is in any other being that is not a
moral agent; as the brightness of the sun, and the ferti-
lity of the earth, are good, but not virtuous, because
these properties are necessary to these bodies, and not
the fruit of self-determining power.

There needs no other confutation of this notion of
God's not being virtuous or praiseworthy, to Christians
acquainted with the Bible, but only stating and particularly representing of it. To bring texts of Scripture,
wherein God is represented as in every respect in the
highest manner virtuous and supremely praise-worthy,

would be endless, and is altogether needless to such as
have been brought up in the light of the Gospel.

It were to be wished that Dr Whitby, and other divines
of the same sort, had explained themselves, when they
have asserted, that that which is necessary, is not deserving of praise; at the same time that they have owned
God's perfection to be necessary, and so in effect representing God as not deserving praise. Certainly, if their
words have any meaning at all, by praise they must
mean the exercise or testimony of some sorts of esteem,
respect, or honourable regard. And will they then say,
that men are worthy of that esteem, respect, and honour,
for their virtue, small and inperfect as it is, which God
is not worthy of, for his infinite righteousnes, holiness,
and goodness? If so, it must be because of some sort of
peculiar excellency in the virtuous man, which is his
prerogative, wherein he really has the preference; some
dignity that is entirely distinguished from any excellency, amiableness, or honourableness in God; not in
imperfection and dependence, but in pre-eminence; which
therefore, he does not receive from God, nor is God the
fountain or pattern of it; nor can God, in that respect,
stand in competition with him as the object of honour
and regard; but man may claim a peculiar esteem, commendation, and glory, that God can have no pretension
to. Yea, God has no right, by virtue of his necessary
holiness, to intermeddle with that grateful respect and
praise due to the virtuous man, who chooses virtue in
the exercise of a freedom *ad utrumque,* any more than a
precious stone, which cannot avoid being hard and beautiful.

And if it be so, let it be explained what that peculiar
respect is that is due to the virtuous man, which differs
in nature and kind, in some way of pre-eminence, from
all that is due to God. What is the name or description
of that peculiar affection? Is it esteem, love, admira-
tion, honour, praise, or gratitude? The Scripture every
where represents God as the highest object of all these:
there we read of the soul's magnifying the Lord, of lov-

ing him with all the heart, with all the soul, with all the mind, and with all the strength; admiring him, and his righteous acts, or greatly regarding them as marvellous and wonderful; honouring, glorifying, exalting, extolling, blessing, thanking, and praising him; giving unto him all the glory of the good which is done or received, rather than unto men; that no flesh should glory in his presence; but that he should be regarded as the Being to whom all glory is due. What, then, is that respect? What passion, affection, or exercise, is it, that Arminians call praise, diverse from all these things which men are worthy of for their virtue, and which God is not worthy of in any degree?

If that necessity which attends God's moral perfections and actions be as inconsistent with a being worthy of praise, as a necessity of coaction, as is plainly implied in, or inferred from, Dr Whitby's discourse; then why should we thank God for his goodness, any more than if he were forced to be good or any more than we should thank one of our fellow-creatures who did us good, not freely, and of good will, or from any kindness of heart, but from mere compulsion or extrinsical necessity? Arminians suppose that God is necessarily a good and gracious being; for this they make the ground of some of their main arguments against many doctrines maintained by Calvinists; they say these are *certainly* false, and it is *impossible* they should be true, because they are not consistent with the goodness of God. This supposes, that it is *impossible* but that God should be good: for if it be possible that he should be otherwise, then that impossibility of the truth of these doctrines ceases, according to their own argument.

That virtue in God is not, in the most proper sense, *rewardable*, is not for want of merit in his moral perfections and actions, sufficient to deserve rewards from his creatures; but because he is infinitely above all capacity of receiving any reward or benefit from the creature; he is already infinitely and unchangeably happy, and we cannot be profitable unto him. But still he is worthy of our supreme benevolence for his virtue; and would be worthy of our beneficence, which is the fruit and expression of benevolence, if our goodness could extend to him. If God deserves to be thanked and praised for his goodness, he would, for the same reason, deserve that we should also *requite* his kindness, if that were possible. " What shall I render to the Lord for all his benefits?" is the natural language of thankfulness : and so far as in us lies, it is our duty to recompense God's goodness, and render again according to benefits received. And that we might have opportunity for so natural an expression of our gratitude to God as beneficence, notwithstanding his being infinitely above our reach, he has appointed others to be his receivers, and to stand in his stead as the objects of our beneficence; such are especially our indigent brethren.

SECTION II.

THE ACTS OF THE WILL OF THE HUMAN SOUL OF JESUS CHRIST NECESSARILY HOLY, YET TRULY VIRTUOUS, PRAISEWORTHY, REWARDABLE, &c.

I HAVE already considered how Dr Whitby insists upon it, that a freedom, not only from co-action, but necessity, is " requisite either to virtue or vice, praise or dispraise, reward or punishment." He also insists on the same freedom as absolutely requisite to a person's being the subject of a law, of precepts, or prohibitions ; in the book before mentioned, (pp. 301, 314, 328, 339, 340, 341, 342, 347, 361, 373, 410.) And of promises and threatenings, (pp. 298, 301, 305, 311, 339, 340, 363.) And as requisite to a state of trial, (p. 297, &c.)

Now, therefore, with an eye to these things, I would inquire into the moral conduct and practices of our Lord Jesus Christ, which he exhibited in his human nature here in his state of humiliation. And, *first*, I would show, that his holy behaviour was necessary; or that it was impossible it should be otherwise than that he should behave himself holily, and that he should be perfectly holy in each individual act of his life. And, *secondly*, that his holy behaviour was properly the nature of virtue, and was worthy of praise; and that he was the subject of law, precepts, or commands, promises, and rewards; and that he was in a state of trial.

I. It was impossible that the acts of the will of the human soul of Christ should, in any instance, degree, or circumstance, be otherwise than holy, and agreeable to God's nature and will. The following things make this evident.

1. God had promised so effectually to preserve and uphold him by his Spirit, under all his temptations, that he could not fail of reaching the end for which he came into the world; which he would have failed of, had he fallen into sin. We have such a promise, Isa. xlii. 1, 2, 3, 4, "Behold my servant, whom I uphold; mine elect, in whom my soul delighteth: I have put my Spirit upon him; he shall bring forth judgment to the Gentiles. He shall not cry, nor lift up, nor cause his voice to be heard in the street.—He shall bring forth judgment unto truth. He shall not fail nor be discouraged, till he have set judgment in the earth; and the isles shall wait for his law." This promise, of Christ's having God's Spirit put upon him, and his not crying and lifting up his voice, &c. relates to the time of Christ's appearance on earth, as is manifest from the nature of the promise, and also the application of it in the New Testament, Matt. xii. 18. And the words imply a promise of his being so upheld by God's Spirit, that he should be preserved from sin; particularly from pride and vain-glory, and from being overcome by any of the temptations he should be under to affect the glory of this world, the pomp of an earthly prince, or the applause and praise of men: and that he should be so upheld, that he should by no means fail of obtaining the end of his coming into the world, of bringing forth judgment unto victory, and establishing his kingdom of grace in the earth,—and in the following verses this promise is confirmed, with the greatest imaginable solemnity: "Thus saith the LORD, HE that created the heavens and stretched them out; he that spread

forth the earth, and that which cometh out of it; he that giveth breath unto the people upon it, and spirit to them that walk therein: I the Lord have called thee in righteousness, and will hold thine hand, and will keep thee, and give thee for a covenant of the people, for a light of the Gentiles; to open the blind eyes, to bring out the prisoners from the prison, and them that sit in darkness out of the prison-house. I am JEHOVAH, that is my name," &c.

Very parallel with these promises is that, Isaiah xlix. 7, 8, 9, which also has an apparent respect to the time of Christ's humiliation on earth: "Thus saith the Lord, the Redeemer of Israel, and his Holy One, to him whom man despiseth, to him whom the nation abhorreth, to a servant of rulers, Kings shall see and arise, princes also shall worship, because of the Lord that is faithful, and the Holy One of Israel, and he shall choose thee. Thus saith the Lord, In an acceptable time have I heard thee, and in a day of salvation have I helped thee; and I will preserve thee, and give thee for a covenant of the people, to establish the earth," &c.

And Isa. l. 5, 6, we have the Messiah expressing his assurance that God would help him, by so opening his ear, or inclining his heart to God's commandments, that he should not be rebellious, but should persevere, and not apostatise or turn his back: that through God's help, he should be immovable, in a way of obedience, under the great trials of reproach and suffering he should meet with; setting his face like a flint: so that he knew he should not be ashamed, or frustrated in his design; and finally should be approved and justified, as having done his work faithfully: "The Lord hath opened mine ear; so that I was not rebellious, neither turned away my back. I gave my back to the smiters, and my cheeks to them that plucked off the hair: I hid not my face from shame and spitting. For the Lord God will help me; therefore shall I not be confounded: therefore have I set my face as a flint, and I know that I shall not be ashamed. He is near that justifieth me; who will contend with me?

let us stand together. Who is mine adversary? let him come near to me. Behold, the Lord God will help me; who is he that shall condemn me? lo, they all shall wax old as a garment; the moth shall eat them up."

2. The same thing is evident from all the promises which God made to the Messiah, of his future glory, kingdom, and success, in his office and character of a Mediator; which glory could not have been obtained if his holiness had failed, and he had been guilty of sin. God's absolute promise of any things makes the things promised *necessary*, and their failing to take place absolutely *impossible :* and, in like manner, it makes those things necessary on which the thing promised depends, and without which it cannot take effect. Therefore it appears, that it was utterly impossible that Christ's holiness should fail, from such absolute promises as those, Psal. cx. 4. "The Lord hath sworn, and will not repent, Thou art a priest for ever, after the order of Melchizedek." And from every other promise in that psalm, contained in each verse of it. And Psal. ii. 7, 8, "I will declare the decree: the Lord hath said unto me, Thou art my Son; this day have I begotten thee. Ask of me and I will give thee the heathen for thine inheritance," &c. Psal. xlv. 3, 4, &c. "Gird thy sword on thy thigh, O most Mighty, with thy glory and thy majesty; and in thy majesty ride prosperously." And so every thing that is said from thence to the end of the psalm. And those promises, Isa. iii. 13, 14, 15; and liii. 10, 11, 12. And all those promises which God makes to the Messiah, of success, dominion, and glory, in the character of a Redeemer, in Isaiah, chap. xlix.

3. It was often promised to the church of God of old, for their comfort, that God would give them a righteous, sinless Saviour. Jer. xxiii. 5, 6, " Behold, the days come, saith the Lord, that I will raise up unto David a righteous Branch, and a King shall reign and prosper, and shall execute judgment and justice in the earth. In his days shall Judah be saved, and Israel shall dwell safely: and this is the name whereby he shall be called,

The Lord our righteousness." So, Jer. xxxiii. 15. " I will cause the Branch of rightousness to grow up unto David; and he shall execute judgment and righteousness in the land." Isa. ix. 6, 7. " For unto us a child is born;— upon the throne of David and of his kingdom, to order it, and to establish it with judgment and justice, from henceforth even for ever. The zeal of the Lord of Hosts will do this." Chap. xi. at the beginning: " There shall come forth a rod out of the stem of Jesse, and a Branch shall grow out of his roots: and the Spirit of the Lord shall rest upon him, the spirit of knowledge, and of the fear of the Lord. With righteousness shall he judge the poor, and reprove with equity. Righteousness shall be the girdle of his loins, and faithfulness the girdle of his reins." Chap. liii. 13, " My servant shall deal prudently." Chap. liii. 9, " Because he had done no violence, neither was guile found in his mouth." If it be impossible that these promises should fail, and if it be easier for heaven and earth to pass away, than one jot or tittle of these promises of God to pass away, then it was impossible that God should commit any sin. Christ himself signified, that it was impossible but that the things which were spoken concerning him should be fulfilled. Luke xiv. 44, " That all things must be fulfilled, which were written in the law of Moses, and in the prophets, and in the Psalms, concerning me." Matt. xxvi. 53, 54, " But how then shall the Scripture be fulfilled, that thus it must be ?" Mark xiv. 49, " But the Scriptures must be fulfilled." And so the Apostle, Acts i. 16, 17, " This Scripture must needs have been fulfilled.

4. All the promises, which were made to the church of old, of the Messiah as a future Saviour, from that made to our first parents in Paradise, to that which was delivered by the prophet Malachi, show it to be impossible that Christ should not have persevered in perfect holiness. The ancient predictions given to God's church, of the Messiah as a Saviour, were of the nature of promises, as is evident by the predictions themselves, and

the manner of delivering them. But they are expressly, and very often, called promises in the New Testament; as in Luke i. 54, 55, 72, 73; Acts xiii. 32, 33; Rom. i. 1, 2, 3; and chap. xv. 8; Heb. vi. 13, &c. These promises were often made with great solemnity, and confirmed with an oath; as in Gen. xxii. 16, 17, " By myself have I sworn, saith the Lord, that in blessing I will bless thee, and in multiplying I will multiply thy seed as the stars of heaven, and as the sand which is upon the sea-shore: and in thy seed shall all the nations of the earth be blessed." Compare Luke i. 72, 73; and Gal. iii. 8, 15, 16. The apostle, in Heb. vi. 17, 18, speaking of this promise to Abraham, says: " Wherein God, willing more abundantly to show to the heirs of promise the immutability of his counsel, confirmed it by an oath; that by two IMMUTABLE things, in which it was IMPOSSIBLE for God to lie, he might have strong consolation." In which words the necessity of the accomplishment, or (which is the same thing) the impossibility of the contrary, is fully declared. So God confirmed the promise of the great salvation of the Messiah, made to David, by an oath, Psal. lxxxix. 3, 4, " I have made a covenant with my chosen, I have sworn unto David my servant: Thy seed will I establish for ever, and build up thy throne to all generations." There is nothing that is so abundantly set forth in Scripture as sure and irrefragable, as this promise and oath to David. See Psal. lxxxix. 34, 35, 36; 2 Sam. xxiii. 5; Isa. lv. 4; Acts ii. 29, 30; and xiii. 34. The Scripture expressly speaks of it as utterly impossible that this promise and oath to David, concerning the everlasting dominion of the Messiah of his seed, should fail. Jer. xxxiii. 15, &c. "In those days, and at that time, I will cause the Branch of righteousness to grow up unto David. For thus saith the Lord, David shall never want a man to sit upon the throne of the house of Israel." Ver. 20, 21, " If you can break my covenant of the day, and my covenant of the night, and that there should not be day and night in their season; then may also my covenant be broken with David my servant, that he should not have a son to reign upon his throne." So in ver. 25, 26. Thus abundant is the Scripture in representing how impossible it was, that the promises made of old concerning the great salvation and kingdom of the Messiah should fail; which implies, that it was impossible that this Messiah, the second Adam, the promised seed of Abraham and of David, should fall from his integrity, as the first Adam did.

5. All the promises that were made to the church of God under the Old Testament, of the great enlargement of the church, and advancement of her glory, in the days of the gospel, after the coming of the Messiah; the increase of her light, liberty, holiness, joy, triumph over her enemies, &c. of which so great a part of the Old Testament consists; which are repeated so often, are so variously exhibited, so frequently introduced with great pomp and solemnity, and are so abundantly sealed with typical and symbolical representations; I say, all these promises imply, that the Messiah should perfect the work of redemption; and this implies that he should persevere in the work which the Father had appointed him, being in all things conformed to his will. These promises were often confirmed by an oath. (See Isa. liv. 9, with the context; chap. lxii. 18.) And it is represented as utterly impossible that these promises should fail. (Isa. xlix. 15, with the context; chap. liv. 10, with the context; chap. li. 4—8; chap. xl. 8, with the context.) And therefore it was impossible that the Messiah should fail, or commit sin.

6. It was impossible that the Messiah should fail of persevering in integrity and holiness, as the first Adam did, because this would have been inconsistent with the promises which God made to the blessed virgin his mother, and to her husband, implying that " he should save his people from their sins;" that " God would give him the throne of his father David;" that " he should reign over the house of Jacob for ever; and that " of his kingdom there shall be no end." These promises were sure, and it was impossible they should fail. And there-

fore the virgin Mary, in trusting fully to them, acted reasonably, having an immoveable foundation of her faith; as Elisabeth observes, Luke i. 45, "And blessed is she that believed; for there shall be a performance of those things which were told her from the Lord."

7. That it should have been possible that Christ should sin, and so fail in the work of our redemption, does not consist with the eternal purpose and decree of God, revealed in the Scriptures, that he would provide salvation for fallen man in and by Jesus Christ, and that salvation should be offered to sinners through the preaching of the Gospel. Such an absolute decree as this Arminians do not deny. Thus much at least (out of all controversy) is implied in such Scriptures as 1 Cor. ii. 7; Eph. i. 4, 5; and chap. iii. 9, 10, 11; 1 Pet. i. 19, 20. Such an absolute decree as this, Arminians allow to be signified in these texts. And the Arminians' election of nations and societies, and general election of the Christian church, and conditional election of particular persons, imply this. God could not decree before the foundation of the world, to save all that should believe in, and obey Christ, unless he had absolutely decreed that salvation should be provided, and effectually wrought out by Christ. And since (as the Arminians themselves strenuously maintain) a decree of God infers *necessity;* hence it became *necessary,* that Christ should persevere, and actually work out salvation for us, and that he should not fail by the commission of sin.

8. That it should have been possible for Christ's holiness to fail, is not consistent with what God promised to his Son, before all ages. For, that salvation should be offered to men, through Christ, and bestowed on all his faithful followers, is what is at least implied in that certain and infallible promise spoken of by the apostle, Tit. i. 2, "In hope of eternal life, which God, that cannot lie, promised before the world began." This does not seem to be controverted by Arminians.*

9. That it should be possible for Christ to fail of doing

* See Dr Whitby on the Five Points, pp. 48—50.

his Father's will, is inconsistent with the promise made
to the Father by the Son, by the Logos that was with
the Father from the beginning, before he took the human
nature: as may be seen in Psal. xl. 6, 7, 8, (compared
with the apostle's interpretation, Heb. x. 5-9:) "Sacrifice and offering thou didst not desire: mine ears hast
thou opened (or bored); burnt-offering and sin-offering
thou hast not required. Then said I, Lo, I come: in the
volume of the book it is written of me, I delight to do
thy will, O my God, and thy law is within my heart,"
—where is a manifest allusion to the covenant, which the
willing servant, who loved his master's service, made
with his master, to be his servant for ever, on the day
wherein he had his ear bored; which covenant was probably inserted in the public records, called the "*volume
of the book*," by the judges, who were called to take cog-
nisance of the transaction, Exod. xxi. If the Logos, who
was with the Father before the world, and who made
the world, thus engaged in covenant to do the will of
the Father in the human nature, and the promise was
as it were recorded, that it might be made sure, doubtless
it was *impossible* that it should fail; and so it was *impossible* that Christ should fail of doing the will of the
Father in the human nature.

10. If it was possible for Christ to have failed of doing
the will of his Father, and so to have failed of effectually
working out redemption for sinners, then the salvation
of all the saints, who were saved from the beginning of
the world to the death of Christ, was not built on a firm
foundation. The Messiah, and the redemption which
he was to work out by his obedience unto death, was
the foundation of the salvation of all the posterity of
fallen man that ever were saved. Therefore, if when
the Old Testament saints had the pardon of their sins and
the favour of God promised them, and salvation bestowed upon them, still it was possible that the Messiah,
when he came, might commit sin, then all this was on a
foundation that was not firm and stable, but liable to
fail; something which it was possible might never be.

God did as it were trust to what his Son had engaged
and promised to do in future time; and depended so
much upon it, that he proceeded actually to save men
on the account of it, as though it had been already done.
But this trust and dependence of God, on the supposition
of Christ's being liable to fail of doing his will, was lean-
ing on a staff that was weak, and might possibly break.
The saints of old trusted on the promises of a future redemption to be wrought out and completed by the Messiah, and built their comfort upon it: Abraham saw
Christ's day, and rejoiced; and he and the other patri-
archs died in the faith of the promise of it, (Heb. xi. 13.)
But on this supposition, their faith, and their comfort,
and their salvation, was built on a moveable, fallible
foundation; Christ was not then a tried stone, a sure
foundation, as in Isa. xxviii. 16.   David entirely rested
on the covenant of God with him, concerning the future
glorious dominion and salvation of the Messiah, of his
seed; says it was " all his salvation, and all his desire;"
and comforts himself that this covenant was an " everlasting covenant, ordered in all things and sure," 2 Sam.
xxiii. 5.   But if Christ's virtue might fail, he was mistaken: his great comfort was not built so sure as he
thought it was, being founded entirely on the determinations of the free-will of Christ's human soul, which
was subject to no necessity, and might be determined
either one way or the other.   Also, the dependence of
those who looked for redemption in Jerusalem, and wait-
ed for the consolation of Israel, (Luke ii. 25, 38,) and
the confidence of the disciples of Jesus, who forsook all
and followed him, that they might enjoy the benefits of
his future kingdom, was built on a sandy foundation.

11. The man Christ Jesus, before he had finished his
course of obedience, and while in the midst of temptations and trials, was abundant in positively predicting
his own future glory in his kingdom, and the enlargement of his church, the salvation of the Gentiles through
him, &c., and in promises of blessings he would bestow
on his true disciples in his future kingdom; on which

promises he required the full dependence of his disciples, (John xiv.) But the disciples would have no ground for such dependence, if Christ had been liable to fail in his work: and Christ himself would have been guilty of presumption, in so abounding in peremptory promises of great things, which depended on a mere contingence, viz., the determinations of his free-will, consisting in a freedom *ad utrumque*, to either sin or holiness, standing in indifference, and incident, in thousands of future instances, to go either one way or the other.

Thus it is evident, that it was *impossible* that the acts of the will of the human soul of Christ should be otherwise than holy, and conformed to the will of the Father; or, in other words, they were necessarily so conformed.

I have been the longer in the proof of this matter, it being a thing denied by some of the greatest Arminians —by Episcopius in particular; and because I look upon it as a point clearly and absolutely determining the controversy between Calvinists and Arminians, concerning the necessity of such a freedom of will as is insisted on by the latter, in order to moral agency, virtue, command or prohibition, promise or threatening, reward or punishment, praise or dispraise, merit or demerit. I now therefore proceed,

II. To consider whether Christ, in his holy behaviour on earth, was not thus a moral agent, subject to commands, promises, &c.

Dr Whitby very often speaks of what he calls a freedom *ad utrumlibet*, without necessity, as requisite to law and commands; and speaks of necessity as entirely inconsistent with injunctions and prohibitions. But yet we read of Christ's being the subject of the commands of his Father, John x. 18, and xv. 10. And Christ tells us, that every thing that he said or did was in compliance with "commandments he had received of the Father," John xii. 49, 50, and xiv. 31. And we often read of Christ's obedience to his Father's commands, Rom. v. 19; Phil. ii. 18; Heb. v. 8.

The fore-mentioned writer represents " promises offer-

ed as motives" to persons to do their duty, or "a being
moved and induced by promises," as utterly inconsistent
with a state wherein persons have not a liberty *ad utrumlibet,* but are necessarily determined to one. (See particularly, pp. 298 and 311.)   But the thing which this
writer asserts is demonstrably false, if the Christian religion be true.   If there be any truth in Christianity or
the Holy Scriptures, the man Christ Jesus had his will
infallibly, unalterably, and unfrustrably determined to
good, and that alone; but yet he had promises of glorious
rewards made to him, on condition of his persevering in,
and perfecting, the work which God had appointed him;
Isa. liii. 10, 11, 12; Psal. ii. and cx.; Isa. xlix. 7, 8, 9.
In Luke xxii. 28, 29, Christ says to his disciples, " Ye
are they which have continued with me in my temptations; and I appoint unto you a kingdom, as my Father
hath appointed unto me."   The word most properly
signifies to appoint by covenant or promise.   The plain
meaning of Christ's words is this: " As you have par-
took of my temptations and trials, and have been steadfast, and have overcome, I promise to make you par-
takers of my reward, and to give you a kingdom; as the
Father hath promised me a kingdom for continuing steadfast, and overcoming in those trials."   And the words
are well explained by those in Rev. iii. 21, " To him
that overcometh will I grant to sit with me in my throne;
even as I also overcame, and am set down with my Father in his throne."   And Christ hath not only promises
of glorious success, and rewards made to his obedience
and sufferings, but the Scriptures plainly represent him
as using these promises for motives and inducements to
obey and suffer; and particularly that promise of a kingdom which the Father had appointed him, or sitting with
the Father on his throne; as in Heb. xii. 1, 2, " Let us
lay aside every weight, and the sin which doth so easily
beset us, and let us run with patience the race that is set
before us, looking unto Jesus, the author and finisher of
our faith, who, for the joy that was set before him, en-

dured the cross, despising the shame, and is set down on the right hand of the throne of God."

And how strange would it be to hear any Christian assert, that the holy and excellent temper and behaviour of Jesus Christ, and that obedience which he performed under such great trials, was not virtuous or praiseworthy, because his will was not free *ad utrumque,* to either holiness or sin, but was unalterably determined to one; that, upon this account, there is no virtue at all in all Christ's humility, meekness, patience, charity, forgiveness of enemies, contempt of the world, heavenly-mindedness, submission to the will of God, perfect obedience to his commands, (though he was obedient unto death, even the death of the cross,) his great compassion to the afflicted, his unparalleled love to mankind, his faithfulness to God and man under such great trials, his praying for his enemies, even when nailing him to the cross; that virtue, when applied to these things, is but an empty name; that there was no merit in any of these things; that is, that Christ was worthy of nothing at all on account of them, worthy of no reward, no praise, no honour or respect from God or man, because his will was not indifferent, and free either to these things or the contrary; but under such a strong inclination or bias to the things that were excellent, as made it impossible that he should choose the contrary; that, upon this account, (to use Dr Whitby's language,) " it would be sensibly unreasonable" that the human nature should be rewarded for any of these things.

According to this doctrine, that creature who is evidently set forth in Scripture as the " first-born of every creature," as having " in all things the pre-eminence," and as the highest of all creatures in virtue, honour, and worthiness of esteem, praise, and glory, on the account of his virtue, is less worthy of reward or praise than the very least of saints; yea, no more worthy than a clock or mere machine, that is purely passive, and moved by natural necessity.

If we judge by Scriptural representations of things, we have reason to suppose that Christ took on him our nature, and dwelt with us in this world, in a suffering state, not only to satisfy for our sins, but that he, being in our nature and circumstances, and under our trials, might be our most fit and proper example, leader, and captain, in the exercise of glorious and victorious virtue, and might be a visible instance of the glorious end and reward of it; that we might see in him the beauty, amiableness, and true honour and glory, and exceeding benefit, of that virtue which it is proper for us human beings to practise; and might thereby learn, and be animated, to seek the like glory and honour, and to obtain the like glorious reward. See Heb. ii. 9—14; with v. 8, 9; and xii. 1, 2, 3. John xv. 10. Rom. viii. 17. 2 Tim. ii. 11, 12. 1 Pet. ii. 19, 20; and iv. 13. But if there was nothing of any virtue or merit, or worthiness of any reward, glory, praise, or commendation at all, in all that he did, because it was all necessary, and he could not help it, then how is there any thing so proper to animate and incite us, free creatures, by patient continuance in well-doing, to seek for honour, glory, and virtue?

God speaks of himself as peculiarly well pleased with the righteousness of this servant of his. Isa. xlii. 21, " The Lord is well pleased for his righteousness' sake." The sacrifices of old are spoken of as a sweet savour to God, but the obedience of Christ as far more acceptable than they. Psal. xl. 6, 7, " Sacrifice and offering thou didst not desire; mine ear hast thou opened [as thy servant performing willing obedience]: burnt-offering and sin-offering hast thou not required. Then said I, Lo, I come [as a servant that cheerfully answers the calls of his master]: I delight to do thy will, O my God, and thy law is within my heart." Matt. xvii. 5, " This is my beloved Son, in whom I am well pleased." And Christ tells us expressly, that the Father loves him for that wonderful instance of his obedience, his voluntary yielding himself to death, in compliance with the Father's

command; John x. 17, 18, " Therefore doth my Father
love me, because I lay down my life. No man taketh
it from me; but I lay it down of myself. This commandment received I of my Father."

And if there was no merit in Christ's obedience unto
death, if it was not worthy of praise and of the most
glorious rewards, the heavenly hosts were exceedingly
mistaken, by the account that is given of them in Rev.
v. 8—12: " The four beasts and the four and twenty
elders fell down before the Lamb, having every one of
them harps, and golden vials full of odours. And they
sung a new song, saying, Thou art WORTHY to take the
book, and to open the seals thereof; for thou wast slain.
And I beheld, and I heard the voice of many angels
round about the throne, and the beasts and the elders:
and the number of them was ten thousand times ten
thousand, and thousands of thousands; saying with a
loud voice, WORTHY is the Lamb that was slain, to receive power, and riches, and wisdom, and strength, and
honour, and glory, and blessing."   ·

Christ speaks of the eternal life which he was to receive as the reward of his obedience to the Father's commandments; John xii. 49, 50, " I have not spoken of myself; but the Father which sent me, he gave me a commandment, what I should say, and what I should speak.
And I know that his commandment is life everlasting:
whatsoever I speak, therefore, even as the Father said
unto me, so I speak." God promises to divide him a
portion with the great, &c. for his being his righteous
servant, for his glorious virtue under such great trials
and afflictions; Isa. liii. 11, 12, " He shall see of the
travail of his soul, and be satisfied: by his knowledge
shall my righteous servant justify many; for he shall
bear their iniquities. Therefore will I divide him a portion with the great, and he shall divide the spoil with
the strong; because he hath poured out his soul unto
death." The Scriptures represent God as rewarding him
far above all his other servants; Phil. ii. 7, 8, 9, " He
took on him the form of a servant, and was made in the

likeness of men: and being found in fashion as a man, he humbled himself, and became obedient unto death, even the death of the cross.   Wherefore God also hath highly exalted him, and given him a name above every name." Psal. xlv. 7, " Thou lovest righteousness, and hatest wickedness; therefore God, thy God, hath anointed thee with the oil of gladness above thy fellows."

There is no room to pretend that the glorious benefits bestowed in consequence of Christ's obedience, are not properly of the nature of a reward.   What is a reward, in the most proper sense, but a benefit bestowed in consequence of something morally excellent in quality or behaviour, in testimony of well-pleasedness in that moral excellency, and respect and favour on that account?   If we consider the nature of a reward most strictly, and make the utmost of it, and add to the things contained in this description proper merit or worthiness, and the bestowment of the benefit in consequence of a promise; still it will be found there is nothing belonging to it, but that the Scripture is most express as to its belonging to the glory bestowed on Christ after his sufferings, as appears from what has been already observed; there was a glorious benefit bestowed in consequence of something morally excellent, being called *righteousness* and *obedience;* there was great favour, love, and well-pleasedness, for this righteousness and obedience, in the bestower; there was proper merit, or worthiness of the benefit, in the obedience; it was bestowed in fulfilment of promises made to that obedience; and was bestowed *therefore,* or *because* he had performed that obedience.

I may add to all these things, that Jesus Christ, while here in the flesh, was manifestly in a state of trial.   The last Adam, as Christ is called, 1 Cor. xv. 45; Rom. v. 14, taking on him the human nature, and so the form of a servant, and being under the law, to stand and act for us, was put into a state of trial, as the first Adam was. Dr Whitby mentions these three things as evidences of persons being in a state of trial (on the Five Points, pp. 298, 299): namely, their afflictions being spoken of as their trials or temptations, their being the subjects of promises, and their being exposed to Satan's temptations. But Christ was apparently the subject of each of these. Concerning promises made to him, I have spoken already. The difficulties and *afflictions* he met with in the course of his obedience, are called his *temptations* or *trials;* Luke xxii. 28, " Ye are they which have continued with me in my *temptations*, [or *trials*.]" Heb. ii. 18, " For in that he himself hath suffered, being *tempted* [or tried], he is able to succour them that are tempted." And chap. iv. 15, " We have not an high priest which cannot be touched with the feeling of our infirmities, but was in all points *tempted* like as we are, yet without sin." And as to his being tempted by Satan, it is what none will dispute.

SECTION III.

THE CASE OF SUCH AS ARE GIVEN UP OF GOD TO SIN, AND OF FALLEN MAN IN GENERAL, PROVES MORAL NECESSITY AND INABILITY TO BE CONSISTENT WITH BLAME-WORTHINESS.

Dr Whitby asserts freedom, not only from co-action, but necessity, to be essential to any thing deserving the name of sin, and to an action's being culpable, in these words (Discourse on the Five Points, edit. 3, p. 348): " If they be thus necessitated, then neither their sins of omission or commission could deserve that name; it being essential to the nature of sin, according to St Austin's definition, that it be an action *à quo liberum est abstinere.* Three things seem plainly necessary to make an action or omission culpable: 1. That it be in our power to perform or forbear it; for, as Origen and all the fathers say, no man is blameworthy for not doing what he could not do." And elsewhere the Doctor insists, that " when any do evil of necessity, what they do is no vice, that they are guilty of no fault,* are worthy of no blame, dispraise,† or dishonour,‡ but are unblameable."‖

---

    * Discourse on the Five Points, pp. 347, 360, 361,, 377.
    † 303, 326, 329, and many other places.   ‡ 371.   ‖ 304, 361.

If these things are true, in Dr Whitby's sense of necessity, they will prove all such to be blameless who are given up of God to sin, in what they commit after they are thus given up. That there is such a thing as men's being judicially given up to sin, is certain, if the Scripture rightly informs us, such a thing being often there spoken of; as in Psal. lxxxi. 12, " So I gave them up to their own hearts' lust, and they walked in their own counsels." Acts vii. 42, " Then God turned, and gave them up to worship the host of heaven." Rom. i. 24, " Wherefore God also gave them up to uncleanness, through the lusts of their own hearts, to dishonour their own bodies between themselves." Ver. 26, " For this cause God gave them up to vile affections." Ver. 28, " And even as they did not like to retain God in their knowledge, God gave them over to a reprobate mind, to do those things that are not convenient."

It is needless to stand particularly to inquire what God's " giving men up to their own hearts' lusts" signifies; it is sufficient to observe, that hereby is certainly meant God's so ordering or disposing things, in some respect or other, either by doing or forbearing to do, as that the consequence should be men's continuing in their sins. So much as men are given up to, so much is the consequence of their being given up, whether that be less or more. If God does not order things so, by action or permission, that sin will be the consequence, then the event proves that they are not given up to that consequence. If good be the consequence, instead of evil, then God's mercy is to be acknowledged in that good; which mercy must be contrary to God's judgment in giving up to evil. If the event must prove that they are given up to evil as the consequence, then the persons who are the subjects of his judgment must be the subjects of such an event, and so the event is necessary.

If not only co-action, but all necessity, will prove men blameless, then Judas was blameless, after Christ had given him over, and had already declared his certain damnation, and that he should verily betray him.

He was guilty of no sin in betraying his Master, on this supposition; though his so doing is spoken of by Christ as the most aggravated sin, more heinous than the sin of Pilate in crucifying him. And the Jews in Egypt in Jeremiah's time, were guilty of no sin, in their not worshipping the true God, after God had " sworn by his great name, that his name should be no more named in the mouth of any man of Judah, in all the land of Egypt," Jer. xliv. 26.

Dr Whitby (Disc. on the Five Points, pp. 302, 303) denies that men, in this world, are ever so given up by God to sin, that their wills should be necessarily determined to evil; though he owns, that hereby it may become exceeding difficult for men to do good, having a strong bent and powerful inclination to what is evil.— But if we should allow the case to be just as he represents, the judgment of giving up to sin will no better agree with his notions of that liberty which is essential to praise or blame, than if we should suppose it to render the avoiding of sin impossible. For if an impossibility of avoiding sin wholly excuses a man, then, for the same reason, its being difficult to avoid it excuses him in part, and this just in proportion to the degree of difficulty. If the influence of *moral* impossibility or inability be the same, to excuse persons in not doing, or not avoiding any thing, as that of natural inability, (which is supposed,) then undoubtedly, in like manner, moral difficulty has the same influence to excuse with natural difficulty. But all allow that natural impossibility wholly excuses, and also that natural difficulty excuses in part, and makes the act or omission less blameable in proportion to the difficulty. All natural difficulty, according to the plainest dictates of the light of nature, excuses in some degree, so that the neglect is not so blameable, as if there had been no difficulty in the case: and so the greater the difficulty is, still the more excusable, in proportion to the increase of the difficulty. And as natural impossibility wholly excuses and excludes all blame, so the nearer the difficulty approaches to impossibility, still the

nearer a person is to blamelessness in proportion to that
approach. And if the case of moral impossibility or necessity be just the same with natural necessity or co-action, as to influence to excuse a neglect, then also, for
the same reason, the case of natural difficulty does not
differ in influence, to excuse a neglect, from moral difficulty, arising from a strong bias or bent to evil, such as
Dr Whitby owns in the case of those that are given up
to their own hearts' lusts. So that the fault of such
persons must be lessened, in proportion to the difficulty,
and approach to impossibility. If ten degrees of moral
difficulty make the action quite impossible, and so wholly
excuse, then if there be nine degrees of difficulty, the
person is in great part excused, and is nine degrees
in ten less blameworthy than if there had been no difficulty at all; and he has but one degree of blameworthiness. The reason is plain, on Arminian principles, viz.
because as difficulty, by antecedent bent and bias on the
will, is increased, liberty of indifference, and self-determination in the will, is diminished: so much hinderance
and impediment is there in the way of the will's acting
freely, by mere self-determination. And if ten degrees
of such hinderance take away all such liberty, then nine
degrees take away nine parts in ten, and leave but one
degree of liberty. And therefore there is but one degree
of blameableness, *cæteris paribus*, in the neglect; the man
being no further blameable in what he does or neglects
than he has liberty in that affair: for blame or praise
(say they) arises wholly from a good use or abuse of
liberty.

From all which it follows, that a strong bent and bias
one way, and difficulty of going the contrary, never
causes a person to be at all more exposed to sin, or any
thing blameable: because, as the difficulty is increased, so
much the less is required and expected. Though in one
respect exposedness to sin or fault is increased, viz. by
an increase of exposedness to the evil action or omission, yet it is diminished in another respect to balance it,
namely, as the sinfulness or blameableness of the action

or omission is diminished in the same proportion. So that, on the whole, the affair, as to exposedness to guilt or blame, is left just as it was.

To illustrate this, let us suppose a scale of a balance to be intelligent, and a free agent, and indued with a self-moving power, by virtue of which it could act and produce effects to a certain degree, *ex. gr.* to move itself up or down with a force equal to a weight of ten pounds; and that it might therefore be required of it, in ordinary circumstances, to move itself down with that force, for which it has power and full liberty, and therefore would be blameworthy if it failed of it. But then let us suppose a weight of ten pounds to be put in the opposite scale, which in force entirely counterbalances its self-moving power, and so renders it impossible for it to move down at all; and therefore wholly excuses it from any such motion. But if we suppose there be only nine pounds in the opposite scale, this renders its motion not impossible, but yet more difficult; so that it can now only move down with the force of one pound; but, however, this is all that is required of it under these circumstances; it is wholly excused from nine parts of its motion: and if the scale, under these circumstances, neglects to move, and remains at rest, all that it will be blamed for, will be its neglect of that one-tenth part of its motion; which it had as much liberty and advantage for, as in usual circumstances it has for the greater motion which in such a case would be required. So that this new difficulty does not at all increase its exposedness to any thing blameworthy.

And thus the very supposition of difficulty in the way of a man's duty, or proclivity to sin, through a being given up to hardness of heart, or indeed by any other means whatsoever, is an inconsistence, according to Dr Whitby's notions of liberty, virtue and vice, blame and praise. The avoiding sin and blame, and the doing what is virtuous and praiseworthy, must be always equally easy.

Dr Whitby's notions of liberty, obligation, virtue,

sin, &c. lead him into another inconsistence. He abundantly insists, that necessity is inconsistent with the nature of sin or fault. He says, in the fore-mentioned treatise, p. 14, " Who can blame a person for doing what he could not help?" And page 15, " It being sensibly unjust to punish any man for doing that which it was never in his power to avoid?" And in p. 341, to confirm his opinion, he quotes one of the fathers, saying, " Why doth God command, if man hath not free will and power to obey?" And again, in the same and the next page, " Who will not cry out, that it is folly to command him that hath not liberty, to do what is commanded; and that it is unjust to condemn him that has it not in his power to do what is required?" And in p. 373, he cites another, saying, " A law is given to him that can turn to both parts; *i. e.* obey or transgress it; but no law can be against him who is bound by nature."

And yet the same Dr Whitby asserts, that fallen man is not able to perform perfect obedience. In p. 165, he has these words : " The nature of Adam had power to continue innocent and without sin; whereas it is certain our nature never had so." But if we have not power to continue innocent and without sin, then sin is inconsistent with necessity, and we may be sinful in that which we have not power to avoid; and those things cannot be true, which he asserts elsewhere, namely, " That if we be necessitated, neither sins of omission nor commission would deserve that name," (p. 348.) If we have it not in our power to be innocent, then we have it not in our power to be blameless; and if so, we are under a necessity of being blameworthy. And how does this consist with what he so often asserts, that necessity is inconsistent with blame or praise? If we have it not in our power to perform perfect obedience to all the commands of God, then we are under a necessity of breaking some commands, in some degree; having no power to perform so much as is commanded. And if so, why does he cry out of the unreasonableness and folly of commanding beyond what men have power to do!

M

And Arminians in general are very inconsistent with themselves in what they say of the inability of fallen man in this respect. They strenuously maintain, that it would be unjust in God to require any thing of us beyond our present power and ability to perform; and also hold, that we are now unable to perform perfect obedience, and that Christ died to satisfy for the imperfections of our obedience, and has made way, that our imperfect obedience might be accepted instead of perfect; wherein they seem insensibly to run themselves into the grossest inconsistence. For (as I have observed elsewhere) " they hold, that God, in mercy to mankind, has abolished that rigorous constitution or law that they were under originally; and instead of it, has introduced a more mild constitution, and put us under a new law, which requires no more than imperfect sincere obedience, in compliance with our poor, infirm, impotent circumstances since the fall."

Now, how can these things be made consistent? I would ask, what law these imperfections of our obedience are a breach of? If they are a breach of no law that we were ever under, then they are not sins. And if they be not sins, what need of Christ's dying to satisfy for them? But if they are sins, and the breach of some law, what law is it? They cannot be a breach of their new law; for that requires no other than imperfect obedience, or obedience with imperfections: and therefore to have obedience attended with imperfections, is no breach of it; for it is as much as it requires. And they cannot be a breach of their old law; for that, they say, is entirely abolished; and we never were under it. They say it would not be just in God to require of us perfect obedience, because it would not be just to require more than we can perform, or to punish us for failing of it. And, therefore, by their own scheme, the imperfections of our obedience do not deserve to be punished. What need, therefore of Christ's dying to satisfy for them? What need of his suffering, to satisfy for that which is no fault, and in its own nature deserves no suffering?

What need of Christ's dying to purchase, that our imperfect obedience should be accepted, when, according to their scheme, it would be unjust in itself, that any other obedience than imperfect should be required? What need of Christ's dying to make way for God's accepting such an obedience, as it would be unjust in him not to accept? Is there any need of Christ's dying to prevail with God not to do unrighteously? If it be said, that Christ died to satisfy that old law for us, that so we might not be under it, but that there might be room for our being under a more mild law; still I would inquire, what need of Christ's dying, that we might not be under a law, which (by their principles) it would be in itself unjust that we should be under, whether Christ had died or no, because, in our present state, we are not able to keep it?

So the Arminians are inconsistent with themselves, not only in what they say of the need of Christ's satisfaction to atone for those imperfections which we cannot avoid, but also in what they say of the grace of God, granted to enable men to perform the sincere obedience of the new law. " I grant," says Dr Stebbing,* " indeed, that by reason of original sin, we are utterly disabled for the performance of the condition, without new grace from God. But I say, then, that he gives such a grace to all of us, by which the performance of the condition is truly possible: and upon this ground he may and doth most righteously require it." If Dr Stebbing intends to speak properly, by *grace* he must mean, that assistance which is of grace, or of free favour and kindness. But yet in the same place he speaks of it as very *unreasonable, unjust,* and *cruel,* for God to require that as the condition of pardon, that is become impossible by original sin. If it be so, what *grace* is there in giving assistance and ability to perform the condition of pardon? Or why is that called by the name of grace, that is an absolute debt, which God is bound to bestow, and which it would be unjust and cruel in him to withhold, seeing

* Treatise of the Operations of the Spirit. Second Edition, pp. 112, 113.

he requires that, as the condition of pardon, which he cannot perform without it?

SECTION IV.

COMMAND AND OBLIGATION TO OBEDIENCE CONSISTENT WITH MORAL INABILITY TO OBEY.

It being so much insisted on by Arminian writers, that necessity is inconsistent with law or command, and particularly, that it is absurd to suppose God by his command should require that of men which they are unable to do—not allowing in this case for any difference that there is between natural and moral inability—I would therefore now particularly consider this matter.

And, for the greater clearness, I would distinctly lay down the following things.

I. The will itself, and not only those actions which are the effects of the will, is the proper object of precept or command. This is, such or such a state or act of men's wills is in many cases properly required of them by commands; and not only those alterations in the state of their bodies or minds that are the consequences of volition. This is most manifest; for it is the soul only that is properly and directly the subject of precepts or commands; that only being capable of receiving or perceiving commands. The motions or state of the body are matter of command, only as they are subject to the soul, and connected with its acts. But now the soul has no other faculty whereby it can, in the most direct and proper sense, consent, yield to, or comply with, any command, but the faculty of the will; and it is by this faculty only that the soul can directly disobey, or refuse compliance; for the very notions of consenting, yielding, accepting, complying, refusing, rejecting, &c. are, according to the meaning of the terms, nothing but certain acts of the will. Obedience, in the primary nature of it, is the submitting and yielding of the will of one to the will of another. Disobedience is the not consenting, not complying of the will of the commanded to the manifested will of the commander. Other acts that are not the acts of the will, as certain motions of the body and alterations in the soul, are obedience or disobedience only indirectly, as they are connected with the state or actions of the will, according to an established law of nature. So that it is manifest, the will itself may be required: and the being of a good will is the most proper, direct, and immediate subject of command; and, if this cannot be prescribed or required by command or precept, nothing can; for other things can be required no otherwise than as they depend upon, and are the fruits of, a good will.

Corol. 1. If there be several acts of the will, or a series of acts, one following another, and one the effect of another, the first and determining act is properly the subject of command, and not only the consequent acts, which are dependent upon it. Yea, it is this more especially which is that which command or precept has a proper respect to; because it is this act that determines the whole affair: in this act the obedience or disobedience lies, in a peculiar manner; the consequent acts being all subject to it, and governed and determined by it. This determining governing act must be the proper object of precept, or none.

Corol. 2. It also follows, from what has been observed, that if there be any sort of act or exertion of the soul, prior to all free acts of the will or acts of choice in the case, directing and determining what the acts of the will shall be,—that act or exertion of the soul cannot properly be subject to any command or precept, in any respect whatsoever, either directly or indirectly, immediately or remotely. Such acts cannot be subject to commands directly, because they are no acts of the will; being by the supposition prior to all acts of the will, determining and giving rise to all its acts: they not being acts of the will, there can be in them no consent to, or compliance with, any command. Neither can they be subject to command or precept indirectly or remotely; for they are not so much as the effects or consequences of the

will, being prior to all its acts. So that if there be any
obedience in that original act of the soul, determining
all volitions, it is an act of obedience wherein the will
has no concern at all; it preceding every act of will.
And, therefore, if the soul either obeys or disobeys in
this act, it is wholly involuntarily; there is no willing obedience or rebellion, no compliance or opposition
of the will in the affair: and what sort of obedience or
rebellion is this?

And thus the Arminian notion of the freedom of the
will consisting in the soul's determining its own acts of
will, instead of being essential to moral agency, and to
men's being the subjects of moral government, is utterly
inconsistent with it. For if the soul determines *all* its
acts of will, it is therein subject to no command or moral government, as has been now observed; because its
original determining act is no act of will or choice, it
being prior, by the supposition, to *every act* of will.
And the soul cannot be the subject of command in the
act of the will itself, which depends on the foregoing determining act, and is determined by it; inasmuch as this
is necessary, being the necessary consequence and effect of
that prior determining act, which is not voluntary. Nor
can the man be the subject of command or government in
his external actions; because these are all necessary, being
the necessary effects of the acts of the will themselves.
So that mankind, according to this scheme, are subjects
of command or moral government in nothing at all; and
all their moral agency is entirely excluded, and no room
for virtue or vice in the world.

So that it is the Arminian scheme, and not the scheme
of the Calvinists, that is utterly inconsistent with moral
government, and with all use of laws, precepts, prohibitions, promises, or threatenings. Neither is there any
way whatsoever to make their principles consist with
these things. For if it be said, that there is no prior
determining act of the soul, preceding the acts of the
will, but that volitions are events that come to pass by
pure accident without any determining cause, this is

most palpably inconsistent with all use of laws and precepts; for nothing is more plain than that laws can be
of no use to direct and regulate perfect accident; which
by the supposition of its being pure accident, is in no
case regulated by any thing preceding; but happens,
this way or that, perfectly by chance, without any cause
or rule. The perfect uselessness of laws and precepts
also follows from the Arminian notion of indifference,
as essential to that liberty which is requisite to virtue
or vice. For the end of laws is to bind to one side: and
the end of commands is to turn the will one way: and
therefore they are of no use unless they turn or bias the
will that way. But if liberty consists in indifference,
then their biassing the will one way only destroys liberty,
as it puts the will out of equilibrium. So that the will,
having a bias, through the influence of binding law, laid
upon it, is not wholly left to itself, to determine itself
which way it will, without influence from without.

II. Having shown that the will itself, especially in
those acts which are original, leading and determining
in any case, is the proper subject of precept and command, and not only those alterations in the body, &c.
which are the effects of the will; I now proceed, in the
second place, to observe, that the very opposition or defect of the will itself, in that act which is its original and
determining act in the case; I say, the will's opposition
in this act to a thing proposed or commanded, or its failing of compliance, implies a moral inability to that thing:
or in other words, whenever a command requires a certain state or act of the will, and the person commanded,
notwithstanding the command and the circumstances
under which it is exhibited, still finds his will opposite
or wanting, in that, belonging to its state or acts, which
is original and determining in the affair, that man is
morally unable to obey that command.

This is manifest from what was observed in the first
part concerning the nature of moral inability, as distinguished from natural: where it was observed, that a
man may then be said to be morally unable to do a

thing, when he is under the influence or prevalence of a contrary inclination; or has a want of inclination, under such circumstances and views. It is also evident, from what has been before proved, that the will is always, and in every individual act, necessarily determined by the strongest motive; and so is always unable to go against the motive, which, all things considered, has now the greatest strength and advantage to move the will. But no further to insist on these things, the truth of the position now laid down, viz. that when the will is opposite *to*, or failing of a compliance with a thing in its original determining inclination or act, it is not able to comply, appears by the consideration of these two things.

1. The will in the time of that diverse or opposite leading act or inclination, and when actually under the influence of it, is not able to exert itself to the contrary, to make an alteration, in order to a compliance. The inclination is unable to change itself; and that for this plain reason, that it is unable to incline to change itself. Present choice cannot at present choose to be otherwise: for that would be at present to choose something diverse from what is at present chosen. If the will, all things now considered, inclines or chooses to go that way; then it cannot choose, all things now considered, to go the other way, and so cannot choose to be made to go the other way. To suppose that the mind is now sincerely inclined to change itself to a different inclination, is to suppose the mind is now truly inclined otherwise than it is now inclined. The will may oppose some future remote act that it is exposed to, but not its own present act.

2. As it is impossible that the will should comply with the thing commanded, with respect to its leading act, by an act of its own in the time of that diverse or opposite leading and original act, or after it has actually come under the influence of that determining choice or inclination; so it is impossible it should be determined to a compliance by any foregoing act; for, by the very supposition, there is no foregoing act; the opposite or

non-complying act being that act which is original and
determining in the case.   Therefore it must be so, that
if this first determining act be found non-complying, on
the proposal of the command, the mind is morally unable to obey.   For, to suppose it to be able to obey, is to
suppose it to be able to determine and cause its first determining act to be otherwise, and that it has power
better to govern and regulate its first governing and re-
gulating act, which is absurd; for it is to suppose a
prior act of the will, determining its first determining
act; that is, an act prior to the first, and leading and
governing the original and governing act of all; which
is a contradiction.

Here, if it should be said, that although the mind has
not any ability to will contrary to what it does will, in
the original and leading act of the will, because there is
supposed to be no prior act to determine and order it
otherwise, and the will cannot immediately change itself, because it cannot at present incline to a change;
yet, the mind has an ability for the present to forbear
to proceed to action, and taking time for deliberation;
which may be an occasion of the change of the inclination.

I answer, (1.) In this objection, that seems to be forgotten which was observed before, viz. that the determining to take the matter into consideration, is itself an
act of the will; and if this be all the act wherein the
mind exercises ability and freedom, then this, by the
supposition, must be all that can be commanded or required by precept.   And if this act be the commanding
act, then all that has been observed concerning the commanding act of the will remains true, that the very
want of it is a moral inability to exert it, &c.   (2.) We
are speaking concerning the first and leading act of the
will in the case, or about the affair; and if a determining to deliberate, or, on the contrary, to proceed immediately without deliberating, be the first and leading
act; or whether it be or no, if there be another act be-

fore it, which determines that; or whatever be the original and leading act; still, the foregoing proof stands good, that the non-compliance of the leading act implies moral inability to comply.

If it should be objected, that these things make all moral inability equal, and suppose men morally unable to will otherwise than they actually do will, in all cases, and equally so in every instance;

In answer to this objection, I desire two things may be observed. *First,* That if by being *equally* unable be meant as *really* unable; then so far as the inability is merely moral, it is true, the will, in every instance, acts by moral necessity, and is morally unable to act otherwise, as truly and properly in one case as another; as, I humbly conceive, has been perfectly and abundantly demonstrated by what has been said in the preceding part of this Essay. But yet, in some respect, the inability may be said to be greater in some instances than others: though the man may be truly unable, (if moral inability can truly be called inability,) yet he may be further from being able to do some things than others; as it is in things which men are naturally unable to do. A person, whose strength is no more than sufficient to lift the weight of one hundred pounds, is as truly and really unable to lift one hundred and one pounds, as ten thousand pounds; but yet he is further from being able to lift the latter weight than the former; and so, according to common use of speech, has a greater inability for it. So it is in moral inability. A man is truly morally unable to choose contrary to a present inclination, which in the least degree prevails; or, contrary to that motive which, all things considered, has strength and advantage now to move the will, in the least degree, superior to all other motives in view: but yet he is further from ability to resist a very strong habit, and a violent and deeply-rooted inclination, or a motive vastly exceeding all others in strength. And again, the inability may, in some respects, be called greater in some instances than others, as it may be more general and extensive to all acts of that kind. So, men may be said to be unable in a different sense, and to be further from moral ability, who have that moral inability which i general and habitual, than they who have only that inability which is occasional and particular.* Thus, in cases of natural inability; he that is born blind may be said to be unable to see, in a different manner, and is, in some respects, further from being able to see, than he whose sight is hindered by a transient cloud or mist.

And besides, that which was observed in the first part of this discourse, concerning the inability which attends a strong and settled habit, should be here remembered; viz. that fixed habit is attended with this peculiar moral inability, by which it is distinguished from occasional volition, namely, that endeavours to avoid future volitions of that kind, which are agreeable to such a habit, much more frequently and commonly prove vain and insufficient. For though it is impossible there should be any true sincere desires and endeavours against a present volition or choice, yet there may be against volitions of that kind, when viewed at a distance. A person may desire and use means to prevent future exercises of a certain inclination; and, in order to it, may wish the habit might be removed; but his desires and endeavours may be ineffectual. The man may be said in some sense to be unable; yea, even as the word *unable* is a relative term, and has relation to ineffectual endeavours; yet not with regard to present, but remote endeavours.

Secondly, It must be borne in mind, according to what was observed before, that indeed no inability whatsoever, which is merely moral, is properly called by the name of *inability;* and that, in the strictest propriety of speech, a man may be said to have a thing in his power, if he has it at his election; and he cannot be said to be unable to do a thing, when he can, if he now pleases, or whenever he has a proper, direct, and immediate desire for it. As to those desires and endeavours that may be against

* See this distinction of moral inability explained in Part I. sect. 4.

the exercises of a strong habit, with regard to which
men may be said to be unable to avoid those exercises,
they are remote desires and endeavours in two respects.
First, as to *time:* they are never against present volitions,
but only against volitions of such a kind, when viewed
at a distance. *Secondly,* as to their *nature:* these opposite desires are not directly and properly against the habit and inclination itself, or the volitions in which it is
exercised; for these, in themselves considered, are agreeable; but against something else that attends them, or is
their consequence: the opposition of the mind is levelled
entirely against this; the inclination or volitions themselves are not at all opposed directly, and for their own
sake; but only indirectly and remotely, on the account
of something alien and foreign.

III. Though the opposition of the will itself, or the
very want of will, to a thing commanded, implies a moral inability to that thing; yet, if it be, as has been
already shown, that the being of a good state or act of
will, is a thing most properly required by command;
then, in some cases, such a state or act of will may properly be required, which at present is not, and which
may also be wanting after it is commanded. And therefore those things may properly be commanded, which
men have a moral inability for.

Such a state, or act of the will may be required by
command as does not already exist. For if that volition
only may be commanded to be which already is, there
could be no use of precept; commands in all cases would
be perfectly vain and impertinent. And not only may
such a will be required, as is wanting before the command is given, but also such as may possibly be wanting
afterwards,—such as the exhibition of the command
may not be effectual to produce or excite. Otherwise,
no such thing as disobedience to a proper and rightful
command is possible in any case: and there is no case
supposable or possible wherein there can be an inexcu-
sable or faulty disobedience,—which Arminians cannot
affirm, consistently with their principles: for this makes

obedience to just and proper commands always *necessary*, and disobedience impossible. And so the Arminian would overthrow himself, yielding the very point we are upon, which he so strenuously denies, viz. that law and command are consistent with necessity.

If merely that inability will excuse disobedience, which is implied in the opposition or defect of inclination remaining after the command is exhibited, then wickedness always carries that in it which excuses it. It is evermore so, that by how much the more wickedness there is in a man's heart, by so much is his inclination to evil the stronger, and by so much the more, therefore, has he of moral inability to the good required. His moral inability, consisting in the strength of his evil inclination, is the very thing wherein his wickedness consists; and yet, according to Arminian principles, it must be a thing inconsistent with wickedness; and by how much the more he has of it, by so much is he the further from wickedness.

Therefore, on the whole, it is manifest, that moral inability alone (which consists in disinclination) never renders any thing improperly the subject matter of precept or command, and never can excuse any person in disobedience or want of conformity to a command.

Natural inability, arising from the want of natural capacity, or external hinderance, (which alone is properly called inability,) without doubt wholly excuses, or makes a thing improperly the matter of command. If men are excused from doing or acting any good thing, supposed to be commanded, it must be through some defect or obstacle that is not in the will itself, but intrinsic to it; either in the capacity of understanding, or body, or outward circumstances.

Here two or three things may be observed:

1. As to spiritual duties or acts, or any good thing in the state or imminent acts of the will itself, or of the affections (which are only certain modes of the exercise of the will,) if persons are justly excused, it must be through want of capacity in the natural faculty of un-

derstanding. Thus, the same spiritual duties, or holy affections and exercises of heart, cannot be required of men as may be of angels; the capacity of understanding being so much inferior. So, men cannot be required to love those amiable persons whom they have had no opportunity to see, or hear, or come to the knowledge of, in any way agreeable to the natural state and capacity of the human understanding. But the insufficiency of motives will not excuse; unless their being insufficient arises not from the moral state of the will or inclination itself, but from the state of the natural understanding. The great kindness and generosity of another may be a motive insufficient to excite gratitude in the person that receives the kindness, through his vile and ungrateful temper; in this case the insufficiency of the motive arises from the state of the will or inclination of heart, and does not at all excuse. But if this generosity is not sufficient to excite gratitude, being unknown, there being no means of information adequate to the state and measure of the person's faculties, this insufficiency is attended with a natural inability, which entirely excuses.

2. As to such motions of body, or exercises and alterations of mind, which do not consist in the imminent acts or state of the will itself, but are supposed to be required as effects of the will; I say, in such supposed effects of the will, in cases wherein there is no want of a capacity of understanding, that inability, and that only, excuses, which consists in want of connexion between them and the will. If the will fully complies, and the proposed effect does not prove, according to the laws of nature, to be connected with his volition, the man is perfectly excused: he has a natural inability to the thing required. For the will itself, as has been observed, is all that can be directly and immediately required by command; and other things only indirectly, as connected with the will. If, therefore, there be a full compliance of will, the person has done his duty; and if

other things do not prove to be connected with his volition, that is not owing to him.

3. Both these kinds of natural inability 'that have
been mentioned, and so all inability that excuses, may
be resolved into one thing; namely, want of natural
capacity or strength; either capacity of understanding,
or external strength. For when there are external de-
fects and obstacles, they would be no obstacles, were it
not for the imperfection and limitations of understanding and strength.

Corol. If things for which men have a moral inability may properly be the matter of precept or command, then they may also of invitation and counsel.
Commands and invitations come very much to the
same thing; the difference is only circumstantial: commands are as much a manifestation of the will of him
that speaks, as invitations, and as much testimonies of
expectation of compliance. The difference between them
lies in nothing that touches the affair in hand. The
main difference between command and invitation consists in the enforcement of the will of him who commands
or invites. In the latter it is his *kindness*, the goodness which his will arises from: in the former it is his
authority. But whatever be the ground of the will of
him that speaks, or the enforcement of what he says,
yet seeing neither his will nor expectation is any more
testified in the one case than the other, therefore a person's being directed *by invitation*, is no more an evidence of insincerity in him that directs, in manifesting
either a will or expectation which he has not, than his
being known to be morally unable to do what he is directed to *by command*. So that all this grand objection
of Arminians against the inability of fallen men to exert faith in Christ, or to perform other spiritual gospel
duties, from the sincerity of God's counsels and invitations, must be without force.

SECTION V.

THAT SINCERITY OF DESIRES AND ENDEAVOURS, WHICH IS SUPPOSED TO EXCUSE IN THE NON-PERFORMANCE OF THINGS IN THEMSELVES GOOD, PARTICULARLY CONSIDERED.

It is what is much insisted on by many, that some men, though they are not able to perform spiritual duties, such as repentance of sin, love to God, a cordial acceptance of Christ as exhibited and offered in the gospel, &c., yet they may sincerely desire and endeavour these things, and therefore must be excused; it being unreasonable to blame them for the omission of those things which they sincerely desire and endeavour to do, but cannot do.

Concerning this matter, the following things may be observed:

1. What is here supposed, is a great mistake, and gross absurdity; even that men may sincerely choose and desire those spiritual duties of love, acceptance, choice, rejection, &c., consisting in the exercise of the will itself, or in the disposition and inclination of the heart; and yet not be able to perform or exert them. This is absurd, because it is absurd to suppose that a man should directly, properly, and sincerely incline to have an inclination, which at the same time is contrary to his inclination; for that is to suppose him not to be inclined to that which he is inclined to. If a man, in the state and acts of his will and inclination, does properly and directly fall in with those duties, he therein performs them: for the duties themselves consist in that very thing, they consist in the state and acts of the will being so formed and directed. If the soul properly and sincerely falls in with a certain proposed act of will or choice, the soul therein makes that choice its own. Even as when a moving body falls in with a proposed direction of its motion, that is the same thing as to move in that direction.

2. That which is called a *desire* and *willingness* for those inward duties, in such as do not perform, has

respect to these duties only indirectly and remotely, and is improperly represented as a willingness for them; not only because (as was observed before) it respects those good volitions only in a distant view, and with respect to future time; but also because evermore, not these things themselves, but something else, that is alien and foreign, is the object that terminates these volitions and desires.

A drunkard, who continues in his drunkenness, being under the power of a love and violent appetite to strong drink, and without any love to virtue, but being also extremely covetous and close, and very much exercised and grieved at the diminution of his estate, and prospect of poverty, may in a sort *desire* the virtue of temperance; and though his present will is to gratify his extravagant appetite, yet he may wish he had a heart to forbear future acts of intemperance, and forsake his excesses, through an unwillingness to part with his money: but still he goes on with his drunkenness; his wishes and endeavours are insufficient and ineffectual: such a man has no proper, direct, sincere willingness to forsake this vice, and the vicious deeds which belong to it; for he acts voluntarily in continuing to drink to excess: his desire is very improperly called a willingness to be temperate; it is no true desire of that virtue, for it is not that virtue that terminates his wishes, nor have they any direct respect at all to it. It is only *the saving his money*, and avoiding poverty, that terminates and exhausts the whole strength of his desire. The virtue of temperance is regarded only very indirectly and improperly, even as a necessary means of gratifying the vice of covetousness.

So, a man of an exceeding corrupt and wicked heart, who has no love to God and Jesus Christ, but, on the contrary, being very profanely and carnally inclined, has the greatest distaste of the things of religion, and enmity against them; yet being of a family that, from one generation to another, have most of them died in youth of an hereditary consumption; and so having

N

little hope of living long, and having been instructed in the necessity of a supreme love to Christ, and gratitude for his death and sufferings, in order to his salvation from eternal misery; if, under these circumstances, he should, through fear of eternal torments, wish he had such a disposition, but his profane and carnal heart remaining, he continues still in his habitual distaste of, and enmity to, God and religion, and wholly without any exercise of that love and gratitude, (as doubtless the very devils themselves, notwithstanding all the devilishness of their temper, would wish for a holy heart, if by that means they could get out of hell:) in this case, there is no sincere willingness to love Christ, and choose him as his chief good: these holy dispositions and exercises are not at all the direct object of the will; they truly share no part of the inclination or desire of the soul; but all is terminated on deliverance from torment: and these graces and pious volitions, notwithstanding this forced consent, are looked upon undesirable; as when a sick man desires a dose he greatly abhors, to save his life. From these things it appears:

3. That this indirect willingness, which has been spoken of, is not that exercise of the will which the command requires, but is entirely a different one; being a volition of a different nature, and terminated altogether on different objects; wholly falling short of that virtue of will which the command has respect to.

4. This other volition, which has only some indirect concern with the duty required, cannot excuse for the want of that good will itself which is commanded; being not the thing which answers and fulfils the command, and being wholly destitute of the virtue which the command seeks.

Further to illustrate this matter. If a child has a most excellent father, that has ever treated him with fatherly kindness and tenderness, and has every way, in the highest degree, merited his love and dutiful regard, being withal very wealthy; but the son is of so vile a disposition, that he inveterately hates his father, and

yet, apprehending that his hatred of him is like to prove
his ruin, by bringing him finally to poverty and abject
circumstances, through his father's disinheriting him,
or otherwise—which is exceeding cross to his avarice
and ambition—he therefore wishes it were otherwise ;
but yet remaining under the invincible power of his vile
and malignant disposition, he continues still in his
settled hatred of his father.   Now, if such a son's indirect willingness to have love and honour towards his
father at all acquits or excuses before God, for his failing of actually exercising those dispositions towards him,
which God requires, it must be on one of these accounts : (1.) Either that it answers and fulfils the
command.   But this it does not, by the supposition ;
because the thing commanded is love and honour to his
worthy parent.   If the command be proper and just, as
is supposed, to the thing commanded ; and so nothing
else but that can answer the obligation.   Or, (2.) It
must be at least, because there is that virtue or goodness in his indirect willingness, that is equivalent to the
virtue required ; and so balances or countervails it, and
makes up for the want of it.   But that also is contrary
to the supposition.   The willingness the son has merely
from a regard to money and honour, has no goodness in
it to countervail the want of the pious filial respect required.

Sincerity and reality, in that indirect willingness
which has been spoken of, does not make it the better.
That which is real and hearty is often called sincere,
whether it be in virtue or vice.   Some persons are sincerely *bad ;* others are sincerely *good ;* and others may
be sincere and hearty in things which are in their own
nature *indifferent ;* as a man may be sincerely desirous
of eating when he is hungry.   But a being sincere,
hearty, and in good earnest, is no virtue, unless it be in
a thing that is virtuous.   A man may be sincere and
hearty in joining a crew of pirates or a gang of robbers.
When the devils cried out, and besought Christ not to
torment them, it was no mere pretence ; they were very

hearty in their desires not to be tormented: but this did not make their will or desires virtues. And if men have sincere desires, which are in their kind and nature no better, it can be no excuse for the want of any required virtue.

And as a man's being sincere in such an indirect desire or willingness to do his duty as has been mentioned, cannot excuse for the want of performance, so it is with endeavours arising from such a willingness. The endeavours can have no more goodness in them than the will which they are the effect and expression of. And, therefore, however sincere and real, and however great a person's endeavours are, yea, though they should be to the utmost of his ability, unless the will which they proceed from be truly good and virtuous, they can be of no avail, influence, or weight, to any purpose whatsoever, in a moral sense or respect. That which is not truly virtuous in God's sight, is looked upon by him as good for nothing; and so can be of no value, weight, or influence in his account, to recommend, satisfy, excuse, or make up for any moral defect. For nothing can counterbalance evil but good. If evil be in one scale, and we put a great deal into the other, sincere and earnest desires, and many and great endeavours; yet, if there be no real goodness in all, there is no weight in it; and so it does nothing towards balancing the real weight which is in the opposite scale. It is only like the subtracting a thousand noughts from before a real number, which leaves the sum just as it was.

Indeed, such endeavours may have a negatively good influence. Those things which have no positive virtue have no positive moral influence; yet they may be an occasion of persons avoiding some positive evils. As, if a man were in the water with a neighbour that he had ill-will to, who could not swim, holding him up by his hand; which neighbour was much in debt to him; and should be tempted to let him sink and drown, but should refuse to comply with the temptation, not from love to his neighbour, but from the love of money, and because by his drowning he should lose his debt, that which he does in preserving his neighbour from drowning is nothing good in the sight of God: yet hereby he avoids the greater guilt that would have been contracted if he had designedly let his neighbour sink and perish. But when Arminians, in their disputes with Calvinists, insist so much on sincere desires and endeavours, as what must excuse men, must be accepted of God, &c., it is manifest they have respect to some positive moral weight or influence of those desires and endeavours. Accepting, justifying, or excusing, on the account of sincere honest endeavours (as they are called,) and men's doing what they can, &c., has relation to some moral value, something that is accepted as good, and, as such, countervailing some defect.

But there is a great and unknown deceit arising from the ambiguity of the phrase, *sincere endeavours.* Indeed, there is a vast indistinctness and unfixedness in most, or at least very many, of the terms used to express things pertaining to moral and spiritual matters. Whence arise innumerable mistakes, strong prejudices, inextricable confusion, and endless controversy.

The word *sincere* is most commonly used to signify something that is good: men are habituated to understand by it the same as *honest* and *upright;* which terms excite an idea of something good in the strictest and highest sense; good in the sight of Him who sees not only the outward appearance, but the heart. And, therefore, men think that if a person be *sincere*, he will certainly be accepted. If it be said that any one is sincere in his endeavours, this suggests to men's minds as much as that his heart and will is good, that there is no defect of duty as to virtuous inclination; he *honestly* and *uprightly* desires and endeavours to do as he is required; and this leads them to suppose, that it would be very hard and unreasonable to punish him only because he is unsuccessful in his endeavours, the thing endeavoured being beyond his power. Whereas it ought to be ob-

served, that the word *sincere* has these different signifi-
cations:

1. *Sincerity*, as the word is sometimes used, signifies
no more than reality of will and endeavour, with respect
to any thing that is professed or pretended, without any
consideration of the nature of the principle or aim
whence this real will and true endeavour arises. If a
man has some real desire to obtain a thing, either direct
or indirect, or does really endeavour after a thing, he is
said sincerely to desire or endeavour it; without any
consideration of the goodness or virtuousness of the principle he acts from, or any excellency or worthiness of
the end he acts for. Thus, a man who is kind to his
neighbour's wife who is sick and languishing, and very
helpful in her case, makes a show of desiring and endeavouring her restoration to health and vigour; and not
only makes such a show, but there is a reality in his
pretence—he does heartily and earnestly desire to have
her health restored, and uses his true and utmost endeavours for it; he is said sincerely to desire and endeavour
it, because he does so truly or really; though perhaps the
principle he acts from is no other than a vile and scan-
dalous passion; having lived in adultery with her, he
earnestly desires to have her health and vigour restored,
that he may return to his criminal pleasures with her.
Or,

2. By *sincerity* is meant, not merely a reality of will
and endeavour of some sort or other, and from some consideration or other, but a virtuous sincerity. That is,
that in the performance of those particular acts that are
the matter of virtue or duty, there be not only the matter, but the form and essence of virtue, consisting in the
aim that governs the act, and the principle exercised in
it. There is not only the reality of the act, that is as it
were the *body* of the duty; but also the *soul*, which
should properly belong to such a body. In this sense, a
man is said to be sincere, when he acts with a pure intention; not from sinister views, or by-ends: he not only

in reality desires and seeks the thing to be done, or qualification to be obtained, for some end or other; but he wills the thing directly and properly, as neither forced nor bribed : the virtue of the thing is properly the object of the will.

In the former sense, a man is said to be sincere, in opposition to a mere pretence and show of the particular thing to be done or exhibited, without any real desire or endeavour at all. In the latter sense, a man is said to be sincere, in opposition to that show of virtue there is in merely doing the matter of duty, without the reality of the virtue itself in the soul, and the essence of it, which there is a show of. A man may be sincere in the former sense, and yet in the latter be in the sight of God, who searches the heart, a vile hypocrite.

In the latter kind of sincerity, only, is there any thing truly valuable or acceptable in the sight of God. And this is the thing which in Scripture is called *sincerity, uprightness, integrity, truth in the inward parts, and a being of a perfect heart.* And if there be such a sincerity, and such a degree of it as there ought to be, and there be any thing further that the man is not able to perform, or which does not prove to be connected with his sincere desires and endeavours, the man is wholly excused and acquitted in the sight of God; his will shall surely be accepted for his deed: and such a sincere will and endeavour is all that in strictness is required of him by any command of God. But as to the other kind of sincerity of desires and endeavours, it, having no virtue in it, (as was observed before,) can be of no avail before God, in any case, to recommend, satisfy, or excuse, and has no positive moral weight or influence whatsoever.

Corol. 1. Hence it may be inferred, that nothing in the reason and nature of things appears from the consideration of any moral weight of that former kind of sincerity, which has been spoken of, at all obliging us to believe, or leading us to suppose, that God has made any positive promises of salvation, or grace, or any saving assistance, or any spiritual benefit whatsoever, to any desires, prayers, endeavours, striving, or obedience of those who hitherto have no true virtue or holiness in their hearts; though we should suppose all the sincerity, and the utmost degree of endeavour, that is possible to be in a person without holiness.

Some object against God's requiring, as the condition of salvation, those holy exercises which are the result of a supernatural renovation: such as a supreme respect to Christ, love to God, loving holiness for its own sake, &c.; that these inward dispositions and exercises are above men's power, as they are by nature; and therefore that we may conclude, that when men are brought to be sincere in their endeavours, and do as well as they can, they are accepted; and that this must be all that God requires in order to men's being received as the objects of his favour, and must be what God has appointed as the condition of salvation: concerning which I would observe, that in such a manner of speaking of " men's being accepted because they are sincere, and do as well as they can," there is evidently a supposition of some virtue, some degree of that which is truly good, though it does not go so far as were to be wished. For if men do what they can, unless their so doing be from some good principle, disposition, or exercise of heart, some virtuous inclination or act of the will, their so doing what they can, is in some respect not a whit better than if they did nothing at all. In such a case, there is no more positive moral goodness in a man's doing what he can, than in the wind-mill's doing what it can; because the action does no more proceed from virtue; and there is nothing in such sincerity of endeavour, or doing what we can, that should render it any more a proper or fit recommendation to positive favour and acceptance, or the condition of any reward or actual benefit, than doing nothing; for both the one and the other are alike nothing, as to any true moral weight or value.

Corol. 2. Hence also it follows, there is nothing that appears in the reason and nature of things which can justly lead us to determine, that God will certainly give the necessary means of salvation, or some way or other bestow true holiness and eternal life on those heathen who are sincere (in the sense above explained) in their endeavours to find out the will of the Deity, and to please him, according to their light, that they may escape his future displeasure and wrath, and obtain happiness in the future state, through his favour.

SECTION VI.

LIBERTY OF INDIFFERENCE NOT ONLY NOT NECESSARY TO VIRTUE, BUT UTTERLY INCONSISTENT WITH IT; AND ALL EITHER VIRTUOUS OR VICIOUS HABITS OR INCLINATIONS INCONSISTENT WITH ARMINIAN NOTIONS OF LIBERTY AND MORAL AGENCY.

To suppose such a freedom of will as Arminians talk of, to be requisite to virtue and vice, is many ways contrary to common sense.

If indifference belongs to liberty of will, as Arminians suppose, and it be essential to a virtuous action that it be performed in a state of liberty, as they also suppose, it will follow, that it is essential to a virtuous action that it be performed in a state of indifference: and if it be performed in a state of indifference, then doubtless it must be performed in the time of indifference. And so it will follow, that in order to the virtuousness of an act, the heart must be indifferent in the time of the performance of that act, and the more indifferent and cold the heart is with relation to the act which is performed, so much the better; because the act is performed with so much the greater liberty. But is this agreeable to the light of nature? Is it agreeable to the notions which mankind, in all ages, have of virtue; that it lies in that which is contrary to indifference, even in the tendency and inclination of the heart to virtuous action; and that the stronger the inclination, and so the further from indifference, the more virtuous the heart, and so much the more praiseworthy the act which proceeds from it?

If we should suppose (contrary to what has been before demonstrated) that there may be an act of will in a state of indifference; for instance, this act, viz. the

will's determining to put itself out of a state of indifference, and give itself a preponderation one way; then
it would follow, on Arminian principles, that this act
or determination of the will is that alone wherein virtue consists, because this only is performed, while the
mind remains in a state of indifference, and so in a state
of liberty; for when once the mind is put out of its equilibrium, it is no longer in such a state: and therefore all
the acts which follow afterwards, proceeding from bias,
can have the nature neither of virtue nor vice. Or if
the thing which the will can do, while yet in a state of
indifference, and so of liberty, be only to suspend acting, and determine to take the matter into consideration,
then this determination is that alone wherein virtue
consists, and not proceeding to action after the scale is
turned by consideration. So that it will follow, from
these principles, all that is done after the mind, by any
means, is once out of its equilibrium, and already possessed by an inclination, and arising from that inclination, has nothing of the nature of virtue or vice, and is
worthy of neither blame nor praise. But how plainly
contrary is this to the universal sense of mankind, and
to the notion they have of sincerely virtuous actions!
which is, that they are actions which proceed from a
heart well disposed and inclined; and the stronger and
the more fixed and determined the good disposition of
the heart, the greater the sincerity of virtue, and so the
more of the truth and reality of it. But if there be any
acts which are done in a state of equilibrium, or spring
immediately from perfect indifference and coldness of
heart, they cannot arise from any good principle or disposition in the heart; and consequently, according to
common sense, have no sincere goodness in them, having no virtue of heart in them. To have a virtuous
heart, is to have a heart that favours virtue, and is
friendly to it, and not one perfectly cold and indifferent
about it.

And besides, the actions that are done in a state of
indifference, or that arise immediately out of such a

state, cannot be virtuous, because, by the supposition, they are not determined by any preceding choice. For if there be preceding choice, then choice intervenes between the act and the state of indifference; which is contrary to the supposition of the act's arising immediately out of indifference. But those acts which are not determined by preceding choice, cannot be virtuous or vicious, by Arminian principles, because they are not determined by the will. So that neither one way nor the other can any actions be virtuous or vicious, according to Arminian principles. If the action be determined by a preceding act of choice, it cannot be virtuous; because the action is not done in a state of indifference, nor does immediately rise from such a state; and so is not done in a state of liberty. If the action be not determined by a preceding act of choice, then it cannot be virtuous; because then the will is not self-determined in it. So that it is made certain, that neither virtue nor vice can ever find any place in the universe.

Moreover, that it is necessary to a virtuous action that it be performed in a state of indifference, under a notion of that being a state of liberty, is contrary to common sense; as it is a dictate of common sense, that indifference itself in many cases is vicious, and so to a high degree. As if, when I see my neighbour or near friend, and one who has in the highest degree merited of me, in extreme distress and ready to perish, I find an indifference in my heart with respect to any thing proposed to be done, which I can easily do, for his relief. So, if it should be proposed to me to blaspheme God, or kill my father, or do numberless other things which might be mentioned, the being indifferent, for a moment, would be highly vicious and vile.

And it may be further observed, that to suppose this liberty of indifference is essential to virtue and vice, destroys the great difference of degrees of the guilt of different crimes, and takes away the heinousness of the most flagitious, horrid iniquities; such as adultery, bestiality, murder, perjury, blasphemy, &c. For according to these principles, there is no harm at all in having the mind in a state of perfect indifference with respect to these crimes; nay, it is absolutely necessary in order to any virtue in avoiding them, or vice in doing them. But for the mind to be in a state of indifference with respect to them, is to be next door to doing them; it is then infinitely near to choosing, and so committing the fact; for equilibrium is the next step to a degree of preponderation; and one, even the least degree of preponderation (all things considered) is choice. And not only so, but for the will to be in a state of perfect equilibrium with respect to such crimes, is for the mind to be in such a state as to be full as likely to choose them as to refuse them, to do them as to omit them. And if our minds must be in such a state, wherein it is as near to choosing as refusing, and wherein it must of necessity, according to the nature of things, be as likely to commit them as to refrain from them, where is the exceeding heinousness of choosing and committing them? If there be no harm in often being in such a state wherein the probability of doing and forbearing are exactly equal, there being an equilibrium, and no more tendency to one than the other, then, according to the nature and laws of such a contingence, it may be expected as an inevitable consequence of such a disposition of things, that we should choose them as often as we reject them; that it should generally so fall out, is necessary, as equality in the effect is the natural consequence of the equal tendency of the cause, or of the antecedent state of things from which the effect arises. Why then should we be so exceedingly to blame if it does so fall out?

It is many ways apparent, that the Arminian scheme of liberty is utterly inconsistent with the being of any such things as either virtuous or vicious habits or dispositions. If liberty of indifference be essential to moral agency, then there can be no virtue in any habitual inclinations of the heart; which are contrary to indifference, and imply in their nature the very destruction and exclusion of it. They suppose nothing can be virtuous in which no liberty is exercised; but how absurd is it to talk of exercising indifference under bias and preponderation!

And if self-determining power in the will be necessary to moral agency, praise, blame, &c., then nothing done by the will can be any further praise or blame-worthy, than so far as the will is moved, swayed, and determined by itself, and the scales turned by the sovereign power the will has over itself. And therefore the will must not be put out of its balance already, the preponderation must not be determined and effected before-hand; and so the self-determining act anticipated. Thus it appears another way, that habitual bias is inconsistent with that liberty which Arminians suppose to be necessary to virtue or vice; and so it follows, that habitual bias itself cannot be either virtuous or vicious.

The same thing follows from their doctrine concerning the inconsistence of necessity with liberty, praise, dispraise, &c. None will deny, that bias and inclination may be so strong as to be invincible, and leave no possibility of the will's determining contrary to it; and so be attended with necessity. This Dr Whitby allows concerning the will of God, angels, and glorified saints, with respect to good; and the will of devils with respect to evil. Therefore, if necessity be inconsistent with liberty; then, when fixed inclination is to such a degree of strength, it utterly excludes all virtue, vice, praise, or blame. And if so, then the nearer habits are to this strength, the more do they impede liberty, and so diminish praise and blame. If very strong habits destroy liberty, the lesser ones proportionably hinder it, according to their degree of strength. And therefore it will follow, that then is the act most virtuous or vicious when performed without any inclination or habitual bias at all, because it is then performed with most liberty.

Every prepossessing fixed bias on the mind brings a degree of moral inability for the contrary; because, so far as the mind is biassed and prepossessed, so much hinderance is there of the contrary. And therefore, if moral inability be inconsistent with moral agency, or the nature of virtue and vice, then, so far as there is any such thing as evil disposition of heart, or habitual depravity of inclination, whether covetousness, pride, malice, cruelty, or whatever else, so much the more excusable persons are, so much the less have their evil acts of this kind the nature of vice. And, on the contrary, whatever excellent dispositions and inclinations they have, so much are they the less virtuous.

It is evident, that no habitual disposition of heart, whether it be to a greater or less degree, can be in any degree virtuous or vicious; or the actions which proceed from them at all praise or blame-worthy. Because, though we should suppose the habit not to be of such strength as wholly to take away all moral ability and self-determining power; or hinder but that, although the act be partly from bias, yet it may be in part from self-determination; yet in this case, all that is from antecedent bias must be set aside, as of no consideration; and in estimating the degree of virtue or vice, no more must be considered than what arises from self-determining power, without any influence of that bias, because liberty is exercised in no more; so that all that is the exercise of habitual inclination, is thrown away, as not belonging to the morality of the action. By which it appears, that no exercise of these habits, let them be stronger or weaker, can ever have any thing of the nature of either virtue or vice.

Here if any one should say, that notwithstanding all these things, there may be the nature of virtue and vice in the habits of the mind, because these habits may be the effects of those acts wherein the mind exercised liberty; that however the fore-mentioned reasons will prove that no habits which are natural, or that are born or created with us, can be either virtuous or vicious, yet they will not prove this of habits which have been acquired and established by repeated free acts.

To such an objector I would say, that this evasion will not at all help the matter. For if freedom of will be essential to the very nature of virtue and vice, then there is no virtue or vice but only in that very thing wherein this liberty is exercised. If a man, in one or more things that he does, exercises liberty, and then by those acts is brought into such circumstances that his liberty ceases, and there follows a long series of acts or events that come to pass necessarily; those consequent acts are not virtuous or vicious, rewardable or punishable; but only the free acts that established this necesity; for in them alone was the man free. The following effects, that are necessary, have no more of the nature of virtue or vice, than health or sickness of body have properly the nature of virtue or vice, being the effects of a course of free acts of temperance or intemperance; or than the good qualities of a clock are of the nature of virtue, which are the effects of free acts of the artificer; or the goodness and sweetness of the fruits of a garden are moral virtues, being the effects of the free and faithful acts of the gardener. If liberty be absolutely requisite to the morality of actions, and necessity wholly inconsistent with it, as Arminians greatly insist; then no necessary effects whatsoever, let the cause be never so good or bad, can be virtuous or vicious; but the virtue or vice must be only in the free cause. Agreeably to this, Dr Whitby supposes the necessity that attends the good and evil habits of the saints in heaven, and damned in hell, which are the consequence of their free acts in their state of probation, are not rewardable or punishable.

On the whole, it appears, that if the notions of Arminians concerning liberty and moral agency be true, it will follow, that there is no virtue in any such habits or qualities as humility, meekness, patience, mercy, gratitude, generosity, heavenly-mindedness; nothing at all praiseworthy in loving Christ above father and mother, wife and children, or our own lives; or in delight in holiness, hungering and thirsting after righteousness, love to enemies, universal benevolence to mankind; and, on the other hand, there is nothing at all vicious, or

worthy of dispraise, in the most sordid, beastly, malignant, devilish dispositions; in being ungrateful, profane,
habitually hating God and things sacred and holy; or in
being most treacherous, envious, and cruel towards
men. For all these things are dispositions and inclinations of the heart. And, in short, there is no such
thing as any virtuous or vicious quality of mind; no such
thing as inherent virtue and holiness, or vice and sin; and
the stronger those habits or dispositions are, which used
to be called virtuous and vicious, the further they are
from being so indeed; the more violent men's lusts are,
the more fixed their pride, envy, ingratitude, and maliciousness, still the further are they from being blameworthy. If there be a man that, by his own repeated
acts, or by any other means, is come to be of the most
hellish disposition, desperately inclined to treat his
neighbours with injuriousness, contempt, and malignity:
the further they should be from any disposition to be
angry with him, or in the least to blame him. So, on
the other hand, if there be a person, who is of a most excellent spirit, strongly inclining him to the most amiable actions, admirably meek, benevolent, &c. so much
is he further from any thing rewardable or commendable. On which principles, the man Jesus Christ was very
far from being praiseworthy for those acts of holiness
and kindness which he performed, these propensities
being strong in his heart. And, above all, the infinitely holy and gracious God is infinitely remote from
any thing commendable, his good inclinations being infinitely strong, and he, therefore, at the utmost possible
distance from being at liberty. And in all cases, the
stronger the inclinations of any are to virtue, and the
more they love it, the less virtuous they are; and the
more they love wickedness, the less vicious.—Whether
these things are agreeable to Scripture, let every Christian, and every man who has read the Bible, judge: and
whether they are agreeable to common sense, let every
one judge that has human understanding in exercise.

And, if we pursue these principles, we shall find that

virtue and vice are wholly excluded out of the world; and that there never was, nor ever can be, any such thing as one or the other, either in God, angels, or men. No propensity, disposition, or habit, can be virtuous or vicious, as has been shown: because they, so far as they take place, destroy the freedom of the will, the foundation of all moral agency, and exclude all capacity of either virtue or vice.—And if habits and dispositions themselves be not virtuous nor vicious, neither can the exercise of these dispositions be so; for the exercise of bias is not the exercise of free self-determining will, and so there is no exercise of liberty in it. Consequently, no man is virtuous or vicious, either in being well or ill disposed, nor in acting from a good or bad disposition. And whether this bias or disposition be habitual or not, if it exists but a moment before the act of will, which is the effect of it, it alters not the case, as to the necessity of the effect. Or if there be no previous disposition at all, either habitual or occasional, that determines the act, then it is not choice that determines it: it is there-fore a contingence, that happens to the man, arising from nothing in him, and is necessary, as to any inclination or choice of his; and, therefore, cannot make him either the better or worse, any more than a tree is better than other trees, because it oftener happens to be lit upon by a swan or nightingale: or a rock more vicious than other rocks, because rattlesnakes have happened oftener to crawl over it. So that there is no virtue nor vice in good or bad dispositions, either fixed or transient; nor any vir-tue or vice in acting from any good or bad previous in-clination; nor yet any virtue or vice, in acting wholly without any previous inclination. Where, then, shall we find room for virtue or vice?

SECTION VII.

ARMINIAN NOTIONS OF MORAL AGENCY INCONSISTENT WITH ALL INFLUENCE
OF MOTIVE AND INDUCEMENT, IN EITHER VIRTUOUS OR VICIOUS ACTIONS.

As Arminian notions of that liberty, which is essential to virtue or vice, are inconsistent with common sense, in their being inconsistent with all virtuous or vicious habits and dispositions; so they are no less so in their inconsistency with all influence of motives in moral actions.

It is equally against those notions of liberty of will, whether there be, previous to the act of choice, a preponderancy of the inclination, or a preponderancy of those circumstances which have a tendency to move the inclination. And, indeed, it comes to just the same thing: to say, the circumstances of the mind are such as to tend to sway and turn its inclination one way, is the same thing as to say, the inclination of the mind, as, under such circumstances, tends that way.

Or if any think it most proper to say, that motives do alter the inclination, and give a new bias to the mind, it will not alter the case, as to the present argument. For if motives operate by giving the mind an inclination, then they operate by destroying the mind's indifference, and laying it under a bias. But to do this, is to destroy the Arminian freedom: it is not to leave the will to its own self-determination, but to bring it into subjection to the power of something extrinsic, which operates upon it, sways and determines it, previous to its own determination. So that what is done from motive, cannot be either virtuous or vicious. And besides, if the acts of the will are excited by motives, those motives are the causes of those acts of the will; which makes the acts of the will necessary as effects necessarily follow the efficiency of the cause. And if the influence and power of the motive causes the volition, then the influence of the motive determines volitions, and volition does not determine itself; and so is not free, in the sense of Arminians, (as has been largely shown already,) and consequently can be neither virtuous nor vicious.

The supposition which has already been taken notice of, as an insufficient evasion in other cases, would be, in like manner, impertinently alleged in this case; namely, the supposition that liberty consists in a power of suspending action for the present, in order to deliberation. If it should be said, though it be true that the will is under a necessity of finally following the strongest motive, yet it may, for the present, forbear to act upon the motive presented, till there has been opportunity thoroughly to consider it, and compare its real weight with the merit of other motives : I answer as follows :

Here, again, it must be remembered, that if determining thus to suspend and consider, be that act of the will, wherein alone liberty is exercised, then in this all virtue and vice must consist; and the acts that follow this consideration, and are the effects of it, being necessary, are no more virtuous or vicious than some good or bad events, which happen when they are fast asleep, and are the consequence of what they did when they were awake. Therefore, I would here observe two things :

1. To suppose that all virtue and vice, in every case, consists in determining, whether to take time for consideration or not, is not agreeable to common sense. For according to such a supposition, the most horrid crimes, adultery, murder, sodomy, blasphemy, &c. do not at all consist in the horrid nature of the things themselves, but only in the neglect of thorough consideration before they were perpetrated; which brings their viciousness to a small matter, and makes all crimes equal. If it be said, that neglect of consideration, when such heinous evils are proposed to choice, is worse than in other cases: I answer, this is inconsistent, as it supposes the very thing to be, which at the same time, is supposed not to be; it supposes all moral evil, all viciousness and

heinousness, does not consist merely in the want of consideration. It supposes some crimes in themselves, in their own nature, to be more heinous than others, antecedent to consideration or inconsideration, which lays the person under a previous obligation to consider in some cases more than others.

2. If it were so, that all virtue and vice, in every case, consisted only in the act of the will, whereby it determines whether to consider or no, it would not alter the case in the least, as to the present argument. For still in this act of the will on this determination, it is induced by some motive, and necessarily follows the strongest motive; and so is necessarily, even in that act wherein alone it is either virtuous or vicious.

One thing more I would observe, concerning the inconsistence of Arminian notions of moral agency with influence of motives. I suppose none will deny, that it is possible for motives to be set before the mind so powerful, and exhibited in so strong a light, and under so advantageous circumstances, as to be invincible; and such as the mind cannot but yield to. In this case, Arminians will doubtless say, liberty is destroyed. And if so, then if motives are exhibited with half so much power, they hinder liberty in proportion to their strength, and go half-way towards destroying it. If a thousand degrees of motive abolish all liberty, then five hundred take it half away. If one degree of the influence of motive does not at all infringe or diminish liberty, then no more do two degrees; for nothing doubled, is still nothing. And if two degrees do not diminish the will's liberty, no more do four, eight, sixteen, or six thousand. For nothing multiplied never so much, comes to but nothing. If there be nothing in the nature of motive or moral suasion, that is at all opposite to liberty, then the greatest degree of it cannot hurt liberty. But if there be any thing in the nature of the thing that is against liberty, then the least degree of it hurts it in some degree, and consequently hurts and diminishes virtue. If invincible motives to that action which is good, take away all the freedom of the act, and so all the virtue of it; then the more forcible the motives are, so much the worse, so much the less virtue; and the weaker the motives are, the better for the cause of virtue; and none is best of all.

Now, let it be considered, whether these things are agreeable to common sense. If it should be allowed, that there are some instances wherein the soul chooses without any motive, what virtue can there be in such a choice? I am sure there is no prudence or wisdom in it. Such a choice is made for no good end; for it is for no end at all. If it were for any end, the view of the end would be the motive exciting to the act; and if the act be for no good end, and so from no good aim, then there is no good intention in it: and, therefore, according to all our natural notions of virtue, no more virtue in it than in the motion of the smoke, which is driven to and fro by the wind, without any aim or end in the thing moved, and which knows not whither, nor why and wherefore, it is moved.

Corol. 1. By these things it appears, that the argument against the Calvinists, taken from the use of counsels, exhortations, invitations, expostulations, &c. so much insisted on by Arminians, is truly against themselves. For these things can operate no other way to any good effect, than as in them is exhibited motive and inducement, tending to excite and determine the acts of the will. But it follows, on their principles, that the acts of will excited by such causes, cannot be virtuous; because, so far as they are from these, they are not from the will's self-determining power. Hence it will follow, that it is not worth the while to offer any arguments to persuade men to any virtuous volition or voluntary action; it is in vain to set before them the wisdom and amiableness of ways of virtue, or the odiousness and folly of ways of vice. This notion of liberty and moral agency frustrates all endeavours to draw men to virtue by instruction or persuasion, precept, or example: for though these things may induce men to what is *materially* virtuous, yet at the same time they take away the *form* of virtue, because they destroy liberty; as they, by their own power, put the will out of its equilibrium, determine and turn the scale, and take the work of self-determining power out of its hands. And the clearer the instructions that are given, the more powerful the arguments that are used, and the more moving the persuasions or examples, the more likely they are to frustrate their own design; because they have so much the greater tendency to put the will out of its balance, to hinder its freedom of self-determination; and so to exclude the very form of virtue, and the essence of whatsoever is praiseworthy.

So, it clearly follows, from these principles, that God has no hand in any man's virtue, nor does at all promote it, either by a physical or moral influence; that none of the moral methods he uses with men to promote virtue in the world, have tendency to the attainment of that end; that all the instructions which he has given to men, from the beginning of the world to this day, by prophets or apostles, or by his Son Jesus Christ; that all his counsels, invitations, promises, threatenings, warnings, and expostulations; that all means he has used with men, in ordinances or providences; yea, all influences of his Spirit, ordinary and extraordinary, have had no tendency at all to excite any one virtuous act of the mind, or to promote any thing morally good and commendable, in any respect. For there is no way that these, or any other means, can promote virtue, but one of these three. Either, (1.) by a physical operation on the heart. But all effects that are wrought in men in this way, have no virtue in them, by the concurring voice of all Arminians. Or, (2.) morally, by exhibiting motives to the understanding, to excite good acts in the will. But it has been demonstrated, that volitions, which are excited by motives, are necessary, and not excited by a self-moving power; and therefore, by their principles, there is no virtue in them. Or, (3.) by merely giving the will an opportunity to determine itself concerning the objects proposed, either to choose or reject, by its own uncaused, unmov-

ed, uninfluenced self-determination.   And if this be all,
then all those means do no more to promote virtue than
vice: for they do nothing but give the will opportunity
to determine itself *either way*, either to good or bad,
without laying it under any bias to either; and so there
is really as much of an opportunity given to determine
in favour of evil as of good.

Thus, that horrid blasphemous consequence will certainly follow from the Arminian doctrine which they
charge on others; namely, that God acts an inconsistent
part in using so many counsels, warnings, invitations,
entreaties, &c. with sinners, to induce them to forsake
sin, and turn to the ways of virtue; and that all are in-
sincere and fallacious.   It will follow, from their doctrine, that God does these things when he knows, at the
same time, that they have no manner of tendency to
promote the effect he seems to aim at; yea, knows that
if they have any influence, this very influence will be
inconsistent with such an effect, and will prevent it.
But what an imputation of insincerity would this fix on
Him who is infinitely holy and true!   So that their's is
the doctrine which, if pursued in its consequences, does
horribly reflect on the Most High, and fix on him the
charge of hypocrisy; and not the doctrine of the Calvinist, according to their frequent and vehement exclamations and invectives.

Corol. 2. From what has been observed in this section, it again appears, that Arminian principles and notions, when fairly examined and pursued in their demonstrable consequences, do evidently shut all virtue
out of the world, and make it impossible that there
should ever be any such thing in any case, or that any
such thing should ever be conceived of.   For, by these
principles, the very notion of virtue or vice implies absurdity and contradiction.   For it is absurd in itself
and contrary to common sense, to suppose a virtuous
act of mind without any good intention or aim; and by
their principles, it is absurd to suppose a virtuous act
with a good intention or aim; for to act for an end, is to

act from a motive.   So that if we rely on these principles, there can be no virtuous act with a good design
and end; and it is self-evident, there can be none without : consequently there can be no virtuous act at all.

Corol. 3. It is manifest, that Arminian notions of moral agency, and the being of a faculty of will, cannot
consist together: and that if there be any such thing as
either a virtuous or vicious act, it cannot be an act of
the will; no will can be at all concerned in it.   For that
act which is performed without inclination, without motive, without end, must be performed without any concern of the will.   To suppose an act of the will without
these, implies a contradiction.   If the soul in its act has
no motive or end; then, in that act (as was observed
before,) it seeks nothing, goes after nothing, exerts no
inclination to any thing; and this implies, that in that
act it desires nothing, and chooses nothing; so that
there is no act of choice in the case: and that is as
much as to say, there is no act of will in the case;—
Which very effectually shuts all vicious and virtuous
acts out of the universe; inasmuch as, according to this,
there can be no virtuous or vicious act wherein the will
is concerned; and according to the plainest dictates of
reason, and the light of nature, and also the principles
of Arminians themselves, there can be no virtuous or
vicious act wherein the will is not concerned.   And
therefore there is no room for any virtuous or vicious
acts at all.

Corol. 4. If none of the moral actions of intelligent
beings are influenced by either previous inclination or
motive, another strange thing will follow; and this is,
that God not only cannot foreknow any of the future
moral actions of his creatures, but he can make no conjecture, can give no probable guess, concerning them.
For, all conjecture in things of this nature must depend
on some discerning or apprehension of these two things,
previous disposition and *motive,* which, as has been observed, Arminian notions of moral agency, in their real
consequence, altogether exclude.

PART IV.

SECTION I.

THE ESSENCE OF THE VIRTUE AND VICE OF DISPOSITIONS OF THE HEART, AND ACTS OF THE WILL, LIES NOT IN THEIR CAUSE, BUT THEIR NATURE.

ONE main foundation of the reasons which are brought to establish the fore-mentioned notions of liberty, virtue, vice, &c. is a supposition, that the virtuousness of the dispositions, or acts of the will, consists not in the nature of these dispositions or acts, but wholly in the origin or cause of them : so that if the disposition of the mind, or acts of the will, be never so good, yet if the cause of the disposition or act be not our virtue, there is nothing vir-tuous or praiseworthy in it; and, on the contrary, if the will, in its inclination or acts, be never so bad, yet unless it arises from something that is our vice or fault, there is nothing vicious or blameworthy in it. Hence their grand objection and pretended demonstration, or self-evidence, against any virtue and commendableness, or vice and blameworthiness, of those habits or acts of the will, which are not from some virtuous or vicious deter-mination of the will itself.

Now, if this matter be well considered, it will appear to be altogether a mistake, yea, a gross absurdity; and that it is most certain, that if there be any such things as a virtuous or vicious disposition, or volition of mind, the virtuousness or viciousness of them consists not in the origin or cause of these things, but in the nature of them.

If the essence of virtuousness or commendableness, and of viciousness or fault, does not lie in the nature of

the dispositions or acts of mind, which are said to be
our virtue or our fault, but in their cause, then it is certain it lies no where at all. Thus, for instance, if the
vice of a *vicious* act of will lies not in the nature of the
act, but the cause; so that its being of a bad nature will
not make it at all our fault, unless it arises from some
faulty determination of ours, as its cause, or something
in us that is our fault; then, for the same reason, neither
can the viciousness of that cause lie in the nature of the
thing itself, but in its cause: that evil determination of
ours is not our fault, merely because it is of a bad nature, unless it arises from some cause in us that is our
fault. And when we are come to this higher cause, still
the reason of the thing holds good; though this cause be
of a bad nature, yet we are not at all to blame on that
account, unless it arises from something faulty in us.
Nor yet can blameworthiness lie in the nature of this
cause but in the cause of that. And thus we must drive
faultiness back from step to step, from a lower cause to
a higher, *in infinitum;* and that is thoroughly to banish
it from the world, and to allow it no possibility of existence any where in the universality of things. On these
principles, vice, or moral evil cannot exist in any thing
that is an *effect;* because *fault* does not consist in the
nature of things, but in their cause; as well as because
effects are necessary, being unavoidably connected with
their cause: therefore the cause only is to blame. And
so it follows, that faultiness can lie only in that cause,
which is a cause only, and no effect of anything. Nor
yet can it lie in this; for then it must lie in the nature
of the thing itself; not in its being from any determination of ours, nor anything faulty in us, which is the
cause, nor indeed from any cause at all; for, by the
supposition, it is no effect, and has no cause. And thus
he that will maintain it is not the nature of habits or
acts of will that makes them virtuous or faulty, but the
cause, must immediately run himself out of his own
assertion; and, in maintaining it, will insensibly contradict and deny it.

This is certain, that if effects are vicious and faulty, not from their nature, or from any thing inherent in them, but because they are from a bad cause, it must be on account of the badness of the cause: a bad effect in the will must be bad, because the cause is bad, or of an evil nature, or has badness as a quality inherent in it: and a good effect in the will must be good, by reason of the goodness of the cause, or its being of a good kind and nature.   And if this be what is meant, the very supposition of fault and praise lying not in the nature of the thing, but the cause, contradicts itself, and does at least resolve the essence of virtue and vice into the nature of things, and supposes it originally to consist in that.— And if a caviller has a mind to run from the absurdity, by saying, "No, the fault of the thing, which is the cause, lies not in this, that the cause itself is of an evil nature, but that the cause is evil in that sense, that it is from another bad cause,"—still the absurdity will follow him; for if so, then the cause before charged is at once acquitted, and all the blame must be laid to the higher cause, and must consist in that's being evil, or of an evil nature.   So now we are come again to lay the blame of the thing blameworthy, to the nature of the thing, and not to the cause.   And if any is so foolish as to go higher still, and ascend from step to step, till he is come to that which is the first cause concerned in the whole affair, and will say, all the blame lies in that; then, at last, he must be forced to own, that the faultiness of the thing which he supposes alone blameworthy, lies wholly in the nature of the thing, and not in the original or cause of it; for the supposition is, that it has no original, it is determined by no act of ours, is caused by nothing faulty in us, being absolutely without any cause.   And so the race is at an end, but the evader is taken in his flight!

It is agreeable to the natural notions of mankind, that moral evil, with its desert of dislike and abhorrence, and all its other ill-deservings, consists in a certain deformity in the nature of certain dispositions of the heart

and acts of the will; and not in the deformity of something else, diverse from the very thing itself, which deserves abhorrence, supposed to be the cause of it;—
which would be absurd, because that would be to suppose a thing that is innocent and not evil, is truly evil
and faulty, because another thing is evil. It implies a
contradiction; for it would be to suppose, the very
thing which is morally evil and blameworthy, is innocent and not blameworthy; but that something else,
which is its cause, is only to blame. To say, that vice
does not consist in the thing which is vicious, but in
its cause, is the same as to say, that vice does not consist in vice, but in that which produces it.

It is true a cause may be to blame for being the cause
of vice: it may be wickedness in the cause that it produces wickedness. But it would imply a contradiction,
to suppose that these two are the same individual wickedness. The wicked act of the cause in producing
wickedness, is one wickedness; and the wickedness produced, if there be any produced, is another. And therefore the wickedness of the latter does not lie in the
former, but is distinct from it; and the wickedness of
both lies in the evil nature of the things which are
wicked.

The thing which makes sin hateful, is that by which
it deserves punishment; which is but the expression of
hatred. And that which renders virtue lovely, is the
same with that on the account of which, it is fit to receive
praise and reward; which are but the expressions of
esteem and love. But that which makes vice hateful,
is its hateful nature; and that which renders virtue
lovely, is its amiable nature. It is a certain beauty or
deformity that are inherent in that good or evil will,
which is the soul of virtue and vice (and not in the occasion of it), which is their worthiness of esteem or disesteem, praise, or dispraise, according to the common
sense of mankind. If the cause or occasion of the rise
of a hateful disposition or act of will, be also hateful,
suppose another antecedent evil will; that is entirely

another sin, and deserves punishment by itself, under a distinct consideration.   There is worthiness of dispraise in the nature of an evil volition, and not wholly in some foregoing act, which is its cause; otherwise the evil volition, which is the effect, is no moral evil, any more than sickness, or some other natural calamity, which arises from a cause morally evil.

Thus, for instance, ingratitude is hateful and worthy of dispraise, according to common sense; not because something as bad, or worse than ingratitude, was the cause that produced it; but because it is hateful in itself, by its own inherent deformity.   So, the love of virtue is amiable and worthy of praise, not merely because something else went before this love of virtue in our minds, which caused it to take place there;—for instance, our own choice; we choose to love virtue, and, by some method or other, wrought ourselves into the love of it;—but because of the amiableness and condescendency of such a disposition and inclination of heart.   If that was the case, that we did choose to love virtue, and so produced that love in ourselves, this choice itself could be no otherwise amiable or praiseworthy, than as love to virtue, or some other amiable inclination, was exercised and implied in it.   If that choice was amiable at all, it must be so on account of some amiable quality in the nature of the choice.   If we chose to love virtue, not in love to virtue, or any thing that was good and exercised no sort of good disposition to the choice, the choice itself was not virtuous nor worthy of any praise, according to common sense, because the choice was not of a good nature.

It may not be improper here to take notice of something said by an author, that has lately made a mighty noise in America.   "A necessary holiness (says he*) is no holiness.   Adam could not be originally created in righteousness and true holiness, because he must choose to be righteous, before he could be righteous.   And therefore he must exist, he must be created; yea, he

* Scrip. Doc. of Original Sin, p. 180, third edit.

must exercise thought and reflection, before he was
righteous." There is much more to the same effect in
that place, and also in pp. 437, 438, 439, 440. If these
things are so, it will certainly follow, that the first
choosing to be righteous is no righteous choice; there is
no righteousness or holiness in it, because no choosing
to be righteous goes before it. For he plainly speaks
of choosing to be righteous, as what must go before
righteousness; and that which follows the choice, being
the effect of the choice, cannot be righteousness or holiness; for an effect is a thing necessary, and cannot prevent the influence or efficacy of its cause; and therefore
is unavoidably dependent upon the cause; and he says a
necessary holiness is no holiness. So that neither can
a choice of righteousness be righteousness or holiness,
nor can any thing that is consequent on that choice, and
the effect of it, be righteousness or holiness; nor can
any thing that is without choice, be righteousness or
holiness. So that by this scheme, all righteousness and
holiness is at once shut out of the world, and no door
left open by which it can ever possibly enter into
the world.

I suppose the way that men came to entertain this
absurd inconsistent notion, with respect to internal inclinations and volitions themselves (or notions that imply it,) viz. that the essence of their moral good or evil
lies not in their nature, but their cause, was, that it is
indeed a very plain dictate of common sense, that it is
so with respect to all outward actions and sensible motions of the body; that the moral good or evil of them
does not lie at all in the motions themselves, which,
taken by themselves, are nothing of a moral nature;
and the essence of all the moral good or evil that concerns them, lies in those internal dispositions and volitions which are the cause of them. Now, being always
used to determine this, without hesitation or dispute,
concerning external actions, which are the things that,
in the common use of language, are signified by such
phrases as men's *actions*, or their *doings;* hence, when

they came to speak of volitions, and internal exercises of their inclinations, under the same denomination of their actions, or what they do, they unwarily determined the case must also be the same with these as with external actions; not considering the vast difference in the nature of the case.

If any shall still object and say, why is it not necessary that the cause should be considered, in order to determine whether any thing be worthy of blame or praise? is it agreeable to reason and common sense, that a man is to be praised or blamed for that which he is not the cause or author of, and has no hand in?

I answer: Such phrases as *being the cause, being the author, having a hand,* and the like, are ambiguous. They are most vulgarly understood for being the designing voluntary cause, or cause by antecedent choice; and it is most certain, that men are not, in this sense, the causes or authors of the first act of their wills, in any case, as certain as any thing is or ever can be; for nothing can be more certain than that a thing is not before it is, nor a thing of the same kind before the first thing of that kind, and so no choice before the first choice.—As the phrase, *being the author,* may be understood, not of being the producer by an antecedent act of will, but as a person may be said to be the author of the act of will itself, by his being the immediate agent, or the being that is acting, or in exercise in that act; if the phrase of *being the author* is used to signify this, then doubtless common sense requires men's being the authors of their own acts of will, in order to their being esteemed worthy of praise or dispraise, on account of them. And common sense teaches, that they must be the authors of external actions, in the former sense, namely, their being the causes of them by an act of will or choice, in order to their being justly blamed or praised: but it teaches no such thing with respect to the acts of the will themselves. But this may appear more manifest by the things which will be observed in the following section.

SECTION II.

ONE thing, that is made very much a ground of argument and supposed demonstration by Arminians, in defence of the fore-mentioned principles concerning moral
agency, virtue, vice, &c., is their metaphysical notion of
agency and action. They say, unless the soul has a
self-determining power, it has no power of action; if its
volitions be not caused by itself, but are excited and determined by some extrinsic cause, they cannot be the
soul's own acts; and that the soul cannot be active, but
must be wholly passive, in those effects which it is the
subject of necessarily, and not from its own free determination.

Mr Chubb lays the foundation of his scheme of liberty, and of his arguments to support it, very much in
this position, that man is an agent, and capable of action,—which doubtless is true: but self-determination
belongs to his notion of action, and is the very essence
of it; whence he infers, that it is impossible for a man
to act and be acted upon, in the same thing, at the same
time; and that nothing that is an action, can be the effect
of the action of another: and he insists, that a necessary
agent, or an agent that is necessarily determined to act,
is a plain contradiction.

But those are a precarious sort of demonstrations,
which men build on the meaning that they arbitrarily
affix to a word; especially when that meaning is abstruse,
inconsistent, and entirely diverse from the original sense
of the word in common speech.

That the meaning of the word *action*, as Mr Chubb
and many others use it, is utterly unintelligible and inconsistent, is manifest, because it belongs to their notion
of an action, that it is something wherein is no passion
or passiveness; that is, (according to their sense of pas-

siveness,) it is under the power, influence, or action of no cause. And this implies, that action has no cause, and is no effect; for to be an effect implies passiveness, or the being subject to the power and action of its cause. And yet they hold, that the mind's action is the effect of its own determination; yea, the mind's free and voluntary determination, which is the same with free choice. So that action is the effect of something preceding, even a preceding act of choice: and consequently, in this effect, the mind is passive, subject to the power and action of the preceding cause, which is the foregoing choice, and therefore cannot be active. So that here we have this contradiction, that action is always the effect of foregoing choice, and therefore cannot be action; because it is passive to the power of that preceding causal choice; and the mind cannot be active and passive in the same thing, at the same time. Again, they say, necessity is utterly inconsistent with action, and a necessary action is a contradiction; and so their notion of action implies contingence, and excludes all necessity. And, therefore, their notion of action implies, that it has no necessary dependence or connexion with any thing foregoing; for such a dependence or connexion excludes contingence, and implies necessity. And yet their notion of action implies necessity, and supposes that it is necessary, and cannot be contingent. For they suppose, that whatever is properly called action, must be determined by the will and free choice; and this is as much as to say, that it must be necessary, being dependent upon, and determined by, something foregoing, namely, a foregoing act of choice. Again, it belongs to their notion of action, of that which is a proper and mere act, that it is the beginning of motion, or of exertion of power; but yet it is implied in their notion of action, that it is not the beginning of motion or exertion of power, but is consequent and dependent on a preceding exertion of power, viz. the power of will and choice; for they say there is no proper action but what is freely chosen, or, which is the same thing, determined by a foregoing act of free choice. But

P

if any of them shall see cause to deny this, and say they hold no such thing, as that every action is chosen or determined by a foregoing choice, but that the very first exertion of will only, undetermined by any preceding act, is properly called action; then I say, such a man's notion of action implies necessity; for what the mind is the subject of, without the determination of its own previous choice, it is the subject of necessarily, as to any hand that free choice has in the affair, and without any ability the mind has to prevent it by any will or election of its own; because, by the supposition, it precludes all previous acts of will or choice in the case, which might prevent it. So that it is again, in this other way, implied in their notion of act, that it is both necessary and not necessary. Again, it belongs to their notion of an *act*, that it is no effect of a predetermining bias or preponderation, but springs immediately out of indifference; and this implies, that it cannot be from foregoing choice, which is foregoing preponderation: if it be not habitual, but occasional, yet if it causes the act, it is truly previous, efficacious, and determining. And yet, at the same time, it is essential to their notion of the act, that it is what the agent is the author of, freely and voluntarily, and that is by previous choice and design.

So that, according to their notion of the act, considered with regard to its consequences, these following things are all essential to it; viz. That it should be necessary, and not necessary; that it should be from a cause, and no cause; that it should be the fruit of choice and design, and not the fruit of choice and design; that it should be the beginning of motion or exertion, and yet consequent on previous exertion; that it should be before it is; that it should spring immediately out of indifference and equilibrium, and yet be the effect of preponderation; that it should be self-originated, and also have its original from something else; that it is what the mind causes itself, of its own will, and can produce or prevent, according to its choice or pleasure, and yet what the mind has no power to prevent, precluding all previous choice in the affair.

So that an act, according to their metaphysical notion of it, is something of which there is no idea; it is nothing but a confusion of the mind, excited by words, without any distinct meaning, and is an absolute nonentity; and that in two respects. (1.) There is nothing in the world that ever was, is, or can be, to answer the things which must belong to its description, according to what they suppose to be essential to it. And (2,) there neither is, nor ever was, nor can be, any notion or idea to answer the word, as they use and explain it. For, if we should suppose any such notion, it would many ways destroy itself. But it is impossible any idea or notion should subsist in the mind, whose very nature and essence which constitutes it, destroys it. If some learned philosopher, who had been abroad, in giving an account of the curious observations he had made in his travels, should say, " he had been in Terra del Fuego, and there had seen an animal, which he calls by a certain name, that begat and brought forth itself, and yet had a sire and dam distinct from itself; that it had an appetite, and was hungry before it had a being; that his master, who led him, and governed him at his pleasure, was always governed by him, and driven by him where he pleased; that when he moved, he always took a step before the first step; that he went with his head first, and yet always went tail foremost; and this, though he had neither tail nor head :" it would be no impudence at all to tell such a traveller, though a learned man, that he himself had no notion or idea of such an animal as he gave an account of, and never had, nor ever would have.

As the fore-mentioned notion of action is very inconsistent, so it is wholly diverse from the original meaning of the word. The more usual signification of it, in vulgar speech, seems to be some motion or exertion of power, that is voluntary, or that is the effect of the will, and is used in the same sense as doing; and most commonly it is used to signify outward actions. So thinking is often distinguished from acting, and desiring and willing from doing.

Besides this more usual and proper signification of the word *action,* there are other ways in which the word is used that are less proper, which yet have place in common speech. Oftentimes it is used to signify some motion or alteration in inanimate things, with relation to some object and effect. So, the spring of a watch is said to act upon the chain and wheels; the sunbeams, to act upon plants and trees; and the fire, to act upon wood. Sometimes the word is used to signify motions, alterations, and exertions of power, which are seen in corporeal things, considered absolutely; especially when these motions seem to arise from some internal cause which is hidden; so that they have a greater resemblance of those motions of our bodies which are the effects of natural volition, or invisible exertions of will. So, the fermentation of liquor, the operations of the loadstone, and of electrical bodies, are called the *action* of these things. And sometimes, the word *action* is used to signify the exercise of thought, or of will and inclination: so meditating, loving, hating, inclining, disinclining, choosing, and refusing, may be sometimes called acting; though more rarely (unless it be by philosophers and metaphysicians) than in any of the other senses.

But the word is never used in vulgar speech in that sense which Arminian divines use it in, namely, for the self-determinate exercise of the will, or an exertion of the soul, that arises without any necessary connexion with any thing foregoing. If a man does something voluntarily, or as the effect of his choice, then, in the most proper sense, and as the word is most originally and commonly used, he is said to *act;* but whether that choice or volition be self-determined, or no; whether it be connected with foregoing habitual bias; whether it be the certain effect of the strongest motive, or some intrinsic cause, never comes into consideration in the meaning of the word.

And if the word *action* is arbitrarily used by some

men otherwise, to suit some scheme of metaphysics or morality, no argument can reasonably be founded on such a use of this term, to prove any thing but their own pleasure. For divines and philosophers strenuously to urge such arguments, as though they were sufficient to support and demonstrate a whole scheme of moral philosophy and divinity, is certainly to erect a mighty edifice on the sand, or rather on a shadow. And though it may now perhaps, through custom, have become natural for them to use the word in this sense, (if that may be called a sense or meaning, which is inconsistent with itself,) yet this does not prove that it is agreeable to the natural notions men have of things, or that there can be any thing in the creation that should answer such a meaning. And though they appeal to experience, yet the truth is, that men are so far from experiencing any such thing, that it is impossible for them to have any conception of it.

If it should be objected, that action and passion are doubtless words of a contrary signification; but to suppose that the agent, in its action, is under the power and influence of something intrinsic, is to confound action and passion, and make them the same thing:

I answer, that action and passion are doubtless, as they are sometimes used, words of opposite signification; but not as signifying opposite existences, but only opposite relations. The words cause and effect are terms of opposite signification; but, nevertheless, if I assert that the same thing may, at the same time, in different respects and relations, be both cause and effect, this will not prove that I confound the terms. The soul may be both active and passive in the same thing in different respects; active with relation to one thing, and passive with relation to another. The word *passion*, when set in opposition to action, or rather activeness, is merely a relative: it signifies no effect or cause, nor any proper existence; but is the same with passiveness, or a being passive, or a being acted upon by something. Which is a mere relation of a thing to some power or force exerted by some cause, producing some effect in it or upon it. And action, when set properly in opposition to passion, or passiveness, is no real existence; it is not the same with *an action*, but is a mere relation: it is the activeness of something on another thing, being the opposite relation to the other, viz. a relation of power, or force, exerted by some cause towards another thing, which is the subject of the effect of that power. Indeed, the word *action* is frequently used to signify something not merely relative, but more absolute, and a real existence; as when we say *an action;* when the word is not used transitively, but absolutely, for some motion or exercise of body or mind, without any relation to any object or effect: and as used thus, it is not properly the opposite of *passion*, which ordinarily signifies nothing absolute, but merely the relation of being acted upon. And therefore, if the word *action* be used in the like relative sense, then action and passion are only two contrary relations. And it is no absurdity to suppose, that contrary relations may belong to the same thing, at the same time, with respect to different things. So, to suppose that there are acts of the soul by which a man voluntarily moves, and acts upon objects, and produces effects which yet themselves are effects of something else, and wherein the soul itself is the object of something acting upon, and influencing that, does not at all confound action and passion. The words may nevertheless be properly of opposite signification: there may be as true and real a difference between acting and being caused to act, though we should suppose the soul to be both in the same volition, as there is between living and being quickened, or made to live. It is no more a contradiction, to suppose that action may be the effect of some other cause besides the agent or being that acts, than to suppose, that life may be the effect of some other cause, besides the liver, or the being that lives, in whom life is caused to be.

The thing which has led men into this inconsistent notion of action, when applied to volition, as though it were essential to this internal action, that the agent should be self-determined in it, and that the will should be the cause of it, was probably this,—that, according to the sense of mankind, and the common use of language, it is so, with respect to men's external actions, which are what originally, and according to the vulgar use and most proper sense of the word, are called actions. Men in these are self-directed, self-determined, and their wills are the cause of the motions of their bodies, and the external things that are done; so that unless men do them voluntarily, and of choice, and the action be determined by their antecedent volition, it is no action or doing of theirs. Hence some metaphysicians have been led unwarily, but exceeding absurdly, to suppose the same concerning volition itself, that *that* also must be determined by the will; which is to be determined by antecedent volition, as the motion of the body is; not considering the contradiction it implies.

But it is very evident, that in the metaphysical distinction between action and passion, (though long since become common and the general vogue,) due care has not been taken to conform language to the nature of things, or to any distinct, clear ideas;—as it is in innumerable other philosophical, metaphysical terms, used in these disputes; which has occasioned inexpressible difficulty, contention, error, and confusion.

And thus probably it came to be thought that necessity was inconsistent with action, as these terms are applied to volition. First, these terms, *action* and *necessity*, are changed from their original meaning, as signifying external voluntary action and constraint, (in which meaning they are evidently inconsistent,) to signify quite other things, viz. volition itself, and certainty of existence. And when the change of signification is made, care is not taken to make proper allowances and abatements for the difference of sense; but still the same things are unwarily attributed to action and necessity, in the new meaning of the words, which plainly belonged to them in their first sense; and on this ground, maxims are established without any real foundation, as though they were the most certain truths, and the most evident dictates of reason.

But, however strenuously it is maintained, that what is necessary cannot be properly called action, and that a necessary action is a contradiction, yet it is probable there are few Arminian divines, who, if thoroughly tried, would stand to these principles. They will allow, that God is, in the highest sense, an active being, and the highest fountain of life and action; and they would not probably deny, that those that are called God's acts of righteousness, holiness, and faithfulness, are truly and properly God's acts, and God is really a holy agent in them; and yet, I trust, they will not deny, that God necessarily acts justly and faithfully, and that it is impossible for him to act unrighteously and unholily.

SECTION III.

THE REASONS WHY SOME THINK IT CONTRARY TO COMMON SENSE, TO SUPPOSE THOSE THINGS WHICH ARE NECESSARY, TO BE WORTHY OF EITHER PRAISE OR BLAME.

It is abundantly affirmed and urged by Arminian writers, that it is contrary to common sense, and the natural notions and apprehensions of mankind, to suppose otherwise than that necessity (making no distinction between natural and moral necessity) is inconsistent with virtue and vice, praise and blame, reward and punishment. And their arguments from hence have been greatly triumphed in; and have been not a little perplexing to many, who have been friendly to the truth, as clearly revealed in the holy Scriptures: it has seemed to them indeed difficult, to reconcile Calvinistic doctrines with the notions men commonly have of justice and equity. And the true reasons of it seem to be these that follow.

I. It is indeed a very plain dictate of common sense, that natural necessity is wholly inconsistent with just praise or blame. If men do things which in themselves are very good, fit to be brought to pass, and very happy effects, properly against their wills, and cannot help it; or do them from a necessity that is without their wills, or with which their wills have no concern or connexion; then it is a plain dictate of common sense, that it is none of their virtue, nor any moral good in them; and that they are not worthy to be rewarded or praised, or at all esteemed, honoured, or loved on that account. And, on the other hand, that if, from like necessity, they do those things which in themselves are very unhappy and pernicious, and do them because they cannot help it; the necessity is such, that it is all one whether they will them or no; and the reason why they are done, is from necessity only, and not from their wills: it is a very plain dictate of common sense, that they are not at all to blame; there is no vice, fault, or moral evil ฿t all in the effect done; nor are they who are thus necessitated, in any wise worthy to be punished, hated, or in the least disrespected, on that account.

In like manner, if things, in themselves good anddesirable, are absolutely impossible, with a natural impossibility, the universal reason of mankind teaches, that this wholly and perfectly excuses persons in their not doing them.

And it is also a plain dictate of common sense, that if the doing things in themselves good, or avoiding things in themselves evil, is not absolutely impossible, with such a natural impossibility, but very difficult, with a natural difficulty, that is, a difficulty prior to, and not at all consisting in, will and inclination itself, and which would remain the same, let the inclination be what it will; then a person's neglect or omission is excused in some measure, though not wholly; his sin is less aggravated than if the thing to be done were easy. And if instead of difficulty and hinderance, there be a contrary natural propensity in the state of things to the thing to be done, or effect to be brought to pass, abstracted from any consideration of the inclination of the heart; though the propensity be not so great as to amount to a natural necessity, yet being some approach to it, so that the doing the good thing be very much from this natural tendency in the state of things, and but little from a good inclination; then it is a dictate of common sense, that there is so much the less virtue in what is done; and so it is less praiseworthy and rewardable. The reason is easy, viz. because such a natural propensity or tendency is an approach to natural necessity; and the greater the propensity, still so much the nearer is the approach to necessity. And, therefore, as natural necessity takes away or shuts out all virtue, so this propensity approaches to an abolition of virtue; that is, it diminishes it. And, on the other hand, natural difficulty, in the state of things, is an approach to natural impossibility. And as the latter, when it is complete and absolute, wholly takes away blame, so such difficulty takes away some blame, or diminishes blame; and makes the thing done to be less worthy of punishment.

II. Men, in their first use of such phrases as these, *must, cannot, cannot help it, cannot avoid it, necessary, unable, impossible, unavoidable, irresistible,* &c., use them to signify a necessity of constraint or restraint, a natural necessity or impossibility; or some necessity that the will has nothing to do in; which may be, whether men will or no; and which may be supposed to be just the same, let men's inclinations and desires be what they will. Such kind of terms, in their original use, I suppose, among all nations, are relative; carrying in their signification (as was before observed) a reference or respect to some contrary will, desire, or endeavour, which, it is supposed, is, or may be, in the case. All men find, and begin to find in early childhood, that there are innumerable things that cannot be done, which they desire to do; and innumerable things, which they are averse to, that must be,—they cannot avoid them, they will be, whether they choose them or no. It is to express this necessity, which men so soon and so often find, and which so greatly and early affects them in innumerable cases, that such terms and phrases are first formed; and it is to signify such a necessity, that they are first used, and that they are most constantly used, in the common affairs of life; and not to signify any such metaphysical, speculative, and abstract notion, as that connexion in the nature or course of things, which is between the subject and predicate of a proposition, and which is the foundation of the certain truth of that proposition; to signify which, they who employ themselves in philosophical inquiries into the first origin and metaphysical relations and dependencies of things, have borrowed these terms, for want of others. But we grow up from our cradles in a use of such terms and phrases entirely different from this, and carrying a sense exceeding diverse from that in which they are commonly used in the controversy between Arminians and Calvinists. And it being, as was said before, a dictate of the universal sense of mankind, evident to us as soon as we begin to think, that the necessity signified by these terms, in the sense in which we first learn .them, does excuse persons and free them from all fault or blame; hence our idea of excusableness or faultlessness is tied to these terms and phrases by a strong habit, which is begun in childhood, as soon as we begin to speak, and grows up with us, and is strengthened by constant use and custom, the connexion growing stronger and stronger.

The habitual connexion which is in men's minds between blamelessness and those forementioned terms, *must, cannot, unable, necessary, impossible, unavoidable,* &c. becomes very strong; because as soon as ever men begin to use reason and speech, they have occasion to excuse themselves, from the natural necessity signified by these terms, in numerous instances—*I cannot do it; I could not help it.* And all mankind have constant and daily occasion to use such phrases in this sense, to excuse themselves and others, in almost all the concerns of life, with respect to disappointments and things that happen, which concern and affect ourselves and others, that are hurtful, or disagreeable to us or them, or things desirable, that we or others fail of.

That a being accustomed to an union of different

ideas, from early childhood, makes the habitual connexion exceeding strong, as though such connexion were owing to nature, is manifest in innumerable instances. It is altogether by such an habitual connexion of ideas, that men judge of the bigness or distance of the objects of sight, from their appearance. Thus, it is owing to such a connexion early established, and growing up with a person, that he judges a mountain, which he sees at ten miles distance, to be bigger than his nose, or further off than the end of it. Having been used so long to join a considerable distance and magnitude with such an appearance, men imagine it is by a dictate of natural sense: whereas, it would be quite otherwise with one that had his eyes newly opened, who had been born blind: he would have the same visible appearance, but natural sense would dictate no such thing, concerning the magnitude or distance of what appeared.

III. When men, after they had been so habituated to connect ideas of innocency or blamelessness with such terms, that the union seems to be the effect of mere nature, come to hear the same terms used, and learn to use them themselves, in the fore-mentioned new and metaphysical sense, to signify quite another sort of necessity, which has no such kind of relation to a contrary supposable will and endeavour; the notion of plain and manifest blamelessness, by this means, is, by a strong prejudice, insensibly and unwarily transferred to a case to which it by no means belongs: the change of the use of the terms, to a signification which is very diverse, not being taken notice of, or adverted to. And there are several reasons why it is not.

1. The terms, as used by philosophers, are not very distinct and clear in their meaning: few use them in a fixed, determined sense. On the contrary, their meaning is very vague and confused,—which is what commonly happens to the words used to signify things intellectual and moral, and to express what Mr Locke calls *mixed modes*. If men had a clear and distinct understanding of what is intended by these metaphysical

terms, they would be able more easily to compare them with their original and common sense; and so would not be so easily led into delusion by any sort of terms in the world, as by words of this sort.

2. The change of the signification of the terms, is the more insensible, because the things signified, though indeed very different, yet do in some generals agree. In necessity, that which is vulgarly so called, there is a strong connexion between the thing said to be necessary, and some thing antecedent to it in the order of nature; so there is also in philosophical necessity. And though in both kinds of necessity the connexion cannot be called by that name, with relation to an opposite will or endeavour, to which it is superior; which is the case in vulgar necessity; yet, in both the connexion is prior to will and endeavour, and so, in some respect, superior. In both kinds of necessity, there is a foundation for some certainty of the proposition that affirms the event.—The terms used being the same, and the things signified agreeing in these and some other general circumstances; and the expressions, as used by philosophers, being not well defined, and so of obscure and loose signification; hence persons are not aware of the great difference: and the notions of innocence or faultiness, which were so strongly associated with them, and were strictly united in their minds, ever since they can remember, remain united with them still, as if the union were altogether natural and necessary; and they that go about to make a separation, seem to them to do great violence, even to nature itself.

IV. Another reason why it appears difficult to reconcile it with reason, that men should be blamed for that which is necessary with a moral necessity, (which, as was observed before, is a species of philosophical necessity,) is, that for want of due consideration, men inwardly entertain that apprehension, that this necessity may be against men's wills and sincere endeavours. They go away with that notion, that men may truly will, and wish, and strive, that it may be otherwise, but that invincible necessity stands in the way.   And many think thus concerning themselves: some, that are wicked men, think they wish that they were good, that they love God and holiness; but yet do not find that their wishes produce the effect.—The reasons why men think so, are as follow: (1.) They find what may be called an *indirect willingness* to have a better will, in the manner before observed.   For it is impossible, and a contradiction, to suppose the will to be directly and properly against itself.   And they do not consider, that this indirect willingness is entirely a different thing from properly willing the thing that is the duty and virtue required; and that there is no virtue in that sort of willingness which they have.   They do not consider, that the volitions which a wicked man may have that he loved God, are no acts of the will at all against the moral evil of not loving God; but only some disagreeable consequences.   But the making the requisite distinction requires more care of reflection and thought than most men are used to.   And men, through a prejudice in their own favour, are disposed to think well of their own desires and dispositions, and to account them good and virtuous, though their respect to virtue be only indirect and remote, and it is nothing at all that is virtuous that truly excites or terminates their inclinations. (2.) Another thing that insensibly leads and beguiles men into a supposition that this moral necessity or impossibility is, or may be, against men's wills and true endeavours, is the derivation and formation of the terms themselves, that are often used to express it, which is such as seems directly to point to, and holds this forth. Such words, for instance, as *unable, unavoidable, impossible, irresistible,* which carry a plain reference to a supposable power exerted, endeavours used, resistance made, in opposition to the necessity; and the persons that hear them, not considering nor suspecting but that they are used in their proper sense; that sense being therefore understood, there does naturally, and as it were necessarily, arise in their minds a supposition, that it may be so indeed, that true desires and endeavours may take place, but that invincible necessity stands in the way, and renders them vain and to no effect.

V. Another thing, which makes persons more ready to suppose it to be contrary to reason, that men should be exposed to the punishments threatened to sin, for doing those things which are morally necessary, or not doing those things morally impossible, is, that imagination strengthens the argument, and adds greatly to the power and influence of the seeming reasons against it, from the greatness of that punishment. To allow that they may be justly exposed to a small punishment, would not be so difficult. Whereas, if there were any good reason in the case, if it were truly a dictate of reason, that such necessity was inconsistent with faultiness, or just punishment, the demonstration would be equally certain with respect to a small punishment, or any punishment at all, as a very great one; but it is not equally easy to the imagination. They that argue against the justice of damning men for those things that are thus necessary, seem to make their argument the stronger, by setting forth the greatness of the punishment in strong expressions:—"That a man should be cast into eternal burnings, that he should be made to fry in hell to all eternity, for those things which he had no power to avoid, and was under a fatal, unfrustrable, invincible necessity of doing."

SECTION IV.

IT IS AGREEABLE TO COMMON SENSE, AND THE NATURAL NOTIONS OF MANKIND, TO SUPPOSE MORAL NECESSITY TO BE CONSISTENT WITH PRAISE AND BLAME, REWARD AND PUNISHMENT.

WHETHER the reasons that have been given, why it appears difficult to some persons to reconcile with common sense the praising or blaming, rewarding or punishing those things which are morally necessary, are thought satisfactory, or not; yet it most evidently appears, by the following things, that if this matter be rightly understood, setting aside all delusion arising from the impropriety and ambiguity of terms, this is not at all inconsistent with the natural apprehensions of mankind, and that sense of things which is found every where in the common people, who are furthest from having their thoughts perverted from their natural channel, by metaphysical and philosophical subtleties; but, on the contrary, altogether agreeable to, and the very voice and dictate of, this natural and vulgar sense.

1. This will appear, if we consider what the vulgar notion of blameworthiness is. The idea which the common people, through all ages and nations, have of faultiness, I suppose to be plainly this; a person's being or doing wrong, with his own will and pleasure; containing these two things: 1. His doing wrong when he does as he pleases: 2. His pleasures being wrong. Or, in other words, perhaps more intelligibly expressing their notion, a person's having his heart wrong; and doing wrong from his heart. And this is the sum total of the matter.

The common people do not ascend up in their reflections and abstractions to the metaphysical sources, relations, and dependencies of things, in order to form their notion of faultiness or blameworthiness. They do not wait till they have decided by their refinings, what first determines the will; whether it be determined by something extrinsic or intrinsic; whether volition determines volition, or whether the understanding determines the will; whether there be any such thing as metaphysicians mean by contingence (if they have any meaning); whether there be a sort of a strange, unaccountable sovereignty in the will, in the exercise of which, by its own sovereign acts, it brings to pass all its own sovereign acts. They do not take any part of their notion of fault or blame from the resolution of any such question. If this were the case, there are multitudes, yea, the far greater part of mankind, nine hundred and ninety-nine out of a thousand, would live and die without having any such notion as that of fault ever entering into their heads, or without so much as one having any conception that any body was to be either blamed or commended for any thing. To be sure it would be a long time before men came to have such notions. Whereas it is manifest, they are some of the first notions that appear in children; who discover, as soon as they can think, or speak, or act at all as rational creatures, a sense of desert. And certainly, in forming their notion of it, they make no use of metaphysics. All the ground they go upon consists in these two things, experience, and a natural sensation of a certain fitness or agreeableness which there is in uniting such moral evil as is above described, viz. a being or doing wrong with the will, and resentment in others, and pain inflicted on the person in whom this moral evil is. Which natural sense is what we call by the name of conscience.

It is true, the common people and children, in their notion of any faulty act or deed, of any person, do suppose that it is the person's own act and deed. But this is all that belongs to what they understand by a thing's being a person's own deed or action; even that it is something done by him of choice. That some exercise or motion should begin of itself, does not belong to their notion of an action or doing. If so, it would belong to their notion of it, that it is something which is the cause of its own beginning; and that is as much as to say, that it is before it begins to be. Nor is their notion of an action, some motion or exercise that begins accidentally, without any cause or reason; for that is contrary to one of the prime dictates of common sense, namely, that every thing that begins to be, has some cause or reason why it is.

The common people, in their notion of a faulty or praiseworthy deed or work done by any one, do suppose that the man does it in the exercise of liberty. But then their notion of liberty is only a person's having opportunity of doing as he pleases. They have no notion of liberty consisting in the will's first acting, and so causing its own acts; and determining, and so causing its own determinations; or choosing, and so causing its own choice. Such a notion of liberty is what none have, but those that have darkened their own minds with confused metaphysical speculation, and abstruse and ambiguous terms. If a man is not restrained from acting as his will determines, or constrained to act otherwise, then he has liberty, according to common notions of liberty, without taking into the idea that grand contradiction of all, the determinations of a man's free will being the effects of the determinations of his free will.—Nor have men commonly any notion of freedom consisting in indifference. For if so, then it would be agreeable to their notion, that the greater indifference men act with, the more freedom they act with; whereas the reverse is true. He that, in acting, proceeds with the fullest inclination, does what he does with the greatest freedom, according to common sense. And so far is it from being agreeable to common sense, that such liberty as consists in indifference is requisite to praise or blame, that, on the contrary, the dictate of every man's natural sense through the world is, that the further he is from being indifferent in his acting good or evil, and the more he does either with full and strong inclination, the more is he esteemed or abhorred, commended or condemned.

II. If it were inconsistent with the common sense of mankind, that men should be either to be blamed or commended in any volitions they have or fail of, in case of moral necessity or impossibility; then it would surely also be agreeable to the same sense and reason of mankind, that the nearer the case approaches to such a moral necessity or impossibility, either through a strong antecedent moral propensity, on the one hand,* or a great antecedent opposition and difficulty on the other, the nearer does it approach to a being neither blame-able nor commendable; so that acts exerted with such preceding propensity, would be worthy of proportion-ably less praise; and when omitted, the act being at-

---

* It is here argued, on the supposition that not all propensity implies moral necessity, but only some very high degree; which none will deny.

tended with such difficulty, the omission would be worthy of less blame. It is so, as was observed before, with natural necessity and impossibility, propensity and difficulty: as it is a plain dictate of the sense of all mankind, that natural necessity and impossibility take away all blame and praise; and therefore, that the nearer the approach is to these, through previous propensity or difficulty, so praise and blame are proportionably diminished. And if it were as much a dictate of common sense, that moral necessity of doing or impossibility of avoiding takes away all praise and blame, as that natural necessity or impossibility does this; then, by a perfect parity of reason, it would be as much the dictate of common sense, that an approach to moral necessity of doing, or impossibility of avoiding, diminishes praise and blame, as that an approach to natural necessity and impossibility does so. It is equally the voice of common sense, that persons are excusable in part in neglecting things difficult against their wills, as that they are excusable wholly in neglecting things impossible against their wills. And if it made no difference, whether the impossibility were natural and against the will, or moral lying in the will, with regard to excusableness; so neither would it make any difference, whether the difficulty, or approach to necessity, be natural against the will, or moral, lying in the propensity of the will.

But it is apparent, that the reverse of these things is true. If there be an approach to a moral necessity in a man's exertion of good acts of will, they being the exercise of a strong propensity to good, and a very powerful love to virtue; it is so far from being the dictate of common sense, that he is less virtuous, and the less to be esteemed, loved, and praised; that it is agreeable to the natural notions of all mankind, that he is so much the better man, worthy of greater respect, and higher commendation. And the stronger the inclination is, and the nearer it approaches to necessity in that respect; or to impossibility of neglecting the virtuous act, or of doing a vicious one; still the more virtuous, and worthy

of higher commendation.   And, on the other hand, if a
man exerts evil acts of mind ; as for instance, acts of
pride or malice, from a rooted and strong habit or principle of haughtiness and maliciousness, and a violent
propensity of heart to such acts; according to the natural sense of men, he is so far from being the less hateful
and blameable on that account, that he is so much the
more worthy to be detested and condemned by all that
observe him.

Moreover, it is manifest that it is no part of the notion, which mankind commonly have of a blameable or
praiseworthy act of the will, that it is an act which is
not determined by an antecedent bias or motive, but by
the sovereign power of the will itself; because, if so, the
greater hand such causes have in determining any acts
of the will, so much the less virtuous or vicious would
they be accounted ; and the less hand, the more virtuous
or vicious.   Whereas the reverse is true: men do not
think a good act to be the less praiseworthy for the
agent's being much determined in it by a good inclination or a good motive, but the more.   And if good inclination or motive has but little influence in determining the agent, they do not think his act so much the
more virtuous, but the less.   And so concerning evil acts,
which are determined by evil motives or inclinations.

Yea, if it be supposed, that good or evil dispositions
are implanted in the hearts of men by nature itself,
(which, it is certain, is vulgarly supposed in innumerable cases,) yet it is not commonly supposed, that men
are worthy of no praise or dispraise for such dispositions; although what is natural is undoubtedly necessary, nature being prior to all acts of the will whatsoever.   Thus, for instance, if a man appears to be of a
very haughty or malicious disposition, and is supposed
to be so by his natural temper, it is no vulgar notion,
no dictate of the common sense and apprehension of
men, that such dispositions are no vices or moral evils,
or that such persons are not worthy of disesteem, or
odium and dishonour; or that the proud or malicious

acts which flow from such natural dispositions, are worthy of no resentment. Yea, such vile natural dispositions, and the strength of them, will commonly be mentioned rather as an aggravation of the wicked acts that come from such a fountain, than an extenuation of them. Its being natural for men to act thus, is often observed by men in the height of their indignation: they will say, " It is his very nature; he is of a vile natural temper; it is as natural to him to act so, as it is to breathe; he cannot help serving the devil," &c. But it is not thus with regard to hurtful, mischievous things, that any are the subjects or occasions of, by natural necessity, against their inclinations. In such a case, the necessity, by the common voice of mankind, will be spoken of as a full excuse.—Thus, it is very plain, that common sense makes a vast difference between these two kinds of necessity, as to the judgment it makes of their influence on the moral quality and desert of men's actions.

And these dictates of men's minds are so natural and necessary, that it may be very much doubted whether the Arminians themselves have ever got rid of them; yea, their greatest doctors, that have gone furthest in defence of their metaphysical notions of liberty, and have brought their arguments to their greatest strength, and, as they suppose, to a demonstration, against the consistence of virtue and vice with any necessity; it is to be questioned, whether there is so much as one of them, but that, if he suffered very much from the injurious acts of a man under the power of an invincible haughtiness and malignancy of temper, would not, from the fore-mentioned natural sense of mind, resent it far otherwise, than if as great sufferings came upon him from the wind that blows, and fire that burns, by natural necessity; and otherwise than he would, if he suffered as much from the conduct of a man perfectly delirious; yea, though he first brought his distraction upon him some way by his own fault.

Some seem to disdain the distinction that we make

between natural and moral necessity, as though it were altogether impertinent in this controversy : "that which is necessary (say they) is necessary; it is that which must be, and cannot be prevented. And that which is impossible, is impossible, and cannot be done : and therefore none can be to blame for not doing it." And such comparisons are made use of, as the commanding of a man to walk who has lost his legs, and condemning and punishing him for not obeying; inviting and calling upon a man who is shut up in a strong prison, to come forth, &c. But, in these things, Arminians are very unreasonable. Let common sense determine whether there be not a great difference between these two cases ; the one, that of a man who has offended his prince, and is cast into prison; and after he has lain there a while, the king comes to him, calls him to come forth to him; and tells him, that if he will do so, and will fall down before him, and humbly beg his pardon, he shall be forgiven and set at liberty, and also be greatly enriched, and advanced to honour; the prisoner heartily repents of the folly and wickedness of his offence against his prince, is thoroughly disposed to abase himself, and accept of the king's offer; but is confined by strong walls, with gates of brass, and bars of iron. The other case is, that of a man who is of a very unreasonable spirit, of a haughty, ungrateful, wilful disposition; and, moreover, has been brought up in traitorous principles, and has his heart possessed with an extreme and inveterate enmity to his lawful sovereign; and for his rebellion is cast into prison, and lies long there, loaden with heavy chains, and in miserable circumstances. At length the compassionate prince comes to the prison, orders his chains to be knocked off, and his prison-doors to be set wide open; calls to him, and tells him, if he will come forth to him, and fall down before him, acknowledge that he has treated him unworthily, and ask his forgiveness; he shall be forgiven, set at liberty, and set in a place of great dignity and profit in his court. But he is stout and stomachful, and full of haughty malignity, that he cannot be willing to accept the offer: his rooted strong pride and malice have perfect power over him, and as it were bind him, by binding his heart: the opposition of his heart has the mastery over him, having an influence on his mind far superior to the king's grace and condescension, and to all his kind offers and promises. Now, is it agreeable to common sense to assert, and stand to it, that there is no difference between these two cases, as to any worthiness of blame in the prisoners; because, forsooth, there is a necessity in both, and the required act in each case is impossible? It is true, a man's evil dispositions may be as strong and immoveable as the bars of a castle. But who cannot see, that when a man, in the latter case, is said to be unable to obey the command, the expression is used improperly, and not in the sense it has originally, and in common speech; and that it may properly be said to be in the rebel's power to come out of prison, seeing he can easily do it if he pleases; though by reason of his vile temper of heart, which is fixed and rooted, it is impossible that it should please him?

Upon the whole, I presume there is no person of good understanding, who impartially considers the things which have been observed, but will allow, that it is not evident, from the dictates of the common sense, or natural notions of mankind, that moral necessity is inconsistent with praise and blame. And, therefore, if the Arminians would prove any such inconsistency, it must be by some philosophical and metaphysical arguments, and not common sense.

There is a grand illusion in the pretended demonstration of Arminians from common sense. The main strength of all these demonstrations lies in that prejudice, that arises through the insensible change of the use and meaning of such terms as *liberty, able, unable, necessary, impossible, unavoidable, invincible, action,* &c. from their original and vulgar sense, to a metaphysical sense, entirely diverse; and the strong connexion of the ideas of blamelessness, &c. with some of these terms, by a habit contracted and established while these terms were used in their first meaning. This prejudice and delusion is the foundation of all those positions they lay down as maxims, by which most of the Scriptures, which they allege in this controversy, are interpreted, and on which all their pompous demonstrations from Scripture and reason depend. From this secret delusion and prejudice they have almost all their advantages; it is the strength of their bulwarks, and the edge of their weapons. And this is the main ground of all the right they have to treat their neighbours in so assuming a manner, and to insult others, perhaps as wise and good as themselves, as weak bigots, men that dwell in the dark caves of superstition, perversely set, obstinately shutting their eyes against the noon-day light, enemies to common sense, maintaining the first-born of absurdities, &c. &c. But perhaps an impartial consideration of the things which have been observed in the preceding parts of this Inquiry, may enable the lovers of truth better to judge, whose doctrine is indeed absurd, abstruse, self-contradictory, and inconsistent with common sense, and many ways repugnant to the universal dictates of the reason of mankind.

Corol. From things which have been observed, it will follow, that it is agreeable to common sense to suppose that the glorified saints have not their freedom at all diminished in any respect: and that God himself has the highest possible freedom according to the true and proper meaning of the term; and that he is, in the highest possible respect, an agent and active in the exercise of his infinite holiness; though he acts therein, in the highest degree necessarily: and his actions of this kind, are in the highest, most absolutely perfect manner, virtuous and praiseworthy; and are so, for that very reason, because they are most perfectly necessary.

SECTION V.

CONCERNING THOSE OBJECTIONS, THAT THIS SCHEME OF NECESSITY REN-
DERS ALL MEANS AND ENDEAVOURS FOR THE AVOIDING OF SIN, OR THE
OBTAINING VIRTUE AND HOLINESS, VAIN AND TO NO PURPOSE; AND
THAT IT MAKES MEN NO MORE THAN MERE MACHINES IN AFFAIRS OF
MORALITY AND RELIGION.

ARMINIANS say, if it be so, that sin and virtue come to
pass by a necessity consisting in a sure connexion of
causes and effects, antecedents and consequents, it can
never be worth the while to use any means or endeavours to obtain the one, and avoid the other; seeing no
endeavours can alter the futurity of the event, which is
become necessary by a connexion already established.

But I desire that this matter may be fully considered;
and that it may be examined with a thorough strictness, whether it will follow, that endeavours and means,
in order to avoid or obtain any future thing, must be
more in vain, on the supposition of such a connexion of
antecedents and consequents than if the contrary be
supposed.

For endeavours to be in vain, is for them not to be
successful; that is to say, for them not eventually to be
the means of the thing aimed at, which cannot be but
in one of these two ways; either, *first*, That although the
means are used, yet the event aimed at does not follow;
or, *secondly*, If the event does follow, it is not because of
the means, or from any connexion or dependence of the
event on the means: the event would have come to pass
as well without the means as with them. If either of
these two things is the case, then the means are not properly successful, and are truly in vain. The successful-
ness or unsuccessfulness of means, in order to an effect,
or their being in vain or not in vain, consists in those
means being connected or not connected with the effect,
in such a manner as this, viz. that the effect is *with* the
means, and not *without* them; or, that the being of the
effect is, on the one hand, connected with means, and
the want of the effect, on the other hand, is connected

with the want of the means. If there be such a connexion as this between means and end, the means are
not in vain; the more there is of such a connexion, the
further they are from being in vain; and the less of such
a connexion, the more they are in vain.

Now, therefore, the question to be answered, (in order
to determine, whether it follows from this doctrine of
the necessary connexion between foregoing things and
consequent ones, that means used in order to any effect
are more in vain than they would be otherwise), is,
whether it follows from it that there is less of the fore-
mentioned connexion between means and effect; that is,
whether, on the supposition of there being a real and
true connexion between means and effect, than on the
supposition of there being no fixed connexion between
antecedent things and consequent ones; and the very
stating of this question is sufficient to answer it. It
must appear to every one that will open his eyes, that
this question cannot be affirmed without the grossest
absurdity and inconsistence. Means are foregoing things,
and effects are following things. And if there were no
connexion between foregoing things and following ones,
there could be no connexion between means and end;
and so all means would be wholly vain and fruitless.
For it is by virtue of some connexion only, that they
become successful. It is some connexion observed or
revealed, or otherwise known, between antecedent things
and following ones, that is what directs in the choice of
means. And if there were no such thing as an established connexion, there could be no choice as to means;
one thing would have no more tendency to an effect than
another; there would be no such thing as tendency in
the case. All those things which are successful means
of other things, do therein prove connected antecedents
of them ; and therefore, to assert that a fixed connexion
between antecedents and consequents makes means vain
and useless, or stands in the way to hinder the connexion between means and end, is just as ridiculous as
to say, that a connexion between antecedents and conse-

quents stands in the way to hinder a connexion between antecedents and consequents.

Nor can any supposed connexion of the succession or train of antecedents and consequents, from the very beginning of all things, the connexion being made already sure and necessary, either by established laws of nature, or by these together with a decree of sovereign immediate interpositions of Divine power, on such and such occasions, or any other way (if any other there be); I say, no such necessary connexion of a series of antecedents and consequents can in the least tend to hinder, but that the means we use may belong to the series; and so may be some of those antecedents which are connected with the consequents we aim at in the established course of things. Endeavours which we use, are things that exist; and therefore they belong to the general chain of events; all the parts of which chain are supposed to be connected; and so endeavours are supposed to be connected with some effects, or some consequent things or other. And certainly this does not hinder but that the events they are connected with, may be those which we aim at, and which we choose, because we judge them most likely to have a connexion with those events from the established order and course of things which we observe, or from something in Divine revelation.

Let us suppose a real and true connexion between a man's having his eyes open in the clear day-light, with good organs of sight, and seeing; so that seeing is connected with his opening his eyes, and not seeing with his not opening his eyes; and also the like connexion between such a man's attempting to open his eyes, and his actually doing it: the supposed established connexion between these antecedents and consequents, let the connexion be never so sure and necessary, certainly does not prove that it is in vain for a man in such circumstances to attempt to open his eyes, in order to seeing: his aiming at that event, and the use of the means, being the effect of his will, does not break the connexion, or hinder the success.

So that the objection we are upon does not lie against the doctrine of the necessity of events by a certainty of connexion and consequence; on the contrary, it is truly forcible against the Arminian doctrine of contingence and self-determination; which is inconsistent with such a connexion. If there be no connexion between those events wherein virtue and vice consist, and any thing antecedent; then there is no connexion between these events and any means or endeavours used in order to them; and if so, then those means must be in vain. The less there is of connexion between foregoing things and following ones, so much the less there is between means and end, endeavours and success; and in the same proportion are means and endeavours ineffectual and in vain.

It will follow from Arminian principles that there is no degree of connexion between virtue or vice, and any foregoing event or thing; or, in other words, that the determination of the existence of virtue or vice does not in the least depend on the influence of any thing that comes to pass antecedently, from which the determination of its existence is, as its cause, means, or ground; because so far as it is so, it is not from self-determination; and, therefore, so far there is nothing of the nature of virtue or vice. And so it follows, that virtue and vice are not at all, in any degree, dependent upon, or connected with, any foregoing event or existence, as its cause, ground, or means. And if so, then all foregoing means must be totally in vain.

Hence it follows, that there cannot, in any consistence with the Arminian scheme, be any reasonable ground of so much as a conjecture concerning the consequence of any means and endeavours, in order to escaping vice, or obtaining virtue, or any choice or preference of means, as having a greater probability of success by some than others; either from any natural connex-

ion or dependence of the end on the means, or through
any divine constitution, or revealed way of God's be-
stowing or bringing to pass these things, in consequence
of any means, endeavours, prayers, or deeds. Conjec-
tures in this latter case, depend on a supposition, that
God himself is the giver, or determining cause, of the
events sought; but if they depend on self-determination,
then God is not the determining or disposing author of
them; and if these things are not of his disposal, then
no conjecture can be made, from any revelation he has
given, concerning any way or method of his disposal of
them.

Yea, on these principles, it will not only follow, that
men cannot have any reasonable ground of judgment or
conjecture that their means and endeavours to obtain virtue, or avoid vice, will be successful, but they may be sure
they will not; they may be certain that they will be in
vain ; and that if ever the thing, which they seek, comes
to pass, it will not be at all owing to the means they use.
For means and endeavours can have no effect at all, in
order to obtain the end, but in one of those two ways;
either (1.) Through a natural tendency and influence to
prepare and dispose the mind more to virtuous acts,
either by causing the disposition of the heart to be more
in favour of such acts, or by bringing the mind more into the view of powerful motives and inducements; or,
(2.) By putting persons more in the way of God's bestowment of the benefit. But neither of these can be
the case. Not the latter; for, as has been just observed,
it does not consist with the Arminian notion of self-determination, which they suppose essential to virtue, that
God should be the bestower, or (which is the same
thing) the determining disposing author of virtue. Not
the former; for natural influence and tendency supposes
causality and connexion, and supposes necessity of event,
which is inconsistent with Arminian liberty. A tendency of means, by biassing the heart in favour of virtue,
or by bringing the will under the influence and power
of motives in its determinations, are both inconsistent

with Arminian liberty of will, consisting in indifference,
and sovereign self-determination, as has been largely demonstrated.

But for the more full removal of this prejudice against
the doctrine of necessity, which has been maintained, as
though it tended to encourage a total neglect of all endeavours as vain; the following things may be considered:—

The question is not, Whether men may not thus improve this doctrine,—we know that many true and
wholesome doctrines are abused; but, whether the doctrine gives any just occasion for such an improvement;
or whether, on the supposition of the truth of the doctrine, such a use of it would be unreasonable? If any
shall affirm, that it would not, but that the very nature
of the doctrine is such as gives just occasion for it, it
must be on this supposition; namely, that such an invariable necessity of all things already settled, must render
the interposition of all means, endeavours, conclusions,
or actions of ours, in order to the obtaining any future
end whatsoever, perfectly insignificant; because they
cannot in the least alter or vary the course and series of
things, in any event or circumstance; all being already
fixed unalterably by necessity; and that therefore it is
folly for men to use any means for any end; but their
wisdom to save themselves the trouble of endeavours,
and take their ease. No person can draw such an infe-
rence from this doctrine, and come to such a conclusion,
without contradicting himself, and going counter to the
very principles he pretends to act upon; for he comes to
a conclusion, and takes a course, in order to an end,
even his ease, or the saving himself from trouble: he
seeks something future, and uses means in order to a future thing, even in his drawing up that conclusion, that
he will seek nothing, and use no means in order to any
thing in future; he seeks his future ease, and the benefit
and comfort of indolence. If prior necessity, that determines all things, makes vain all actions or conclusions of

ours, in order to any thing future ; then it makes vain all conclusions and conduct of ours, in order to our future ease. The measure of our ease, with the time, manner, and every circumstance of it, is already fixed, by all-determining necessity, as much as any thing else. If he says within himself, " What future happiness or misery I shall have, is already, in effect, determined by the necessary course and connexion of things; therefore, I will save myself the trouble of labour and diligence which cannot add to my determined degree of happiness, or diminish my misery; but will take my ease, and will enjoy the comfort of sloth and negligence,"—such a man contradicts himself; he says, the measure of his future happiness and misery is already fixed, and he will not try to diminish the one, nor add to the other ; but yet, in his very conclusion, he contradicts this; for, he takes up this conclusion, to add to his future happiness, by the ease and comfort of his negligence, and to diminish his future trouble and misery by saving himself the trouble of using means and taking pains.

Therefore, persons cannot reasonably make this improvement of the doctrine of necessity, that they will go into a voluntary negligence of means for their own happiness. For the principles they must go upon, in order to this, are inconsistent with their making any improvement at all of the doctrine; for to make some improvement of it, is to be influenced by it, to come to some voluntary conclusion, in regard to their own conduct, with some view or aim ; but this, as has been shown, is inconsistent with the principles they pretend to act upon. In short, the principles are such as cannot be acted upon at all, or, in any respect, consistently. And therefore, in every pretence of acting upon them, or making any improvement at all of them, there is a self-contradiction.

As to that objection against the doctrine, which I have endeavoured to prove, that it makes men no more. than mere machines; I would say, that notwithstanding this doctrine, man is entirely, perfectly, and unspeakably different from a mere machine, in that he has reason and understanding, and has a faculty of will, and is so capable of volition and choice; and in that his will is guided by the dictates or views of his understanding; and in that his external actions and behaviour, and in many respects also his thoughts, and the exercises of his mind, are subject to his will; so that he has liberty to act according to his choice, and do what he pleases; and, by means of these things, is capable of moral habits and moral acts, such inclinations and actions, as, according to the common sense of mankind, are worthy of praise, esteem, love, and reward; or, on the contrary, of disesteem, detestation, indignation, and punishment.

In these things is all the difference from mere machines, as to liberty and agency, that would be any perfection, dignity, or privilege, in any respect; all the difference that can be desired, and all that can be conceived of; and indeed all that the pretensions of the Arminians themselves come to, as they are forced often to explain themselves. (Though their explications overthrow and abolish the things asserted, and pretended to be explained.) For they are forced to explain a self-determining power of will, by a power in the soul to determine as it chooses or wills; which comes to no more than this, that a man has a power of choosing, and in many instances, can do as he chooses,—which is quite a different thing from that contradiction, his having power of choosing his first act of choice in the case.

Or, if their scheme makes any other difference than this between men and machines, it is for the worse; it is so far from supposing men to have a dignity and privilege above machines, that it makes the manner of their being determined still more unhappy. Whereas machines are guided by an understanding cause, by the skilful hand of the workman or owner; the will of man is left to the guidance of nothing but absolute blind contingence.

SECTION VI.

CONCERNING THAT OBJECTION AGAINST THE DOCTRINE WHICH HAS BEEN
MAINTAINED, THAT IT AGREES WITH THE STOICAL DOCTRINE OF FATE,
AND THE OPINIONS OF MR HOBBES.

WHEN Calvinists oppose the Arminian notion of the
freedom of will, and contingence of volition, and insist
that there are no acts of the will, nor any other event
whatsoever, but what are attended with some kind of
necessity; their opposers cry out of them, as agreeing
with the ancient Stoics in their doctrine of fate, and with
Mr Hobbes in his opinion of necessity.

It would not be worth while to take notice of so impertinent an objection, had it not been urged by some of
the chief Arminian writers. There were many important truths maintained by the ancient Greek and Roman
philosophers, and especially the Stoics, that are never
the worse for being held by them. The Stoic philosophers, by the general agreement of Christian divines, and
even Arminian divines, were the greatest, wisest, and
most virtuous of all the heathen philosophers; and in
their doctrine and practice came the nearest to Christianity of any of their sects. How frequently are the say-
ings of these philosophers, in many of the writings and
sermons, even of Arminian divines, produced, not as arguments of the falseness of the doctrines which they delivered, but as a confirmation of some of the greatest
truths of the Christian religion, relating to the unity and
perfections of the Godhead, a future state, the duty and
happiness of mankind, &c., as observing how the light
of nature, and reason, in the wisest and best of the heathen, harmonized with and confirms the gospel of Jesus
Christ.

And it is very remarkable, concerning Dr Whitby,
that although he alleges the agreement of the Stoics
with us, wherein he supposes they maintained the like
doctrine with us, as an argument against the truth of
our doctrine; yet this very Dr Whitby alleges the

R

agreement of the Stoics with the Arminians, wherein he
supposes they taught the same doctrine with them, as an
argument for the truth of their doctrine.* So that, when
the Stoics agree with them, this (it seems) is a confirmation of their doctrine, and a confutation of ours, as showing that our opinions are contrary to the natural sense
and common reason of mankind: nevertheless, when the
Stoics agree with us, it argues no such thing in our favour; but, on the contrary, is a great argument against
us, and shows our doctrine to be heathenish.

It is observed by some Calvinistic writers, that the
Arminians symbolise with the Stoics in some of those
doctrines wherein they are opposed by the Calvinists;
particularly in their denying an original, innate, total
corruption and depravity of heart; and in what they
held of man's ability to make himself truly virtuous
and conformed to God; and in some other doctrines.

It may be further observed, it is certainly no better
objection against our doctrine, that it agrees, in some
respects, with the doctrine of the ancient Stoic philosophers, than it is against theirs, wherein they differ from
us, that it agrees, in some respects, with the opinion of
the very worst of the heathen philosophers, the followers of Epicurus, that father of atheism and licentiousness, and with the doctrine of the Sadducees and Jesuits.

I am not much concerned to know precisely what the
ancient Stoic philosophers held concerning fate, in order
to determine what is truth; as though it were a sure
way to be in the right, to take good heed to differ from
them. It seems that they differed among themselves;
and probably the doctrine of fate, as maintained by
most of them, was, in some respects, erroneous. But
whatever their doctrine was, if any of them held such a
fate as is repugnant to any liberty, consisting in our doing as we please, I utterly deny such a fate. If they
held any such fate as is not consistent with the common
and universal notions that mankind have of liberty, ac-

* Whitby on the " Five Points," p. 325—327, ed. 3.

tivity, moral agency, virtue and vice; I disclaim any such thing, and think I have demonstrated that the scheme I maintain is no such scheme. If the Stoics, by *fate*, meant any thing of such a nature as can be supposed to stand in the way of the advantage and benefit of the use of means and endeavours, or make it less worth the while for men to desire and seek after any thing wherein their virtue and happiness consists; I hold no doctrine that is clogged with any such inconvenience, any more than any other scheme whatsoever; and by no means so much as the Arminian" scheme of contingence; as has been shown. If they held any such doctrine of universal fatality as is inconsistent with any kind of liberty, that is or can be any perfection, dignity, privilege or benefit, or any thing desirable, in any respect, for any intelligent creature, or indeed with any liberty that is possible or conceivable; I embrace no such doctrine. If they held any such doctrine of fate as is inconsistent with the world's being in all things subject to the disposal of an intelligent wise Agent, that presides, not as the *soul* of the world, but as the sovereign *Lord* of the universe, governing all things by proper will, choice, and design, in the exercise of the most perfect liberty conceivable, without subjection to any constraint, or being properly under the power or influence of any thing before, above, or without himself; I wholly renounce any such doctrine.

As to Mr Hobbes's maintaining the same doctrine concerning necessity; I confess it happens I never read Mr Hobbes. Let his opinion be what it will, we need not reject all truth which is demonstrated by clear evidence, merely because it was once held by some bad man. This great truth, that Jesus is the Son of God, was not spoiled because it was once and again proclaimed with a loud voice by the devil. If truth is so defiled, because it is spoken by the mouth, or written by the pen, of some ill-minded mischievous man, that it must never be received, we shall never know when we hold any of the most precious and evident truths by a sure tenure,

And if Mr Hobbes has made a bad use of this truth, that is to be lamented; but the truth is not to be thought worthy of rejection on that account. It is common for the corruptions of the hearts of evil men to abuse the best things to vile purposes.

I might also take notice of its having been observed, that the Arminians agree with Mr Hobbes* in many more things than the Calvinists;—as, in what he is said to hold concerning original sin, in denying the necessity of supernatural illumination, in denying infused grace, in denying the doctrine of justification by faith alone; and other things.

SECTION VII.

CONCERNING THE NECESSITY OF THE DIVINE WILL.

Some may possibly object against what has been supposed of the absurdity and inconsistence of a self-determining power in the will, and the impossibility of its being otherwise than that the will should be determined in every case by some motive, and by a motive which (as it stands in the view of the understanding) is of superior strength to any appearing on the other side; that if these things are true, it will follow, that not only the will of created minds, but the will of God himself, is necessary in all its determinations. Concerning which, says the author of the Essay on the Freedom of Will in God and in the Creature, (pp. 85, 86) "What strange doctrine is this, contrary to all our ideas of the dominion of God? does it not destroy the glory of his liberty of choice, and take away from the Creator and Governor and Benefactor of the world, that most free and sovereign agent, all the glory of this sort of freedom? does it not seem to make him a kind of mechanical medium of fate, and introduce Mr Hobbes's doctrine of fatality and necessity into all things that God hath to do with? Does it not seem to represent the blessed God as a being of vast understanding, as well as power and efficiency, but still to leave him without a will to choose

* Dr Gill, in his answer to Dr Whitby. Vo l. iii. p. 33, &c.

among all the objects within his view? In short, it
seems to make the blessed God a sort of almighty minister of fate, under its universal and supreme influence;
as it was the professed sentiment of some of the ancients, that fate was above the gods."

This is declaiming, rather than arguing; and an application to men's imaginations and prejudices, rather than
to mere reason. But I would calmly endeavour to consider, whether there be any reason in this frightful re-
presentation.—But before I enter upon a particular consideration of the matter, I would observe this: that it is
reasonable to suppose, it should be much more difficult
to express or conceive things according to exact metaphysical truth, relating to the nature and manner of the
existence of things in the Divine understanding and will,
and the operation of these faculties (if I may so call
them) of the Divine mind, than in the human mind;
which is infinitely more within our view, and nearer to
a proportion to the measure of our comprehension, and
more commensurate to the use and import of human
speech. Language is indeed very deficient in regard of
terms to express precise truth concerning our own minds,
and their faculties and operations. Words were first
formed to express external things; and those that are
applied to express things internal and spiritual, are
almost all borrowed, and used in a sort of figurative
sense. Whence they are, most of them, attended with a
great deal of ambiguity and unfixedness in their signification, occasioning innumerable doubts, difficulties, and
confusions, in inquiries and controversies about things of
this nature. But language is much less adapted to express things in the mind of the incomprehensible Deity
precisely as they are.

We find a great deal of difficulty in conceiving exactly
of the nature of our own souls. And notwithstanding
all the progress which has been made, in past and present ages, in this kind of knowledge, whereby our metaphysics, as it relates to these things, is brought to greater perfection than once it was; yet, here is still work

enough left for future inquiries and researches, and room
for progress still to be made, for many ages and generations. But we had need to be infinitely able metaphysicians, to conceive with clearness, according to strict, proper, and perfect truth, concerning the nature of the Divine Essence, and the modes of the action and operation
of the powers of the Divine Mind.

And it may be noted particularly, that though we are
obliged to conceive of some things in God as consequent
and dependent on others, and of some things pertaining
to the Divine nature and will as the foundation of others,
and so before others in the order of nature; as, we must
conceive of the knowledge and holiness of God as prior,
in the order of nature, to his happiness; the perfection
of his understanding, as the foundation of his wise purposes and decrees; the holiness of his nature, as the cause
and reason of his holy determinations. And yet, when
we speak of cause and effect, antecedent and consequent,
fundamental and dependent, determining and determined,
in the first Being, who is self-existent, independent,
of perfect and absolute simplicity and immutability, and
the first cause of all things; doubtless there must be less
propriety in such representations, than when we speak
of derived dependent beings, who are compounded, and
liable to perpetual mutation and succession.

Having premised this, I proceed to observe concerning
the fore-mentioned author's exclamation about the necessary determination of God's will, in all things, by
what he sees to be fittest and best.

That all the seeming force of such objections and exclamations must arise from an imagination that there is
some sort of privilege or dignity in being without such
a moral necessity as will make it impossible to do any
other than always choose what is wisest and best; as
though there were some disadvantage, meanness, and
subjection, in such a necessity; a thing by which the
will was confined, kept under, and held in servitude by
something, which, as it were, maintained a strong and
invincible power and dominion over it, by bonds that

held him fast, and that he could, by no means, deliver himself from. Whereas, this must be all mere imagination and delusion. It is no disadvantage or dishonour to a being, necessarily to act in the most excellent and happy manner, from the necessary perfection of his own nature. This argues no imperfection, inferiority, or dependence, nor any want of dignity, privilege, or ascendancy.* It is not inconsistent with the absolute

* " It might have been objected, with more plausibleness, that the Supreme Cause cannot be free, because he must needs do always what is best in the whole. But this would not at all serve Spinoza's purpose; for this is a necessity, not of nature and of fate, but of fitness and wisdom; a necessity consistent with the greatest freedom and most perfect choice. For the only foundation of this necessity is such an unalterable rectitude of will, and perfection of wisdom, as makes it impossible for a wise being to act foolishly."—CLARKE's *Demonstration of the Being and Attributes of God.* Edit. 6. p. 64.

" Though God is a most perfect free agent, yet he cannot but do always what is best and wisest in the whole. The reason is evident; because perfect wisdom and goodness are as steady and certain principles of action as necessity itself; and an infinitely wise and good Being, endued with the most perfect liberty, can no more choose to act in contradiction to wisdom and goodness, than a necessary agent can act contrary to the necessity by which it is acted; it being as great an absurdity and impossibility in choice, for Infinite Wisdom to choose to act unwisely, or Infinite Goodness to choose what is not good, as it would be in nature, for absolute necessity to fail of producing its necessary effect. There was, indeed, no necessity in nature, that God should at first create such beings as he has created, or indeed any being at all; because he is, in himself, infinitely happy and all-sufficient. There was, also, no necessity in nature, that he should preserve and continue things in being, after they were created; because he would be self-sufficient without their continuance, as he was before their creation. But it was fit, and wise, and good, that Infinite Wisdom should manifest, and Infinite Goodness communicate itself; and therefore it was necessary, in the sense of necessity I am now speaking of, that things should be made, *at such a time,* and continued *so long,* and indeed with various perfections in such degrees, as Infinite Wisdom and Goodness saw it wisest and best that they should."—Ibid. pp. 112, 113.

" It is not a fault, but a perfection of our nature, to desire, will, and act, according to the last result of a fair examination. This is so far from being a restraint or diminution of freedom, that it is the very improvement and benefit of it: it is not an abridgment, it is the end and use of our liberty; and the further we are removed from such a determination, the nearer we are to misery and slavery. A perfect indifference in the mind, not determinable by its last judgment, of the good or evil that is thought to attend its choice, would be so far from being an advantage and excellency of any intellectual nature, that it would be as great an imperfection as the want of indifference to act, or not to act, till determined by the will, would be an imperfection on the other side. It is as much a perfection, that desire, or the power of preferring, should be determined by the good, as that the power of acting should be determined by the will: and the certainer such

and most perfect sovereignty of God. The sovereignty
of God is his ability and authority to do whatever
pleases him; whereby " he doth according to his will in

determination is, the greater the perfection. Nay, were we determined by
any thing but the last result of our own minds, judging of the good or evil
of any action, we were not free. This very end of our freedom being, that
we might attain the good we choose; and therefore every man is brought
under a necessity by his constitution, as an intelligent being, to be determined in willing, by his own thought and judgment, what is best for him to
do; else he would be under the determination of some other than himself,
which is want of liberty. And to deny that a man's will, in every determination, follows his own judgment, is to say, that a man wills and acts for
an end that he would not have, at the same time that he wills and acts for
it. For if he prefers it in his present thoughts before any other, it is plain
he then thinks better of it, and would have it before any other ; unless he
can have, and not have it, will, and not will it, at the same time,—a contradiction too manifest to be admitted. If we look upon those superior beings
above us who enjoy perfect happiness, we shall have reason to judge, that
they are more steadily determined in their choice of good than we; and yet
we have no reason to think they are less happy, or less free, than we are.
And if it were fit f or such poor finite creatures as we are, to pronounce
what Infinite Wisdom and Goodness could do, I think we might say, that
God himself cannot choose what is not good. The freedom of the Almighty hinders not his being determined by what is best. But, to give a right
view of this mistaken part of liberty, let me ask, Would any one be a chan-
geling, because he is less determined by wise determination than a wise
man? Is it worth the name of freedom, to be at liberty to play the fool,
and draw shame and misery upon a man's self? If to break loose from the
conduct of reason, and to want that restraint of examination and judgment
that keeps us from doing or choosing the worse, be liberty, true liberty,
madmen and fools are the only free men. Yet I think nobody would
choose to be mad, for the sake of such liberty, but he that is mad already."
—Locke *on the Hum. Und.* vol. i. edit. 7. pp. 215, 216.

" This Being, having all things always necessarily in view, must always, and
eternally will, according to his infinite comprehension of things ; that is, must
will all things that are wisest and best to be done. There is no getting free
of this consequence. If it can will at all, it must will this way. To be capable of knowing, and not capable of willing, is not to be understood. And
to be capable of willing otherwise than what is wisest and best, contradicts
that knowledge which is infinite. Infinite knowledge must direct the will
without error. Here, then, is the origin of moral necessity, and that is really
of freedom. Perhaps it may be said, when the Divine will is determined,
from the consideration of the eternal aptitudes of things, it is as necessarily
determined as if it were physically impelled, if that were possible. But it is
unskilfulness to suppose this an objection. The great principle is once established, viz. that the Divine will is determined by the eternal reason and
aptitudes of things, instead of being physically impelled; and after that, the
more strong and necessary this determination is, the more perfect the Deity
must be allowed to be ; it is this that makes him an amiable and adorable Being, whose will and power are constantly, immutably determined by the consideration of what is wisest and best ; instead of a surd Being, with power,
but without discerning and reason. It is the beauty of this necessity, that it
is strong as fate itself, with all the advantage of reason and goodness. It is

the armies of heaven, and amongst the inhabitants of the earth; and none can stay his hand, or say unto him, What dost thou?"—The following things belong to the *sovereignty* of God: viz. (1.) Supreme, universal, and infinite *power:* whereby he is able to do what he pleases, without control, without any confinement of that power, without any subjection, in the least measure, to any other power; and so without any hindrance or restraint, that it should be either impossible, or at all difficult, for him to accomplish his will; and without any dependance of his power on any other power, from whence it should be derived, or which it should stand in any need of; so far from this, that all other power is derived from him, and is absolutely dependent on him. (2.) That he has supreme *authority;* absolute and most perfect right to do what he wills, without subjection to any superior authority, or any derivation of authority from any other, or limitation by any distinct independent authority, either superior, equal, or inferior; he being the head of all dominion, and fountain of all authority; and also without restraint by any obligation, implying either subjection, derivation, or dependence, or proper limitation.   (3.) That his *will* is supreme, underived, and independent on any thing without himself; being in every thing determined* by his own counsel, having no other rule but his own wisdom; his will not being subject to, or restrained by, the will of any other, and other wills being perfectly subject to his. (4.) That his *wisdom,* which determines his will, is supreme, perfect, underived, self-sufficient, and independent; so that it may be said, as in Isaiah xl. 14, " With whom took he counsel, and who instructed him, and taught him in the path of judgment, and taught him knowledge, and showed to him the way of understanding?"—There is no other Divine sovereignty but this;

strange to see men contend, that the Deity is not free, because he is necessarily rational, immutably good and wise; when a man is allowed still the perfecter being, the more fixedly and constantly his will is determined by reason and truth."--*Inquiry into the Nature of the Human Soul.* Edit. 3, vol. ii. pp. 403, 404.

and this is properly absolute sovereignty: no other is desirable; nor would any other be honourable or happy and, indeed, there is no other conceivable or possible: It is the glory and greatness of the Divine Sovereign, that God's will is determined by his own infinite, all-sufficient wisdom in every thing; and in nothing at all is either directed by any inferior wisdom, or by no wisdom; whereby it would become senseless arbitrariness, determining and acting without reason, design, or end.

If God's will is steadily and surely determined in every thing by supreme wisdom, then it is in every thing necessarily determined to that which is most wise. And, certainly, it would be a disadvantage and indignity to be otherwise. For if the Divine will was not necessarily determined to that which, in every case, is wisest and best, it must be subject to some degree of undesigning contingence; and so in the same degree liable to evil. To suppose the Divine will liable to be carried hither and thither at random, by the uncertain wind of blind contingence, which is guided by no wisdom, no motive, no intelligent dictate whatsoever, (if any such thing were possible,) would certainly argue a great degree of imperfection and meanness, infinitely unworthy of the Deity. If it be a disadvantage for the Divine will to be attended with this moral necessity, then the more free from it, and the more left at random, the greater dignity and advantage. And, consequently, to be perfectly free from the direction of understanding, and universally and entirely left to senseless, uumeaning contingence, to act absolutely at random, would be the supreme glory.

It no more argues any dependence of God's will, that his supremely wise volition is necessary, than it argues a dependence of his being, that his existence is necessary. If it be something too low for the Supreme Being to have his will determined by moral necessity, so as necessarily, in every case, to will in the highest degree holily and happily; then why is it not also something too low for him to have his existence, and the infinite perfection of his nature, and his infinite happiness, determined by necessity ? It is no more to God's dishonour to be necessarily wise, than to be necessarily holy. And if neither of them be to his dishonour, then it is not to his dishonour necessarily to act holily and wisely. And if it be not dishonourable to be necessarily holy and wise, in the highest possible degree, no more is it mean and dishonourable, necessarily to act holily and wisely in the highest possible degree ; or, which is the same thing, to do that, in every case, which, above all other things, is wisest and best.

The reason why it is not dishonourable to be necessarily *most* holy, is, because holiness in itself is an excellent and honourable thing. For the same reason, it is no dishonour to be necessarily *most* wise, and, in every case, to act most wisely, or do the thing which is the wisest of all ; for wisdom is also in itself excellent and honourable.

The fore-mentioned author of the "Essay on the Freedom of Will," &c. as has been observed, represents that doctrine of the Divine will's being in every thing necessarily determined by a superior fitness, as making the blessed God a kind of almighty minister and mechanical medium of fate ; and he insists, (pp. 93, 94,) that this moral necessity and impossibility is, in effect, the same thing with physical and natural necessity and impossibility ; and in pp. 54, 55, he says, "The scheme which determines the will always and certainly by the understanding, and the understanding by the appearance of things, seems to take away the true nature of vice and virtue. For the sublimest of virtues, and the vilest of vices, seem rather to be matters of fate and necessity, flowing naturally and necessarily from the existence, the circumstances, and present situation of persons and things ; for this existence and situation necessarily makes such an appearance to the mind ; from this appearance flows a necessary perception and judgment concerning these things : this judgment necessarily determines the will ; and thus, by this chain of necessary causes, virtue

and vice would lose their nature, and become natural
ideas, and necessary things, instead of moral and free
actions."

And yet this same author allows, (pp. 30, 31,) that a
perfectly wise being will constantly and certainly choose
what is most fit; and says, pp. 102, 103, "I grant, and
always have granted, that wheresoever there is such
antecedent superior fitness of things, God acts according
to it, so as never to contradict it; and, particularly, in
all his judicial proceedings as a governor, and distributor
of rewards and punishments." Yea, he says expressly,
(p. 42,) "That it is not possible for God to act otherwise than according to this fitness and goodness in
things."

So that, according to this author, putting these several
passages of this essay together, there is no virtue, nor
any thing of a moral nature, in the most sublime and
glorious acts and exercises of God's holiness, justice, and
faithfulness; and he never does any thing which is in
itself supremely worthy, and, above all other things, fit
and excellent, but only as a kind of mechanical medium
of fate; and in what he does as the judge and moral
governor of the world, he exercises no moral excellency,
exercising no freedom in these things, because he acts
by moral necessity, which is, in effect, the same with
physical or natural necessity; and therefore he only acts
by an Hobbistical fatality; "as a being indeed of vast
understanding, as well as power and efficiency, (as he
said before,) but without a will to choose, being a kind
of almighty minister of fate, acting under its supreme
influence." For he allows, that in all these things, God's
will is determined constantly and certainly by a superior
fitness, and that it is not possible for him to act otherwise. And if these things are so, what glory or praise
belongs to God for doing holily and justly, or taking the
most fit, holy, wise, and excellent course, in any one
instance? Whereas, according to the Scriptures, and
also the common sense of mankind, it does not, in the
least, derogate from the honour of any being, that

through the moral perfection of his nature he necessarily acts with supreme wisdom and holiness; but on the contrary, his praise is the greater; herein consists the height of his glory.

The same author (p. 56,) supposes that herein appears the excellent " character of a wise and good man, that though he can choose contrary to the fitness of things, yet he does not; but suffers himself to be directed by fitness;" and that, in this conduct, " he imitates the blessed God." And yet he supposes it is contrariwise with the blessed God; not that he suffers himself to be directed by fitness, when he can choose, contrary to the fitness of things, but that he cannot choose contrary to the fitness of things; as he says, (p. 42,) " that it is not possible for God to act otherwise than according to this fitness, where there is any fitness or goodness in things." Yea, he supposes, (p. 31,) that if a man " were perfectly wise and good, he could not do otherwise than be constantly and certainly determined by the fitness of things."

One thing more I would observe, before I conclude this section; and that is, that if it derogates nothing from the glory of God to be necessarily determined by superior fitness in some things, then neither does it to be thus determined in all things; from any thing in the nature of such necessity, as at all detracting from God's freedom, independence, absolute supremacy, or any dignity or glory of his nature, state, or manner of acting; or as implying any infirmity, restraint, or subjection. And if the thing be such as well consists with God's glory, and has nothing tending at all to detract from it; then we need not be afraid of ascribing it to God in too many things, lest thereby we should detract from God's glory too much.

SECTION VIII.

THE author last cited, as has been observed, owns that God, being perfectly wise, will constantly and certainly choose what appears most fit, where there is a superior fitness and goodness in things; and that it is not possible for him to do otherwise. So that it is in effect confessed, that in those things where there is any real preferableness, it is no dishonour, nothing in any respect unworthy of God, for him to act from necessity: notwithstanding all that can be objected from the agreement of such a necessity with the fate of the Stoics, and the necessity maintained by Mr Hobbes. From which it will follow, that if it were so, that in all the different things among which God chooses, there were evermore a superior fitness or preferableness on one side, then it would be no dishonour, or any thing, in any respect, unworthy or unbecoming of God, for his will to be necessarily determined in every thing. And if this be allowed, it is a giving up entirely the argument, from the unsuitableness of such a necessity to the liberty, supremacy, independence, and glory of the Divine Being; and a resting the whole weight of the affair on the decision of another point wholly diverse, viz. *whether it be so indeed,* that in all the various possible things which are in God's view, and may be considered as capable objects of his choice, there is not evermore a preferableness in one thing above another. This is denied by this author, who supposes that, in many instances, between two or more possible things which come within the view of the Divine mind, there is a perfect indifference and equality, as to fitness or tendency, to attain any good end which God can have in view, or to answer any of his designs. Now, therefore, I would consider whether this be evident.

The arguments brought to prove this are of two

kinds.   (1.) It is urged, that, in many instances, we must suppose there is absolutely no difference between various possible objects of choice, which God has in view : and, (2.) That the difference between many things is so inconsiderable, or of such a nature, that it would be unreasonable to suppose it to be of any consequence, or to suppose that any of God's wise designs would not be answered in one way as well as the other.   Therefore,

I. The first thing to be considered is, whether there are any instances wherein there is a perfect likeness, and absolutely no difference between different objects of choice, that are proposed to the Divine understanding?

And here, in the *first* place, it may be worthy to be considered, whether the contradiction there is in the terms of the question proposed, does not give reason to suspect that there is an inconsistence in the thing supposed.   It is inquired, whether different objects of choice may not be absolutely without difference?   If they are absolutely without difference, then how are they different objects of choice?   If there be absolutely no difference, in any respect, then there is no variety or distinction; for distinction is only by some difference.   And if there be no variety among proposed objects of choice, then there is no opportunity for variety of choice, or difference of determination.   For that determination of a thing, which is not different in any respect, is not a different determination, but the same.   That this is no quibble, may appear more fully anon.

The arguments to prove that the Most High, in some instances, chooses to do one thing rather than another, where the things themselves are perfectly without difference, are two.

1. That the various parts of infinite time and space, absolutely considered, are perfectly alike, and do not differ at all one from another; and that therefore, when God determined to create the world in such a part of infinite duration and space, rather than others, he determined and preferred, among various objects, between

which there was no preferableness, and absolutely no difference.

Answ. This objection supposes an infinite length of time before the world was created, distinguished by successive parts, properly and truly so; or a succession of limited and unmeasurable periods of time, following one another, in an infinitely long series: which must needs be a groundless imagination. The eternal duration which was before the world, being only the eternity of God's existence; which is nothing else but his immediate, perfect, and invariable possession of the whole of his unlimited life, together and at once; *vitæ interminabilis, tota, simul et perfecta possessio.* Which is so generally allowed, that I need not stand to demonstrate it.*

So, this objection supposes an extent of space beyond the limits of the creation, of an infinite length, breadth,

---

* " If all created beings were taken away, all possibility of any mutation or succession of one thing to another, would appear to be also removed. Abstract succession in eternity is scarce to be understood. What is it that succeeds? One minute to another, perhaps, *velut unda supervenit undam.* But when we imagine this, we fancy that the minutes are things separately existing. This is the common notion; and yet it is a manifest prejudice. Time is nothing but the existence of created successive beings, and eternity the necessary existence of the Deity. Therefore, if this necessary Being hath no change or succession in his nature, his existence must of course be unsuccessive. We seem to commit a double oversight in this case; *first*, we find succession in the necessary nature and existence of the Deity himself; which is wrong, if the reasoning above be conclusive. And *then* we ascribe this succession to eternity, considered abstractly from the Eternal Being; and suppose it, one knows not what, a thing subsisting by itself, and flowing one minute after another. This is the work of pure imagination, and contrary to the reality of things. Hence the common metaphorical expression; *Time runs apace, let us lay hold on the present minute,* and the like. The philosophers themselves mislead us by their illustration. They compare eternity to the motion of a point running on for ever, and making a traceless infinite line. Here the point is supposed a thing actually subsisting, representing the present minute; and then they ascribe motion or succession to it; that is, they ascribe motion to a mere nonentity, to illustrate to us a successive eternity, made up of finite successive parts.—If once we allow an all-perfect Mind, which hath an eternal, immutable, and infinite comprehension of all things always, (and allow it we must,) the distinction of past and future vanishes with respect to such a Mind. In a word, if we proceed step by step, as above, the eternity or existence of the Deity will appear to be *vitæ interminabilis, tota, simul et perfecta possessio;* how much soever this may have been a paradox hitherto."—*Inquiry into the Nature of the Human Soul,* vol. ii. pp. 409—411, Edit. 3.

and depth, truly and properly distinguished into different measurable parts, limited at certain stages, one beyond another, in an infinite series. Which notion of
absolute and infinite space is doubtless as unreasonable
as that now mentioned of absolute and infinite duration.
It is as improper to imagine that the immensity and
omnipresence of God is distinguished by a series of miles
and leagues, one beyond another, as that the infinite
duration of God is distinguished by months and years,
one after another. A diversity and order of distinct
parts, limited by certain periods, is as conceivable, and
does as naturally obtrude itself on our imagination, in
one case as the other; and there is equal reason in each
case, to suppose that our imagination deceives us. It is
equally improper to talk of months and years of the
Divine existence, and mile-squares of Deity: and we
equally deceive ourselves when we talk of the world's
being differently fixed, with respect to either of these
sorts of measures. I think we know not what we mean,
if we say, the world might have been differently placed
from what it is, in the broad expanse of infinity; or,
that it might have been differently fixed in the long line
of eternity: and all arguments and objections, which
are built on the imaginations we are apt to have of infinite extension or duration, are buildings founded on
shadows, or castles in the air.

II. The second argument to prove that the Most High
wills one thing rather than another, without any superior fitness or preferableness in the thing preferred, is
God's actually placing in different parts of the world
particles or atoms of matter that are perfectly equal and
alike. The fore-mentioned author says, p. 78, &c. "If
one would descend to the minute specific particles of
which different bodies are composed, we should see
abundant reason to believe that there are thousands of
such little particles, or atoms of matter, which are perfectly equal and alike, and could give no distinct determination to the will of God where to place them." He
there instances in particles of water, of which there are

s

such immense numbers, which compose the rivers and
oceans of this world: and the infinite myriads of the
luminous and fiery particles which compose the body of
the sun, so many, that it would be very unreasonable to
suppose no two of them should be exactly equal and
alike.

Answ. (1.) To this I answer; that as we must suppose matter to be infinitely divisible, it is very unlikely
that any two of all these particles are exactly equal and
alike; so unlikely, that it is a thousand to one, yea, an
infinite number to one, but it is otherwise; and that although we should allow a great similarity between the
different particles of water and fire, as to their general
nature and figure; and however small we suppose those
particles to be, it is infinitely unlikely that any two of
them should be exactly equal in dimensions and quantity
of matter. If we should suppose a great many globes
of the same nature with the globe of the earth, it
would be very strange if there were any two of them
that had exactly the same number of particles of dust
and water in them: But infinitely less strange than
that two particles of light should have just the same
quantity of matter. For a particle of light, according
to the doctrine of the infinite divisibility of matter, is
composed of infinitely more assignable parts than there are
particles of dust and water in the globe of the earth.
And as it is infinitely unlikely that any two of these
particles should be *equal;* so it is, that they should be
alike in other respects: to instance in the configuration
of their surfaces. If there were very many globes, of
the nature of the earth, it would be very unlikely that
any two should have exactly the same number of particles of dust, water, and stone, in their surfaces, and all
posited exactly alike, one with respect to another, without any difference, in any part discernible either by the
naked eye or microscope; but infinitely less strange
than that two particles of light should be perfectly of
the same figure. For there are infinitely more assignable
real parts on the surface of a particle of light, than there

are particles of dust, water, and stone, on the surface of
the terrestrial globe.

Ans. (2.) But then, supposing that there are two
particles, or atoms of matter, perfectly equal and alike,
which God has placed in different parts of the creation;
as I will not deny it to be possible for God to make two
bodies perfectly alike, and put them in different places;
yet it will not follow, that two different or distinct acts
or effects of the Divine power have exactly the same fitness for the same end. For these two different bodies
are not different or distinct, in any other respects than
those wherein they differ; they are two in no other respects than those wherein there is a difference. If they
are perfectly equal and alike in themselves, then they
can be distinguished, or be distinct, only in those things
which are called circumstances: as place, time, rest,
motion, or some other present or past circumstances or
relations. For it is difference only that constitutes
distinction. If God makes two bodies in themselves
every way equal and alike, and agreeing perfectly in
all other circumstances and relations but only their
place; then in this only is there any distinction or du-
plicity. The figure is the same, the measure is the same,
the solidity and resistance are the same, and every thing
the same but only the place. Therefore what the will of
God determines is this, namely, that there should be the
same figure, the same extension, the same resistance,
&c. in two different places. And for this determination
he has some reason. There is some end, for which such
a determination and act has a peculiar fitness, above all
other acts. Here is no one thing determined without
an end, and no one thing without a fitness for that end,
superior to any thing else. If it be the pleasure of
God to cause the same resistance and the same figure to
be in two different places and situations, we can no more
justly argue from it that here must be some determination or act of God's will that is wholly without motive
or end, than we can argue, that whenever, in any case,
it is a man's will to speak the same words, or make the

same sounds, at two different times, there must be some determination or act of his will, without any motive or end. The difference of place, in the former case, proves no more than the difference of time does in the other. If any one should say, with regard to the former case, that there must be something determined without an end; viz. that of those two similar bodies, this in particular should be made in this place and the other in the other, and should inquire why the Creator did not make them in a transposition, when both are alike, and each would equally have suited either place? The inquiry supposes something that is not true; namely, that the two bodies differ and are distinct in other respects besides their place. So that, with this distinction *inherent* in them, they might, in their first creation, have been transposed, and each might have begun its existence in the place of the other.

Let us, for clearness sake, suppose that God had, at the beginning, made two globes, each of an inch diameter, both perfect spheres, and perfectly solid, without pores, and perfectly alike in every respect, and placed them near one to another, one towards the right hand, and the other towards the left, without any difference as to time, motion, or rest, past or present, or any circumstance but only their place; and the question should be asked, Why God in their creation placed them so? why that which is made on the right hand, was not made on the left, and *vice versâ?* Let it be well considered, whether there be any sense in such a question; and whether the inquiry does not suppose something false and absurd. Let it be considered, what the Creator must have done otherwise than he did, what different act of will or power he must have exerted, in order to the thing proposed. All that could have been done, would have been to have made two spheres, perfectly alike, in the same places where he has made them, without any difference of the things made, either in themselves or in any circumstance; so that the whole effect would have been without any difference, and there-

fore just the same. By the supposition, the two spheres
are different in no other respect but their place ; and
therefore in other respects they are the same. Each has
the same roundness; it is not a distinct rotundity, in
any other respects but its situation. There are also the
same dimensions, differing in nothing but their place.
And so of their resistance, and every thing else that belongs to them.

Here, if any chooses to say, " that there is a difference
in another respect, viz. that they are not *numerically*
the same; that it is thus with all the qualities that belong to them; that it is confessed they are, in some
respects, the same, that is, they are both exactly alike;
but yet numerically they differ. Thus the roundness
of one is not the same numerical individual roundness
with that of the other." Let this be supposed; then the
question about the determination of the Divine will in
the affair, is, why did God will that this individual
roundness should be at the right hand, and the other
individual roundness at the left? why did not he make
them in a contrary position? Let any rational person
consider, whether such questions be not words without
a meaning; as much as if God should see fit, for some
ends, to cause the same sounds to be repeated, or made
at two different times ; the sounds being perfectly the same
in every other respect, but only one was a minute after the
other ; and it should be asked, upon it, why God caused
these sounds, numerically different, to succeed one the
other in such a manner? Why he did not make that
individual sound, which was in the first minute, to be in
the second? and the individual sound of the last minute
to be in the first; which inquiries would be even ridiculous; as I think every person must see at once, in the
case proposed of two sounds, being only the same repeated, absolutely without any difference but that one
circumstance of time. If the Most High sees it will
answer some good end, that the same sound should be
made by lightning at two distinct times, and therefore

wills that it should be so, must it needs therefore be, that
herein there is some act of God's will without any motive or end? God saw fit often, at distinct times, and
on different occasions, to say the very same words to
Moses; namely, those, *I am Jehovah.* And would it
not be unreasonable to infer, as a certain consequence,
from this, that here must be some act or acts of the
Divine will, in determining and disposing these words
exactly alike, at different times, wholly without aim or
inducement? But it would be no more unreasonable,
than to say, that there must be an act of God's without
any inducement, if he sees it best, and for some reasons,
determines that there shall be the same resistance, the
same dimensions, and the same figure, in several distinct
places.

If, in the instance of the two spheres perfectly alike,
it be supposed possible that God might have made them
in a contrary position; that which is made at the right
hand being made at the left; then I ask, whether it is
not evidently equally possible, if God had made but one
of them, and that in the place of the right-hand globe,
that he might have made that numerically different
from what it is, and numerically different from what
he did make it; though perfectly alike, and in the same
place; and at the same time, and in every respect, in the
same circumstances and relations? Namely, whether he
might not have made it numerically the same with that
which he has now made at the left hand; and so have
left that which is now created at the right hand in a
state of non-existence? And if so, whether it would
not have been possible to have made one in that place,
perfectly like these, and yet numerically differing from
both? And let it be considered, whether, from this notion
of a numerical difference in bodies perfectly equal and
alike, which numerical difference is something inherent
in the bodies themselves, and diverse from the difference
of place or time, or any circumstance whatsoever, it will
not follow that there is an infinite number of numeri-

cally different possible bodies, perfectly alike, among which God chooses, by a self-determining power, when he goes about to create bodies.

Therefore let us put the case thus: Supposing that God in the beginning had created but one perfectly solid sphere, in a certain place; and it should be inquired, Why God created that individual sphere, in that place, at that time? And why he did not create another sphere perfectly like it, but numerically different, in the same place, at the same time? Or why he chose to bring into being there that very body, rather than any of the infinite number of other bodies perfectly like it; either of which he could have made there as well, and would have answered his end as well? Why he caused to exist, at that place and time, that individual roundness, rather than any other of the infinite number of individual rotundities just like it? Why that individual resistance, rather than any other of the infinite number of possible resistances just like it? And it might as reasonably be asked, Why, when God first caused it to thunder, he caused that individual sound then to be made, and not another just like it? Why did he make choice of this very sound, and reject all the infinite number of other possible sounds just like it, but numerically differing from it, and all differing one from another? I think every body must be sensible of the absurdity and nonsense of what is supposed in such inquiries. And if we calmly attend to the matter, we shall be convinced, that all such kinds of objections as I am answering, are founded on nothing but the imperfection of our manner of conceiving things, and the obscureness of language, and great want of clearness and precision in the signification of terms.

If any shall find fault with this reasoning, that it is going a great length into metaphysical niceties and subtilties, I answer, The objection which they are in reply to is a metaphysical subtilty, and must be treated according to the nature of it.*

* " For men to have recourse to subtilties in raising difficulties, and then

II. Another thing alleged is, that innumerable things which are determined by the Divine will, and chosen and done by God, rather than others, differ from those that are not chosen, in so inconsiderable a manner, that it would be unreasonable to suppose the difference to be of any consequence, or that there is any superior fitness or goodness that God can have respect to in the determination.

To which I answer: it is impossible for us to determine, with any certainty or evidence, that because the difference is very small, and appears to us of no consideration, therefore there is absolutely no superior goodness, and no valuable end, which can be proposed by the Creator and Governor of the world, in ordering such a difference. The fore-mentioned author mentions many instances. One is, there being one atom in the whole universe more or less. But I think it would be unreasonable to suppose, that God made one atom in vain, or without any end or motive. He made not one atom but what was a work of his almighty power, as much as the whole globe of the earth, and requires as much of a constant exertion of almighty power to uphold it; and was made and is upheld understandingly, and on design, as much as if no other had been made but that. And it would be as unreasonable to suppose that he made it without any thing really aimed at in so doing, as much as to suppose, that he made the planet Jupiter without aim or design.

It is possible that the most minute effects of the Creator's power, the smallest assignable difference between the things which God has made, may be attended, in the whole series of events, and the whole compass and extent of their influence, with very great and important consequences. If the laws of motion and gravitation laid down by Sir Isaac Newton hold universally, there is not one atom, nor the least assignable part of an atom,

complain, that they should be taken off by minutely examining these subtilties, is a strange kind of procedure."—*Nature of the Human Soul,* vol. ii., p. 331.

but what has influence, every moment, throughout the whole material universe, to cause every part to be otherwise than it would be, if it were not for that particular corporeal existence.   And however the effect is insensible for the present, yet it may, in length of time, become great and important.

To illustrate this, let us suppose two bodies moving the same way, in straight lines, perfectly parallel one to another ; but to be diverted from this parallel course, and drawn one from another, as much as might be by the attraction of an atom, at the distance of one of the furthest of the fixed stars from the earth; these bodies being turned out of the lines of their parallel motion, will, by degrees, get further and further distant one from the other; and though the distance may be imperceptible for a long time, yet at length it may become very great.   So, the revolution of a planet round the sun being retarded or accelerated, and the orbit of its revolution made greater or less, and more or less elliptical, and so its periodical time longer or shorter, no more than may be by the influence of the least atom, might, in length of time, perform a whole revolution sooner or later than otherwise it would have done; which might make a vast alteration with regard to millions of important events. So, the influence of the least particle may, for aught we know, have such effect on something in the constitution of some human body, as to cause another thought to arise in the mind at a certain time, than otherwise would have been; which, in length of time, (yea, and that not very great), might occasion a vast alteration through the whole world of mankind.   And so innumerable other ways might be mentioned, wherein the least assignable alteration may possibly be attended with great consequences.

Another *argument,* which the fore-mentioned author brings against a necessary determination of the Divine will, by a superior fitness, is, that such doctrine derogates from the freeness of God's grace and goodness, in choosing the objects of his favour and bounty, and from the obligation upon men to thankfulness for s ecial benefits. Page 89, &c.

In answer to this objection, I would observe:

1. That it derogates no more from the goodness of God, to suppose the exercise of the benevolence of his nature to be determined by wisdom, than to suppose it determined by chance, and that his favours are bestowed altogether at random, his will being determined by nothing but perfect accident, without any end or design whatsoever; which must be the case, as has been demonstrated, if volition be not determined by a prevailing motive. That which is owing to perfect contingence, wherein neither previous inducement nor antecedent choice has any hand, is not owing more to goodness or benevolence, than that which is owing to the influence of a wise end.

2. It is acknowledged, that if the motive that determines the will of God in the choice of the objects of his favours, be any moral quality in the object, recommending that object to his benevolence above others, his choosing that object is not so great a manifestation of the freeness and sovereignty of his grace, as if it were otherwise. But there is no necessity of supposing this, in order to our supposing that he has some wise end in view, in determining to bestow his favours on one person rather than another. We are to distinguish between the merit of the object of God's favour, or a moral qualification of the object attracting that favour and recommending to it, and the natural fitness of such a determination of the act of God's goodness, to answer some wise design of his own, some end in the view of God's omniscience. It is God's own act that is the proper and immediate object of his volition.

3. I suppose that none will deny, but that, in some instances, God acts from wise design in determining the particular subjects of his favours: none will say, I presume, that when God distinguishes, by his bounty, particular societies or persons, he never, in any instance, exercises any wisdom in so doing, aiming at some happy

consequence.   And, if it be not denied to be so in some instances, then I would inquire, whether, in these instances, God's goodness is less manifested than in those wherein God has no aim or end at all? and whether the subjects have less cause of thankfulness? And if so, who shall be thankful for the bestowment of distinguishing mercy, with that enhancing circumstance of the distinctions being made without an end? How shall it be known when God is influenced by some wise aim, and when not? It is very manifest, with respect to the apostle Paul, that God had wise ends in choosing him to be a Christian and an apostle, who had been a persecutor, &c. 1 Tim. i. 15, 16, " Christ Jesus came into the world to save sinners; of whom I am chief. Howbeit, for this cause I obtained mercy, that in me first, Jesus Christ might shew forth all long-suffering, for a pattern to them who should hereafter believe on him to life everlasting." But yet the apostle never looked on it as a diminution of the freedom and riches of Divine grace in his election, which he so often and so greatly magnifies.   This brings me to observe :

4. Our supposing such a moral necessity in the acts of God's will as has been spoken of, is so far from necessarily derogating from the riches of God's grace to such as are the chosen objects of his favour, that in many instances this moral necessity may arise from goodness, and from the great degree of it.   God may choose this object rather than another, as having a superior fitness to answer the ends, designs, and inclinations of his goodness; being more sinful, and so more miserable and necessitous than others, the inclinations of Infinite Mercy and Benevolence may be more gratified, and the gracious design of God's sending his Son into the world, may be more abundantly answered, in the exercises of mercy towards such an object, rather than another.

One thing more I would observe, before I finish what I have to say on the head of the necessity of the acts of God's will; and that is, that something much more like a servile subjection of the Divine Being to fatal necessity, will follow from Arminian principles, than from the doctrines which they oppose. For they (at least most of them) suppose, with respect to all events that happen in the moral world, depending on the volitions of moral agents, which are the most important events of the universe, to which all others are subordinate; I say, they suppose, with respect to these, that God has a certain foreknowledge of them, antecedent to any purposes or decrees of his about them. And if so, they have a fixed certain futurity, prior to any designs or volitions of his, and independent on them, and to which his volitions must be subject, as he would wisely accommodate his affairs to this fixed futurity of the state of things in the moral world. So that here, instead of a moral necessity of God's will, arising from, or consisting in, the infinite perfection and blessedness of the Divine Being, we have a fixed, unalterable state of things, properly distinct from the perfect nature of the Divine Mind, and the state of the Divine will and design, and entirely independent on these things, and which they have no hand in, because they are prior to them; and which God's will is truly subject to, being obliged to conform or accommodate himself to it, in all his purposes and decrees, and in every thing he does in his disposals and government of the world; the moral world being the end of the natural; so that all is in vain, that is not accommodated to that state of the moral world, which consists in, or depends upon, the acts and state of the wills of moral agents, which had a fixed futurition from eternity. Such a subjection to necessity as this, would truly argue an inferiority and servitude, that would be unworthy of the Supreme Being; and is much more agreeable to the notion which many of the heathen had of fate, as above the gods, than that moral necessity of fitness and wisdom which has been spoken of; and is truly repugnant to the absolute sovereignty of God, and inconsistent with the supremacy of his will; and really subjects the will of the Most High to the will of his creatures, and brings him into dependence upon them.

SECTION IX.

CONCERNING THAT OBJECTION AGAINST THE DOCTRINE WHICH HAS BEEN
MAINTAINED, THAT IT MAKES GOD THE AUTHOR OF SIN.

IT is urged by Arminians, that the doctrine of the
necessity of men's volitions, or their necessary connexion with antecedent events and circumstances, makes
the First Cause, and Supreme Ordainer of all things,
the author of sin ; in that he has so constituted the
state and course of things, that sinful volitions become
necessary, in consequence of his disposal. Dr Whitby,
in his " Discourse on the Freedom of the Will,"* cites
one of the ancients as on his side, declaring that this
opinion of the necessity of the will " absolves sinners,
as doing nothing of their own accord which was evil,
and would cast all the blame of all the wickedness committed in the world upon God, and upon his providence,
if that were admitted by the assertors of this fate; whether he himself did necessitate them to do these things,
or ordered matters so that they should be constrained to
do them by some other cause." And the Doctor says,
in another place,† " In the nature of the thing, and in
the opinion of the philosophers, *causa deficiens, in rebus
necessariis, ad causam per se efficientem reducenda est*—
in things necessary, the deficient cause must be reduced
to the efficient. And in this case the reason is evident;
because the not doing what is required, or not avoiding
what is forbidden, being a defect, must follow from the
position of the necessary cause of that deficiency."

Concerning this, I would observe the following things:

I. If there be any difficulty in this matter, it is nothing peculiar to this scheme; it is no difficulty or disadvantage, wherein it is distinguished from the scheme
of Arminians, and, therefore, not reasonably objected to
by them.

Dr Whitby supposes, that if sin necessarily follows

---

* On the Five Points, p. 361.　　　　　† Ibid. p. 436.

from God's withholding assistance, or if that assistance be not given, which is absolutely necessary to the avoiding of evil; then, in the nature of the thing, God must be as properly the author of that evil, as if he were the efficient cause of it. From whence, according to what he himself says of the devils and damned spirits, God must be the proper author of their perfect unrestrained wickedness: he must be the efficient cause of the great pride of the devils, and of their perfect malignity against God, Christ, his saints, and all that is good, and of the insatiable cruelty of their disposition. For he allows, that God has so forsaken them, and does so withhold his assistance from them, that they are incapacitated from doing good, and determined only to evil.* Our doctrine, in its consequence, makes God the author of men's sin in this world, no more, and in no other sense, than his doctrine, in its consequence, makes God the author of the hellish pride and malice of the devils. And, doubtless, the latter is as odious an effect as the former.

Again, if it will follow at all, that God is the author of sin, from what has been supposed of a sure and infallible connection between antecedents and consequents, it will follow because of this, viz., that for God to be the author or orderer of those things which he knows beforehand, will infallibly be attended with such a consequence, is the same thing, in effect, as for him to be the author of that consequence. But if this be so, this is a difficulty which equally attends the doctrine of Arminians themselves; at least, of those of them who allow God's certain foreknowledge of all events. For, on the supposition of such a foreknowledge, this is the case with respect to every sin that is committed: God knew, that if he ordered and brought to pass such and such events, such sins would infallibly follow. As, for instance, God certainly foreknew, long before Judas was born, that if he ordered things so, that there should be

---

* On the Five Points, pp. 302, 305.

such a man born, at such a time and at such a place, and that his life should be preserved, and that he should, in Divine providence, be led into acquaintance with Jesus, and that his heart should be so influenced by God's Spirit or providence, as to be inclined to be a follower of Christ, and that he should be one of those twelve, which should be chosen constantly to attend him as his family; and that his health should be preserved, so that he should go up to Jerusalem, at the last passover in Christ's life; and it should be so ordered, that Judas should see Christ's kind treatment of the woman who anointed him at Bethany, and have that reproof from Christ which he had at that time, and see and hear other things which excited his enmity against his Master, and other circumstances should be ordered as they were ordered; it would be what would most certainly and infallibly follow, that Judas would betray his Lord, and would soon after hang himself, and die impenitent, and be sent to hell for his horrid wickedness.

" Therefore, this supposed difficulty ought not to be brought as an objection against the scheme which has been maintained, as disagreeing with the Arminian scheme, seeing it is no difficulty owing to such a disagreement, but a difficulty wherein the Arminians share with us. That must be unreasonably made an objection against our differing from them, which we should not escape or avoid at all by agreeing with them.

And therefore I would observe:—

II. They who object, that this doctrine makes God the author of sin, ought distinctly to explain what they mean by that phrase, *the author of sin*. I know the phrase, as it is commonly used, signifies something very ill. If, by *the author of sin*, be meant the sinner, the agent, or actor of sin, or the doer of a wicked thing; so it would be a reproach and blasphemy to suppose God to be the author of sin. In this sense, I utterly deny God to be the author of sin; rejecting such an imputation on the Most High, as what is infinitely to be abhorred; and deny any such thing to be the consequence

of what I have laid down. But if, by *the author of sin,*
is meant the permitter, or not a hinderer of sin, and, at
the same time, a disposer of the state of events, in such
a manner, for wise, holy, and most excellent ends and
purposes, that sin, if it be permitted, or not hindered,
will most certainly and infallibly follow;—I say, if this
be all that is meant by being the author of sin, I do not
deny that God is the author of sin, (though I dislike
and reject the phrase, as that which by use and custom
is apt to carry another sense), it is no reproach for the
Most High to be thus the author of sin. This is not to
be the actor of sin, but on the contrary, of holiness.
What God doth herein is holy, and a glorious exercise
of the infinite excellency of his nature. And I do not
deny, that God's being thus the author of sin follows
from what I have laid down; and I assert, that it equally
follows from the doctrine which is maintained by most
of the Arminian divines.

That it is most certainly so, that God is in such a
manner the disposer and orderer of sin, is evident, if any
credit is to be given to the Scripture; as well as because
it is impossible, in the nature of things, to be otherwise.
In such a manner God ordered the obstinacy of Pharaoh, in his refusing to obey God's commands, to let
the people go. Exod. iv. 21: "I will harden his heart,
and he shall not let the people go." Chap. vii. 2—5:
"Aaron thy brother shall speak unto Pharaoh, that he
send the children of Israel out of his land. And I will
harden Pharaoh's heart, and multiply my signs and my
wonders in the land of Egypt. But Pharaoh shall not
hearken unto you; that I may lay mine hand upon
Egypt, by great judgments," &c. Chap. ix. 12: "And
the Lord hardened the heart of Pharaoh, and he hear-
kened not unto them, as the Lord had spoken unto Moses." Chap. x. 1, 2: "And the Lord said unto Moses,
Go in unto Pharaoh; for I have hardened his heart, and
the heart of his servants, that I might show these my
signs before him; and that thou mayest tell it in the
ears of thy son, and thy son's son, what things I have

wrought in Egypt, and my signs which I have done amongst them; that ye may know that I am the Lord." Chap. xiv. 4: "And I will harden Pharaoh's heart, that he shall follow after them; and I will be honoured upon Pharaoh and upon all his host." Verse 8: " And the Lord hardened the heart of Pharaoh king of Egypt, and he pursued after the children of Israel." And it is certain that, in such a manner, God, for wise and good ends, ordered that event, Joseph's being sold into Egypt by his brethren. Gen. xlv. 5: " Now, therefore, be not grieved, nor angry with yourselves, that ye sold me hither; for God did send me before you to preserve life." Verse 7, 8: " God did send me before you to preserve a posterity in the earth, and to save your lives by a great deliverance: so that now it was not you that sent me hither, but God." Psalm cvii. 17: " He sent a man before them, even Joseph, who was sold for a servant." It is certain, that thus God ordered the sin and folly of Sihon king of the Amorites, in refusing to let the people of Israel pass by him peaceably. Deut. ii. 30: " But Sihon king of Heshbon would not let us pass by him; for the Lord thy God hardened his spirit, and made his heart obstinate, that he might deliver him into thine hand." It is certain, that God thus ordered the sin and folly of the kings of Canaan, that they attempted not to make peace with Israel, but, with a stupid boldness and obstinacy, set themselves violently to oppose them and their God. Josh. xi. 20: " For it was of the Lord, to harden their hearts, that they should come against Israel in battle, that he might destroy them utterly, and that they might have no favour; but that he might destroy them, as the Lord commanded Moses." It is evident, that thus God ordered the treacherous rebellion of Zedekiah against the king of Babylon. Jer. lii. 3: " For through the anger of the Lord it came to pass in Jerusalem and Judah, until he 'had cast them out from his presence, that Zedekiah rebelled against the king of Babylon." So, 2 Kings xxiv. 20. And it is exceeding manifest, that God thus ordered the rapine

T

and unrighteous ravages of Nebuchadnezzar, in spoiling and ruining the nations round about. Jer. xxv. 9: "Behold, I will send and take all the families of the north, saith the Lord, and Nebuchadnezzar my servant, and will bring them against this land, and against all the nations round about; and will utterly destroy them, and make them an astonishment, and a hissing, and perpetual desolations." Chap. xliii. 10, 11: "I will send and take Nebuchadnezzar the king of Babylon, my servant; and I will set his throne upon these stones that I have hid, and he shall spread his royal pavilion over them. And when he cometh, he shall smite the land of Egypt, and deliver such as are for death to death, and such as are for captivity to captivity, and such as are for the sword to the sword." Thus God represents himself as sending for Nebuchadnezzar, and taking of him and his armies, and bringing him against the nations which were to be destroyed by him, to that very end, that he might utterly destroy them, and make them desolate; and as appointing the work that he should do, so particularly, that the very persons were designed that he should kill with the sword, and those that should be killed with famine and pestilence, and those that should be carried into captivity; and that in doing all these things he should act as his servant; by which, less cannot be intended, than that he should serve his purposes and designs. And in Jer. xxvii. 4—6, God declares how he would cause him thus to serve his designs, viz., by bringing this to pass in his sovereign disposals, as the great Possessor and Governor of the universe, that disposes all things just as pleases him. "Thus saith the Lord of Hosts, the God of Israel: I have made the earth, the man and the beast that are upon the ground, by my great power, and by my out-stretched arm, and have given it unto whom it seemed meet unto me. And now I have given all these lands into the hands of Nebuchadnezzar, MY SERVANT; and the beasts of the field have I given also to serve him." And Nebuchadnezzar is spoken of as doing these things, by having his "arms strengthened" by God, and having "God's sword put into his hands, for this end." Ezek. xxx. 24—26. Yea, God speaks of his terribly ravaging and wasting the nations, and cruelly destroying all sorts, without distinction of sex or age, as the weapon in God's hand, and the instrument of his indignation, which God makes use of to fulfil his own purposes, and execute his own vengeance. Jer. li. 20, &c. " Thou art my battle-axe and weapons of war: for with thee will I break in pieces the nations; and with thee I will destroy kingdoms; and with thee I will break in pieces the horse and his rider; and with thee I will break in pieces the chariot and his rider; with thee also will I break in pieces man and woman; and with thee will I break in pieces old and young; and with thee will I break in pieces the young man and the maid," &c. It is represented, that the designs of Nebuchadnezzar, and those that destroyed Jerusalem, never could have been accomplished, had not God determined them as well as they. Lam. iii. 37: " Who is he that saith, and it cometh to pass, and the Lord commandeth it not ?" And yet the king of Babylon's thus destroying the nations, and especially the Jews, is spoken of as his great wickedness, for which God finally destroyed him. Isa. xiv. 4, 5, 6, 12. Hab. ii. 5—12, and Jer. l. and li. It is most manifest, that God, to serve his own designs, providentially ordered Shimei's cursing David. 2 Sam. xvi. 10, 11 : " The Lord hath said unto him, Curse David.—Let him curse: for the Lord hath bidden him."

It is certain, that God thus, for excellent, holy, gracious, and glorious ends, ordered the fact which they committed who were concerned in Christ's death, and that therein they did but fulfil God's designs: as, I trust, no Christian will deny it was the design of God, that Christ should be crucified, and that for this end he came into the world. It is very manifest, by many Scriptures, that the whole affair of Christ's crucifixion, with its circumstances, and the treachery of Judas, that made way for it, was ordered in God's providence, in pursuance of his purpose; notwithstanding the violence that is used with those plain Scriptures, to obscure and pervert the sense of them. Acts ii. 23: "Him, being delivered by the determinate counsel and foreknowledge of God,* ye have taken, and by wicked hands have crucified and slain." Luke xxii. 21, 22:† "But, behold, the hand of him that betrayeth me is with me on the table. And truly the Son of Man goeth, as it was determined." Acts iv. 27, 28: "For of a truth, against thy holy child Jesus, whom thou hast anointed, both Herod and Pontius Pilate, with the Gentiles and the people of Israel, were gathered together, for to do whatsoever thy hand and thy counsel determined before to be done." Acts iii. 17, 18: " And now, brethren, I wot that through ignorance ye did it, as did also your rulers. But those things, which God before had showed by the mouth of all his prophets, that Christ should suffer, he hath so fulfilled." So that what these murderers of Christ did, is spoken of as what God brought to pass, or ordered, and that by which he fulfilled his own word.

In Rev. xvii. 17, "the agreeing of the kings of the earth to give their kingdom to the beast," though it was a very wicked thing in them, is spoken of as " a fulfilling God's will," and what " God had put into their hearts to do." It is manifest, that God sometimes permits sin to be committed, and at the same time orders things so, that if he permits the fact, it will come to pass, because, on some accounts, he sees it needful and of importance that it should come to pass.

---

* " Grotius, as well as Beza, observes, προγνωσις must here signify *decree;* and Elsner has shown that it has that signification in approved Greek writers. And it is certain εκδοτος signifies one given up into the hands of an enemy."—DODDRIDGE *in loc.*

† " As this passage is not liable to the ambiguities which some have apprehended in Acts ii. 23, and iv. 28, (which yet seem, on the whole, to be parallel to it, in their most natural construction), I look upon it as an evident proof, that those things are, in the language of Scripture, said to be determined or decreed (or exactly bounded and marked out by God, as the word ὁριζω most naturally signifies,) which he sees in fact will happen, in consequence of his volitions, without any necessitating agency; as well as those events of which he is properly the author."—*Idem in loc.*

Matt. xviii. 7: "It must needs be that offences come; but wo to that man by whom the offence cometh." With 1 Cor. xi. 19: "For there must also be heresies among you, that they which are approved may be made manifest among you."

Thus it is certain and demonstrable, from the holy Scriptures, as well as the nature of things, and the principles of Arminians, that God permits sin; and at the same time, so orders things in his providence, that it certainly and infallibly will come to pass, in consequence of his permission.

I proceed to observe in the next place:

III. That there is a great difference between God's being concerned thus, by his permission, in an event and act, which, in the inherent subject and agent of it, is sin, (though the event will certainly follow on his permission,) and his being concerned in it by producing it and exerting the act of sin; or between his being the orderer of its certain existence, by not hindering it, under certain circumstances, and his being the proper actor or author of it, by a positive agency or efficiency. And this, notwithstanding what Dr Whitby offers about a saying of philosophers, that *causa deficiens, in rebus necessariis, ad causam per se efficientem reducenda est.* As there is a vast difference between the sun's being the cause of the lightsomeness and warmth of the atmosphere, and brightness of gold and diamonds, by its presence and positive influence; and its being the occasion of darkness and frost in the night, by its motion, whereby it descends below the horizon. The motion of the sun is the occasion of the latter kind of events; but it is not the proper cause efficient, or producer of them; though they are necessarily consequent on that motion, under such circumstances: no more is any action of the Divine Being the cause of the evil of men's wills. If the sun were the proper cause of cold and darkness, it would be the fountain of these things, as it is the fountain of light and heat; and then something might be argued from the nature of cold and darkness, to a like-

ness of nature in the sun; and it might be justly inferred, that the sun itself is dark and cold, and that his
beams are black and frosty. But from its being the
cause no otherwise than by its departure, no such thing
can be inferred, but the contrary: it may justly be
argued, that the sun is a bright and hot body, if cold
and darkness are found to be the consequence of its
withdrawment; and the more constantly and necessarily these effects are connected with and confined to its
absence, the more strongly does it argue the sun to be
the fountain of light and heat. So, inasmuch as sin is
not the fruit of any positive agency or influence of the
Most High, but, on the contrary, arises from the withholding of his action and energy, and, under certain circumstances, necessarily follows on the want of his influence; this is no argument that he is sinful, or his operation evil, or has anything of the nature of evil; but, on
the contrary, that he, and his agency, are altogether
good and holy, and that he is the fountain of all holiness. It would be strange arguing, indeed, because men
never commit sin, but only when God leaves them to
themselves, and necessarily sin when he does so, that
therefore their sin is not from themselves, but from
God; and so, that God must be a sinful being: as
strange as it would be to argue, because it is always
dark when the sun is gone, and never dark when the
sun is present, that therefore all darkness is from the
sun, and that his disc and beams must needs be black.

IV. It properly belongs to the supreme and absolute
Governor of the universe, to order all important events
within his dominion by his wisdom; but the events in
the moral world are of the most important kind; such
as the moral actions of intelligent creatures, and their
consequences.

These events will be ordered by something. They
will either be disposed by wisdom, or they will be disposed by chance; that is, they will be disposed by blind
and undesigning causes, if that were possible, and could
be called a disposal. Is it not better that the good and

evil which happen in God's world, should be ordered,
regulated, bounded, and determined, by the good pleasure of an infinitely wise Being, who perfectly comprehends within his understanding and constant view
the universality of things, in all their extent and duration, and sees all the influence of every event, with
respect to every individual thing and circumstance
throughout the grand system, and the whole of the
eternal series of consequences,—than to leave these
things to fall out by chance, and to be determined by
those causes which have no understanding or aim?
Doubtless, in these important events, there is a better
and a worse, as to the time, subject, place, manner, and
circumstances of their coming to pass, with regard to
their influence on the state and course of things. And
if there be, it is certainly best that they should be determined to that time, place, &c. which is best. And
therefore it is in its own nature fit, that wisdom and not
chance, should order these things. So that it belongs to
the Being who is the Possessor of infinite wisdom, and
is the Creator and Owner of the whole system of created
existences, and has the care of all; I say it belongs to
him to take care of this matter; and he would not do
what is proper for him if he should neglect it. And it
is so far from being unholy in him to undertake this
affair, that it would rather have been unholy to neglect
it; as it would have been a neglecting what fitly apper-
tains to him; and so it would have been a very unfit
and unsuitable neglect.

Therefore the sovereignty of God doubtless extends to
this matter; especially considering, that if it should be
supposed to be otherwise, and God should leave men's
volitions, and all moral events, to the determination and
disposition of blind unmeaning causes, or they should
be left to happen perfectly without a cause; this would
be no more consistent with liberty, in any notion of it,
and particularly not in the Arminian notion of it, than
if these events were subject to the disposal of Divine
Providence, and the will of man were determined by

circumstances which are ordered and disposed by Divine wisdom, as appears by what has been already observed. But it is evident, that such a providential disposing and determining men's moral actions, though it infers a moral necessity of those actions, yet it does not in the least infringe the real liberty of mankind; the only liberty that common sense teaches to be necessary to moral agency, which, as has been demonstrated, is not inconsistent with such necessity.

On the whole it is manifest, that God may be, in the manner which has been described, the orderer and disposer of that event, which, in the inherent subject and agent, is moral evil; and yet his so doing may be no moral evil. He may will the disposal of such an event, and its coming to pass, for good ends, and his will not be an immoral or sinful will, but a perfectly holy will. And he may actually, in his providence, so dispose and permit things, that the event may be certainly and infallibly connected with such disposal and permission, and his act therein not be an immoral or unholy, but a perfectly holy act. Sin may be an evil thing; and yet that there should be such a disposal and permission as that it should come to pass, may be a good thing. This is no contradiction or inconsistence. Joseph's brethren's selling him into Egypt, consider it only as it was acted by them, and with respect to their views and aims, which were evil, was a very bad thing; but it was a good thing, as it was an event of God's ordering, and considered with respect to his views and aims, which were good. Gen. l. 20, "As for you, ye thought evil against me; but God meant it unto good." So the crucifixion of Christ, if we consider only those things which belong to the event as it proceeded from his murderers, and are comprehended within the compass of the affair considered as their act, their principles, dispositions, views, and aims; so it was one of the most heinous things that ever was done, in many respects the most horrid of all acts: but consider it as it was willed and ordered of God, in the extent of his designs and

views, it was the most admirable and glorious of all
events; and God's willing the event was the most holy
volition of God that ever was made known to men; and
God's act in ordering it was a divine act, which, above
all others, manifests the moral excellency of the Divine
Being.

The consideration of these things may help us to a
sufficient answer to the cavils of Arminians, concerning
what has been supposed by many Calvinists, of a distinction between a secret and revealed will of God, and
their diversity one from the other; supposing that the
Calvinists herein ascribe inconsistent wills to the Most
High: which is without any foundation. God's secret
and revealed will, or, in other words, his disposing and
perceptive will, may be diverse, and exercised in dissimilar acts, the one in disapproving and opposing, the
other in willing and determining, without any inconsistence. Because, although these dissimilar exercises of
the Divine will may, in some respects, relate to the
same things, yet, in strictness, they have different and
contrary objects, the one evil, and the other good. Thus,
for instance, the crucifixion of Christ was a thing contrary to the revealed or perceptive will of God; because,
as it was viewed and done by his malignant murderers,
it was a thing infinitely contrary to the holy nature of
God, and so necessarily contrary to the holy inclination
of his heart, revealed in his law. Yet this does not at
all hinder but that the crucifixion of Christ, considered
with all those glorious consequences which were within
the view of the Divine Omniscience, might be indeed,
and therefore might appear to God to be, a glorious
event; and consequently be agreeable to his will, though
this will may be secret, i. e. not revealed in God's law.
And thus considered, the crucifixion of Christ was not
evil, but good. If the secret exercises of God's will
were of a kind that is dissimilar, and contrary to his revealed will respecting the same or like objects; if the
objects of both were good, or both evil; then, indeed, to
ascribe contrary kinds of volition or inclination to God

respecting these objects, would be to ascribe an inconsistent will to God: but to ascribe to him different and
opposite exercises of heart respecting different objects,
and objects contrary one to another, is so far from supposing God's will to be inconsistent with itself, that it
cannot be supposed consistent with itself any other way.
For any being to have a will of choice respecting good,
and at the same time, a will of rejection and refusal respecting evil, is to be very consistent; but the contrary,
viz. to have the same will towards these contrary objects, and to choose and love both good and evil at the
same time, is to be very inconsistent.

There is no inconsistence in supposing, that God may
hate a thing as it is in itself, and considered simply as
evil, and yet that it may be his will it should come to
pass, considering all consequences. I believe there is no
person of good understanding, who will venture to say,
he is certain that it is impossible it should be best, taking in the whole compass and extent of existence, and
all consequences in the endless series of events, that
there should be such a thing as moral evil in the world.*

---

* Here are worthy to be observed some passages of a late noted writer, of
our nation, that nobody who is acquainted with will suspect to be very
favourable to Calvinism. " It is difficult," says he, " to handle the necessity of evil in such a manner as not to stumble such as are not above being
alarmed at propositions which have an uncommon sound. But if philosophers will but reflect calmly on the matter, they will find, that, consistently with the unlimited power of the Supreme Cause, it may be said,
that in the best-ordered system, evils must have place."—TURNBULL'S
Principles of Moral Philosophy, pp. 327, 328. He is there speaking of moral
evils, as may be seen.

Again, the same author, in his second volume, entitled " Christian Philosophy," p. 35, has these words : " If the Author and Governor of all things
be infinitely perfect, then whatever is is right ; of all possible systems he
hath chosen the best ; and consequently there is no absolute evil in the universe. This being the case, all the seeming imperfections or evils in it are
such only in a partial view ; and, with respect to the whole system, they are
goods."

" Whence, then, comes evil ? is the question that hath, in all ages, been
reckoned the Gordian knot in philosophy. And indeed, if we own the existence of evil in the world in an absolute sense, we diametrically contradict
what hath been just now proved of God. For if there be any evil in the
system, that is not good with respect to the whole, then is the whole not
good, but evil, or, at best, very imperfect ; and an author must be as his

And if so, it will certainly follow, that an infinitely wise Being, who always chooses what is best, must choose that there should be such a thing. And if so, then such a choice is not an evil, but a wise and holy choice. And if so, then that providence which is agreeable to such a choice, is a wise and holy providence. Men do *will* sin as sin, and so are the authors and actors of it: they love it as sin, and for evil ends and purposes. God does not will sin as sin, or for the sake of any thing evil; though it be his pleasure so to order things, that, he permitting, sin will come to pass; for the sake of the great good that by his disposal shall be the consequence. His willing to order things so that evil should come to pass, for the sake of the contrary good, is no argument that he does not hate evil as evil: and if so, then it is no reason why he may not reasonably forbid evil as evil, and punish it as such.

The Arminians themselves must be obliged, whether they will or no, to allow a distinction of God's will, amounting to just the same thing that Calvinists intend by their distinction of a *secret and revealed will.* They must allow a distinction of those things which God thinks best should be, considering all circumstances and consequences, and so are agreeable to his disposing

workmanship is; as is the effect, such is the cause. But the solution of this difficulty is at hand; that there is no evil in the universe. What! are there no pains, no imperfections? Is there no misery, no vice, in the world? or, are not these evils? Evils indeed they are; that is, those of one sort are hurtful, and those of the other sort are equally hurtful and abominable; but they are not evil or mischievous with respect to the whole."—*Ibid.*, p. 37.

" But he is, at the same time, said to create evil, darkness, confusion : and yet to do no evil, but to be the Author of good only. He is called the ' Father of lights;' the Author of 'every perfect and good gift, with whom there is no variableness nor shadow of turning;' who ' tempteth no man,' but ' giveth to all men liberally, and upbraideth not.' And yet by the prophet Isaiah, He is introduced saying of himself, ' I form light, and create darkness ; I make peace and create evil ; I the Lord do all these things. What is the meaning, the plain language of all this, but that the Lord delighteth in goodness, and (as the Scripture speaks) evil is ' his strange work ?' He intends and pursues the universal good of his creation : and the evil which happens is not permitted for its own sake, or through any pleasure in evil, but because it is requisite to the greater good pursued."—*Ibid.*, p. 42.

will, and those things which he loves, and are agreeable to his nature, in themselves considered. Who is there that will dare to say, that the hellish pride, malice, and cruelty of devils, are agreeable to God, and what he likes and approves? And yet, I trust, there is no Christian divine but what will allow, that it is agreeable to God's will so to order and dispose things concerning them, so to leave them to themselves, and give them up to their own wickedness, that this perfect wickedness should be a necessary consequence. Be sure Dr Whitby's words do plainly suppose and allow it.*

These following things may be laid down as maxims of plain truth, and indisputable evidence.

1. That God is a *perfectly happy* being in the most absolute and highest sense possible.

2. That it will follow from hence, that God is free from every thing that is *contrary to happiness;* and so, that in strict propriety of speech, there is no such thing as any pain, grief, or trouble in God.

3. When any intelligent being is really crossed and disappointed, and things are contrary to what he truly desires, he is the less pleased, or has less pleasure, his pleasure and happiness is diminished, and he suffers what is disagreeable to him, or is the subject of something that is of a nature contrary to joy and happiness, even pain and grief.†

From this last axiom it follows, that if no distinction is to be admitted between God's hatred of sin, and his will with respect to the event and the existence of sin, as the all-wise determiner of all events, under the view of all consequences through the whole compass and series of things; I say, then, it certainly follows, that the coming to pass of every individual act of sin is truly, all things

---

* Whitby on the Five Points, edit. 2. pp, 300, 305, 309.

† Certainly it is not less absurd and unreasonable to talk of God's will and desires being truly and properly crossed, without his suffering any uneasiness, or any thing grievous or disagreeable, than it is to talk of something that may be called a revealed will, which may, in some respects, be different from a secret purpose; which purpose may be fulfilled, when the other is opposed.

considered, contrary to his will, and that his will is really
crossed in it; and this in proportion as he hates it.
And as God's hatred of sin is infinite, by reason of the
infinite contrariety of his holy nature to sin; so his will
is infinitely crossed in every act of sin that happens.
Which is as much as to say : He endures that which is
infinitely disagreeable to him, by means of every act of
sin that he sees committed. And therefore, as appears by
the preceding positions, he endures truly and really infinite grief or pain from every sin. And so he must be
infinitely crossed, and suffer infinite pain every day, in
millions of millions of instances : he must continually be
the subject of an immense number of real and truly infinitely great crosses and vexations. Which would be to
make him infinitely the most miserable of all beings.

If any objector should say: all that these things
amount to is, that God may do evil that good may come,
which is justly esteemed immoral and sinful in men;
and therefore may be justly esteemed inconsistent with
the moral perfections of God. I answer : that for God to
dispose and permit evil, in the manner that has been
spoken of, is not to do evil that good may come ; for it
is not to do evil at all. In order to a thing's being morally evil, there must be one of these things belonging to
it : either it must be a thing unfit and unsuitable in its
own nature ; or it must have a bad tendency; or it must
proceed from an evil disposition, and be done for an evil
end. But neither of these things can be attributed to
God's ordering and permitting such events, as the immoral acts of creatures for good ends. (1.) It is not unfit in its own nature, that he should do so. For it is in its
own nature fit that infinite wisdom, and not blind chance,
should dispose moral good and evil in the world. And
it is fit that the Being who has infinite wisdom, and is the
Maker, Owner, and supreme Governor of the world,
should take care of that matter. And therefore there is
no unfitness or unsuitableness in his doing it. It may be
unfit, and so immoral, for any other beings to go about
to order this affair; because they are not possessed of a

wisdom, that in any manner fits them for it; and, in other respects, they are not fit to be trusted with this affair; nor does it belong to them, they not being the owners and lords of the universe.

We need not be afraid to affirm, that if a wise and good man knew with absolute certainty, it would be best, all things considered, that there should be such a thing as moral evil in the world, it would not be contrary to his wisdom and goodness, {for him to choose that it should be so. It is no evil desire to desire good, and to desire that which, all things considered, is best. And it is no unwise choice to choose that that should be, which it is best should be; and to choose the existence of that thing concerning which this is known, viz. that it is best it should be, and so is known in the whole to be most worthy to be chosen. On the contrary, it would be a plain defect in wisdom and goodness, for him not to choose it. And the reason why he might not order it, if he were able, would not be because he might not desire it, but only the ordering of that matter does not belong to him. But it is no harm for him who is, by right, and in the greatest propriety, the supreme orderer of all things, to order every thing in such a manner, as it would be a point of wisdom in him to choose that they should be ordered. If it would be a plain defect of wisdom and goodness in a being, not to choose that that should be, which he certainly knows it would, all things considered, be best should be, (as was but now observed), then it must be impossible for a being who has no defect of wisdom and goodness, to do otherwise than choose it should be; and that for this very reason, because he is perfectly wise and good. And if it be agreeable to perfect Wisdom and Goodness for him to choose that it should be, and the ordering of all things supremely and perfectly belongs to him, it must be agreeable to infinite Wisdom and Goodness to order that it should be. If the choice is good, the ordering and disposing things according to that choice must also be good. It can be no harm in one to whom it belongs, " to do his will in the armies of hea-

ven, and amongst the inhabitants of the earth," to execute a good volition. If this will be good, and the object of his will be, all things considered, good and best,
then the choosing or willing it, is not willing evil that
good may come. And if so, then his ordering according to that will, is not doing evil that good may come. '

2. It is not of a bad tendency, for the Supreme Being
thus to order and permit that moral evil to be, which it
is best should come to pass. For that it is of good tendency, is the very thing supposed in the point now in
question. Christ's crucifixion, though a most horrid
fact in them that perpetrated it, was of most glorious
tendency, as permitted and ordered of God.

3. Nor is there any need of supposing it proceeds from
any evil disposition or aim; for by the supposition, what
is aimed at is good, and good is the actual issue, in the
final result of things.

SECTION X.

CONCERNING SIN'S FIRST ENTRANCE INTO THE WORLD.

The things which have already been offered may serve
to obviate or clear many of the objections which might
be raised concerning sin's first coming into the world;
as though it would follow from the doctrine maintained,
that God must be the author of the first sin, through
his so disposing things, that it should necessarily follow
from his permission, that the sinful act should be committed, &c. I need not, therefore, stand to repeat what
has been said already about such a necessity's not proving God to be the author of sin, in any ill sense, or in
any such sense as to infringe any liberty of man, concerned in his moral agency, or capacity of blame, guilt,
and punishment.

But, if it should nevertheless be said, supposing the
case so, that God, when he had made man, might so
order his circumstances, that, from these circumstances,
together with his withholding further assistance and Divine influence, his sin would infallibly follow, why might

not God as well have first made man with a fixed prevailing principle of sin in his heart?

I answer, 1. It was meet, if sin did come into existence, and appear in the world, it should arise from the
imperfection which properly belongs to a creature, as
such, and should appear so to do, that it might appear
not to be from God, as the efficient or fountain. But
this could not have been, if man had been made at first
with sin in his heart; nor unless the abiding principle
and habit of sin were first introduced by an evil act of
the creature. If sin had not arisen from the imperfection of the creature, it would not have been so visible,
that it did not arise from God, as the positive cause, and
real source of it.—But it would require room that cannot be here allowed, fully to consider all the difficulties
which have been started concerning the first entrance of
sin into the world.

And therefore,

2. I would observe, that objections against the doctrine that has been laid down, in opposition to the Arminian notion of liberty, from these difficulties, are altogether impertinent; because no additional difficulty is
incurred by adhering to a scheme in this manner differing from theirs, and none would be removed or avoided,
by agreeing with, and maintaining theirs. Nothing that
the Arminians say about the contingence, or self-determining power of man's will, can serve to explain, with
less difficulty, how the first sinful volition of mankind
could take place, and man be justly charged with the
blame of it. To say, the will was self-determined, or
determined by free choice, in that sinful volition,—which
is to say, that the first sinful volition was determined
by a foregoing sinful volition,—is no solution of the difficulty. It is an odd way of solving difficulties, to advance greater, in order to it. To say two and two make
nine, or that a child begat his father, solves no difficulty: no more does it, to say, the first sinful act of
choice was before the first sinful act of choice, and chose
and determined it, and brought it to pass. Nor is it any

better solution to say, the first sinful volition chose, determined, and produced itself; which is to say, it was before it was. Nor will it go any further towards helping us over the difficulty, to say, the first sinful volition arose accidentally, without any cause at all, any more than it will solve that difficult question, How the world could be made out of nothing? to say, it came into being out of nothing, without any cause, as has been already observed. And if we should allow that that could be, that the first evil volition should arise by perfect accident, without any cause, it would relieve no difficulty, about God's laying the blame of it to man. For how was man to blame for perfect accident, which had no cause, and which, therefore, he (to be sure) was not the cause of, any more than if it came by some external cause?—Such kind of solutions are no better, than if some person, going about to solve some of the strange mathematical paradoxes about infinitely great and small quantities, as, that some infinitely great quantities are infinitely greater than some other infinitely great quantities; and also that some infinitely small quantities are infinitely less than others, which yet are infinitely little; in order to a solution, should say, that mankind have been under a mistake, in supposing a greater quantity to exceed a smaller; and that a hundred multiplied by ten makes but a single unit.

SECTION XI.

OF A SUPPOSED INCONSISTENCE OF THESE PRINCIPLES WITH GOD'S MORAL CHARACTER.

THE things which have been already observed may be sufficient to answer most of the objections, and silence the great exclamations of Arminians against the Calvinists, from the supposed inconsistence of Calvinistic principles with the moral perfections of God, as exercised in his government of mankind. The consistence of such a doctrine of necessity as has been maintained, with the fitness and reasonableness of God's commands, promises

U

and threatenings, rewards and punishments, has been
particularly considered: the cavils of our opponents, as
though our doctrine of necessity made God the author of
sin, have been answered; and also their objection against
these principles, as inconsistent with God's sincerity in
his counsels, invitations, and persuasions, has been already obviated, in what has been observed respecting
the consistence of what Calvinists suppose concerning
the secret and revealed will of God: by that it appears,
there is no repugnance in supposing it may be the secret
will of God, that his ordination and permission of events
should be such, that it shall be a certain consequence,
that a thing never will come to pass, which yet it is
man's duty to do, and so God's perceptive will that he
should do; and this is the same thing as to say, God
may sincerely command and require him to do it. And
if he may be sincere in commanding him, he may, for
the same reason, be sincere in counselling, inviting, and
using persuasions with him to do it. Counsels and invitations are manifestations of God's perceptive will, or of
what God loves, and what is in itself, and as man's act,
agreeable to his heart; and not of his disposing will, and
what he chooses as a part of his own infinite scheme of
things. It has been particularly shown, Part III. sect.
iv. that such a necessity as has been maintained, is not
inconsistent with the propriety and fitness of Divine
commands; and for the same reason, not inconsistent
with the sincerity of invitations and counsels, in the
corollary at the end of that section. Yea, it hath been
shown, Part III. sect. vii. corol. 1. that this objection
of Arminians, concerning the sincerity and use of Divine
exhortations, invitations, and counsels, is demonstrably
against themselves.

Notwithstanding, I would further observe, that the
difficulty of reconciling the sincerity of counsels, invitations, and persuasions, with such an antecedent known
fixedness of all events as has been supposed, is not peculiar to this scheme, as distinguished from that of the
generality of Arminians, which acknowledge the absolute

foreknowledge of God: and therefore it would be unreasonably brought as an objection against my differing
from them. The main seeming difficulty in the case is
this: that God, in counselling, inviting, and persuading,
makes a show of aiming at, seeking, and using endeavours for the thing exhorted and persuaded to; whereas,
it is impossible for any intelligent being truly to seek,
or use endeavours for a thing, which he at the same time
knows, most perfectly, will not come to pass; and that
it is absurd to suppose, he makes the obtaining of a thing
his end, in his calls and counsels, which he, at the same
time, infallibly knows will not be obtained by these
means. Now, if God knows this, in the utmost certainty
and perfection, the way by which he comes by this
knowledge makes no difference. If he knows it is by
the necessity which he sees in things, or by some other
means, it alters not the case. But it is in effect allowed
by Arminians themselves, that God's inviting and persuading men to do things, which he, at the same time,
certainly knows will not be done, is no evidence of insincerity; because they allow, that God has a certain
foreknowledge of all men's sinful actions and omissions.
And as this is thus implicitly allowed by most Arminians, so all that pretend to own the Scriptures to be
the word of God, must be constrained to allow it.—God
commanded and counselled Pharaoh to let his people go,
and used arguments and persuasions to induce him to it;
he laid before him arguments taken from his infinite
greatness and almighty power, (Exod. vii. 16,) and fore-
warned him of the fatal consequences of his refusal, from
time to time; (chap. viii. 1, 2, 20, 21 ; chap. ix. 1—5,
13—17; and x. 3, 6.) He commanded Moses, and the
elders of Israel, to go and beseech Pharaoh to let the
people go; and at the same time told them, he knew
surely that he would not comply to it. Exod. iii. 18,
19: " And thou shalt come, thou and the elders of
Israel, unto the king of Egypt, and you shall say unto
him; The Lord God of the Hebrews hath met with us;
and now let us go, we beseech thee, three days' journey

into the wilderness, that we may sacrifice unto the Lord
our God." And, "I am sure that the king of Egypt
will not let you go." So our blessed Saviour, the even-
ing wherein he was betrayed, knew that Peter would
shamefully deny him before the morning; for he declares it to him with asseverations, to show the certainty
of it; and tells the disciples, that all of them should be
offended because of him that night; Matt. xxvi. 31—35;
John xiii. 38; Luke xxii. 31—34; John xvi. 32. And
yet it was their duty to avoid these things; they were
very sinful things, which God had forbidden, and which
it was their duty to watch and pray against; and they
were obliged to do so from the counsels and persuasions
Christ used with them, at that very time, so to do;
Matt. xxvi. 41. " Watch and pray, that ye enter not
into temptation." So that whatever difficulty there can
be in this matter, it can be no objection against any
principles which have been maintained in opposition to
the principles of Arminians; nor does it any more concern me to remove the difficulty, than it does them, or
indeed all that call themselves Christians, and acknowledge the Divine authority of the Scriptures. Nevertheless, this matter may possibly (God allowing) be more
particularly and largely considered, in some future discourse on the doctrine of predestination.

But I would here observe, that however the defenders
of that notion of liberty of will which I have opposed,
exclaim against the doctrine of Calvinists, as tending to
bring men into doubts concerning the moral perfections
of God; it is their scheme, and not the scheme of Calvinists, that indeed is justly chargeable with this. For
it is one of the most fundamental points of their scheme
of things, that a freedom of will, consisting in self-determination, without all necessity, is essential to moral
agency. This is the same thing as to say, that such a
determination of the will, without all necessity, must be
in all intelligent beings, in those things wherein they are
moral agents, or in their moral acts : and from this it
will follow, that God's will is not necessarily determined

in any thing he does, as a moral agent, or in any of his acts that are of a moral nature : so that in all things, wherein he acts holily, justly, and truly, he does not act necessarily; or his will is not necessarily determined to act holily and justly; because, if it were necessarily determined, he would not be a moral agent in thus acting; his will would be attended with necessity, which, they say, is inconsistent with moral agency :—" He can act no otherwise; he is at no liberty in the affair; he is determined by unavoidable, invincible necessity; therefore such agency is no moral agency; yea, no agency at all, properly speaking : a necessary agent is no agent : he being passive, and subject to necessity, what he does is no act of his, but an effect of a necessity prior to any act of his." This is agreeable to their manner of arguing. Now then, what is become of all our proof of the moral perfections of God ? How can we prove that God certainly will, in any one instance, do that which is just and holy, seeing his will is determined in the matter by no necessity ? We have no other way of proving that any thing certainly will be, but only by the necessity of the event. Where we can see no necessity, but that the thing may be, or may not be, there we are unavoidably left at a loss. We have no other way properly and truly to demonstrate the moral perfections of God, but the way that Mr Chubb proves them in pp. 252, 261, 262, 263, of his Tracts, viz. that God must necessarily perfectly know what is most worthy and valuable in itself, which, in the nature of things, is best and fittest to be done. And as this is most eligible in itself, the being omniscient, must see it to be so ; and being both omniscient and self-sufficient, cannot have any temptation to reject it ; and so must necessarily will that which is best. And thus, by this necessity of the determination of God's will to what is good and best, we demonstrably establish God's moral character.

Corol. From things which have been observed, it appears, that most of the arguments from Scripture, which Arminians make use of to support their scheme, are no

other than begging the question. For in these their
arguments, they determine in the first place, that without such a freedom of will as they hold, men cannot be
proper moral agents, nor the subjects of command,
counsel, persuasion, invitation, promises, threatenings,
expostulations, rewards, and punishments ; and that
without such freedom, it is to no purpose for men to
take any care, or use any diligence, endeavours, or means,
in order to their avoiding sin, or becoming holy, escaping punishment, or obtaining happiness : and having
supposed these things, which are grand things in question in the debate, then they heap up Scriptures, containing commands, counsels, calls, warnings, persuasions,
expostulations, promises, and threatenings, (as doubtless, they may find enough such : the Bible is confessedly
full of them, from the beginning to the end;) and then
they glory how full the Scripture is on their side, how
many more texts there are that evidently favour their
scheme, than such as seem to favour the contrary. But
let them first make manifest the things in question,
which they suppose and take for granted, and show them
to be consistent with themselves, and produce clear evidence of their truth; and they have gained their point,
as all will confess, without bringing one Scripture. For
none denies, that there are commands, counsels, promises, threatenings, &c. in the Bible. But unless they
do these things, their multiplying such texts of Scripture is insignificant and vain.

It may further be observed, that such Scriptures as
they bring are really against them, and not for them.
As it has been demonstrated, that it is their scheme, and
not ours, that is inconsistent with the use of motives
and persuasives, or any moral means whatsoever, to induce men to the practice of virtue, or abstaining from
wickedness: their principles, and not ours, are repugnant to moral agency, and inconsistent with moral government, with law or precept, with the nature of virtue
or vice, reward or punishment, and with every thing
whatsoever of a moral nature, either on the part of a

moral governor, or in the state, actions, or conduct of the subject.

SECTION XII.

OF A SUPPOSED TENDENCY OF THESE PRINCIPLES TO ATHEISM AND LICENTIOUSNESS.

IF any object against what has been maintained, that it tends to atheism, I know not on what grounds such an objection can be raised, unless it be, that some atheists have held a doctrine of necessity, which they suppose to be like this. But if it be so, I am persuaded the Arminians would not look upon it just, that their notion of freedom and contingence should be charged with a tendency to all the errors that ever any embraced who have held such opinions. The Stoic philosophers, whom the Calvinists are charged with agreeing with, were no atheists, but the greatest theists, and nearest akin to Christians in their opinions concerning the unity and the perfections of the Godhead, of all the heathen philosophers. And Epicurus, that chief father of atheism, maintained no such doctrine of necessity, but was the greatest maintainer of contingence.

The doctrine of necessity, which supposes a necessary connexion of all events, on some antecedent ground and reason of their existence, is the only medium we have to prove the being of God. And the contrary doctrine of contingence, even as maintained by Arminians (which certainly implies or infers that events may come into existence, or begin to be, without dependence on any thing foregoing, as their cause, ground, or reason,) takes away all proof of the being of God; which proof is summarily expressed by the apostle in Rom. i. 20. And this is a tendency to atheism with a witness. So that, indeed, it is the doctrine of Arminians, and not of the Calvinists, that is justly charged with a tendency to atheism; it being built on a foundation that is the utter subversion of every demonstrative argument for the proof of a Deity; as has been shown, Part II. sect. iii.

And whereas it has often been said, that the Calvinistic doctrine of necessity saps the foundations of all religion and virtue, and tends to the greatest licentiousness of practice; this objection is built on the pretence, that our doctrine renders vain all means and endeavours in order to be virtuous and religious. Which pretence has been already particularly considered in the fifth section of this Part; where it has been demonstrated, that this doctrine has no such tendency: but that such a tendency is truly to be charged on the contrary doctrine; inasmuch as the notion of contingence, which their doctrine implies, in its certain consequences, overthrows all connexion, in every degree, between endeavour and event, means and end.

And besides, if many other things, which have been observed to belong to the Arminian doctrine, or to be plain consequences of it, be considered, there will appear just reason to suppose that it is *that* which must rather tend to licentiousness. Their doctrine excuses all evil inclinations, which men find to be natural; because in such inclinations they are not self-determined, as such inclinations are not owing to any choice or determination of their own wills:—which leads men wholly to justify themselves in all their wicked actions, so far as natural inclination has had a hand in determining their wills to the commission of them. Yea, these notions, which suppose moral necessity and inability to be inconsistent with blame or moral obligation, will directly lead men to justify the vilest acts and practices, from the strength of their wicked inclinations of all sorts; strong inclinations inducing a moral necessity; yea, to excuse every degree of evil inclination, so far as this has evidently prevailed, and been the thing which has determined their wills: because, so far as antecedent inclination determined the will, so far the will was without liberty of indifference and self-determination. Which, at last, will come to this, that men will justify themselves in all the wickedness they commit. It has been observed already, that this scheme of things does ex-

ceedingly diminish the guilt of sin, and the difference
between the greatest and smallest offences ;* and if it
be pursued in its real consequences, it leaves room for
no such thing as either virtue or vice, blame or praise, in
the world.† And then, again, how naturally does this
notion of the sovereign self-detemrining power of the
will, in all things, virtuous or vicious, and whatsoever
deserves either reward or punishment, tend to encourage
men to put off the work of religion and virtue, and
turning from sin to God ; it being that which they have
a sovereign power to determine themselves to, just when
they please; or if not, they are wholly excusable in going
on in sin because of their inability to do any other.

  If it should be said, that the tendency of this doctrine
of necessity to licentiousness appears by the improvement
many at this day actually make of it, to justify themselves in their dissolute courses ; I will not deny that
some men do unreasonably abuse this doctrine, as they
do many other things which are true and excellent in
their own nature : but I deny that this proves the doctrine itself has any tendency to licentiousness. I think,
the tendency of doctrines, by what now appears in the
world, and in our nation in particular, may much more
justly be argued from the general effect which has been
seen to attend the prevailing of the principles of Arminians, and the contrary principles; as both have had their
turn of general prevalence in our nation. If it be indeed
as is pretended, that Calvinistic doctrines undermine the
very foundation of all religion and morality, and ener-
vate and disannul all rational motives to holy and virtuous practice ; and that the contrary doctrines give the
inducements to virtue and goodness their proper force,
and exhibit religion in a rational light, tending to recommend it to the reason of mankind, and enforce it in
a manner that is agreeable to their natural notions of
things : I say, if it be thus, it is remarkable that virtue
and religious practice should prevail most, when the for-

* Part III. sect vi.

† Part III. sect. iii. corol. 1. after the first head, sect. vi. and vii. ; Part
IV. sect i,

mer doctrines, so inconsistent with it, prevailed almost
universally : and that ever since the latter doctrines, so
happily agreeing with it, and of so proper and excellent
a tendency to promote it, have been gradually prevailing, vice, profaneness, luxury, and wickedness of all sorts,
and contempt of all religion, and of every kind of serious-
ness and strictness of conversation, should proportion-
ably prevail ; and that these things should thus accom-
pany one another, and rise and prevail one with another,
now for a whole age together.   It is remarkable, that this
happy remedy (discovered by the free inquiries, and
superior sense and wisdom of this age) against the
pernicious effects of Calvinism, so inconsistent with
religion, and tending so much to banish all virtue from
the earth, should, on so long a trial, be attended with no
good effect; but that the consequence should be the
reverse of amendment; that in proportion as the remedy
takes place, and is thoroughly applied, so the disease
should prevail; and the very same dismal effect take
place, to the highest degree, which Calvinistic doctrines
are supposed to have so great a tendency to; even the
banishing of religion and virtue, and the prevailing of
unbounded licentiousness of manners.   If these things
are truly so, they are very remarkable, and matter of
very curious speculation.

SECTION XIII.

CONCERNING THAT OBJECTION AGAINST THE REASONING BY WHICH THE
CALVINISTIC DOCTRINE IS SUPPORTED, THAT IT IS METAPHYSICAL
AND ABSTRUSE.

It has often been objected against the defenders of
Calvinistic principles, that in their reasonings they run
into nice scholastic distinctions, and abstruse metaphysical subtleties, and set these in opposition to common
sense.   And it is possible, that, after the former manner, it may be alleged against the reasoning by which I
have endeavoured to confute the Arminian scheme of liberty and moral agency, that it is very abstracted and meta-

physical. Concerning this, I would observe the following things.

I. If that be made an objection against the foregoing reasoning, that it is metaphysical, or may properly be reduced to the science of metaphysics, it is a very impertinent objection; whether it be so or no, is not worthy of any dispute or controversy. If the reasoning be good, it is as frivolous to inquire what science it is properly reduced to, as what language it is delivered in: and for a man to go about to confute the arguments of his opponent, by telling him his arguments are metaphysical, would be as weak as to tell him, his arguments could not be substantial, because they were written in French or Latin. The question is not, whether what is said be metaphysics, physics, logic, or mathematics, Latin, French, English, or Mohawk? But, whether the reasoning be good, and the arguments truly conclusive? The foregoing arguments are no more metaphysical, than those which we use against the Papists, to disprove their doctrine of transubstantiation; alleging, it is inconsistent with the notion of corporeal identity, that it should be in ten thousand places at the same time. It is by metaphysical arguments only we are able to prove, that the rational soul is not corporeal; that lead or sand cannot think; that thoughts are not square or round, or do not weigh a pound. The arguments by which we prove the being of God, if handled closely and distinctly, so as to show their clear and demonstrative evidence, must be metaphysically treated. It is by metaphysics only, that we can demonstrate that God is not limited to a place, or is not mutable; that he is not ignorant or forgetful; that it is impossible for him to lie, or be unjust; and that there is one God only, and not hundreds or thousands. And, indeeed, we have no strict demonstration of any thing, excepting mathematical truths, but by metaphysics. We can have no proof, that is properly demonstrative, of any one proposition, relating to the being and nature of God, his creation of

the world, the dependence of all things on him, the
nature of bodies or spirits, the nature of our own souls,
or any of the great truths of morality and natural religion, but what is metaphysical. I am willing my arguments should be brought to the test of the strictest and
justest reason, and that a clear, distinct, and determinate
meaning of the terms I use, should be insisted on; but
let not the whole be rejected, as if all were confuted, by
fixing on it the epithet metaphysical.

II. If the reasoning which has been made use of, be
in some sense metaphysical, it will not follow, that
therefore it must needs be abstruse, unintelligible, and
akin to the jargon of the schools. I humbly conceive
the foregoing reasoning, at least as to those things which
are most material belonging to it, depends on no abstruse
definitions or distinctions, or terms without a meaning,
or of very ambiguous and undetermined signification, or
any points of such abstraction and subtlety, as tends to
involve the attentive understanding in clouds and darkness. There is no high degree of refinement and abstruse speculation, in determining that a thing is not before it is, and so cannot be the cause of itself ; or that
the first act of free choice has not another act of free
choice going before that, to excite or direct it ; or in determining, that no choice is made, while the mind remains in a state of absolute indifference ; that preference and equilibrium never co-exist; and that therefore
no choice is made in a state of liberty consisting in indifference : and that so far as the will is determined by
motives, exhibited and operating previous to the act
of the will, so far it is not determined by the act of the
will itself ; that nothing can begin to be, which before
was not, without a cause, or some antecedent ground or
reason, why it then begins to be; that effects depend on
their causes, and are connected with them; that virtue
is not the worse, nor sin the better, for the strength of
inclination with which it is practised, and the difficulty
which thence arises of doing otherwise; that when it is
already infallibly known that the thing will be, it is not

a thing contingent whether it will ever be or no; or that it can be truly said, notwithstanding, that it is not necessary it should be, but it either may be, or may not be. And the like might be observed of many other things which belong to the foregoing reasoning.

If any shall still stand to it, that the foregoing reasoning is nothing but metaphysical sophistry; and that it must be so, that the seeming force of the arguments all depends on some fallacy and wile that is hid in the obscurity which always attends a great degree of metaphysical abstraction and refinement ; and shall be ready to say, " Here is indeed something that tends to confound the mind, but not to satisfy it : for who can ever be truly satisfied in it, that men are fitly blamed or commended, punished or rewarded, for those volitions which are not from themselves, and of whose existence they are not the causes. Men may refine as much as they please, and advance their abstract notions, and make out a thousand seeming contradictions, to puzzle our understandings; yet there can be no satisfaction in such doctrine as this : the natural sense of the mind of man will always resist it."* I humbly conceive that

* A certain noted author of the present age says, the arguments for necessity are nothing but quibbling, or logomachy, using words without a meaning, or begging the question. I do not know what kind of necessity any authors he may have reference to are advocates for, or whether they have managed their arguments well or ill. As to the arguments I have made use of, if they are quibbles, they may be shown so: such knots are capable of being untied, and the trick and cheat may be detected and plainly laid open. If this be fairly done, with respect to the grounds and reasons I have relied upon, I shall have just occasion, for the future, to be silent, if not to be ashamed of my argumentations. I am willing my proofs should be thoroughly examined ; and if there be nothing but begging the question, or mere logomachy, or dispute of words, let it be made manifest, and shown how the seeming strength of the argument depends on my using words without a meaning, or arises from the ambiguity of terms, or my making use of words in an indeterminate and unsteady manner; and that the weight of my reasons rests mainly on such a foundation ; and then I shall either be ready to retract what I have urged, and thank the man that has done the kind part, or shall be justly exposed for my obstinacy.

The same author is abundant in appealing, in this affair, from what he calls logomachy and sophistry, to experience. A person can experience only what passes in his own mind. But yet, as we may well suppose that all men have the same human faculties. so a man may well argue from his own experience to that of others, in things that show the nature of those such an objector, if he has capacity, and humility, and calmness of spirit, sufficient impartially and thoroughly to examine himself, will find that he knows not really what he would be at ; and, indeed, his difficulty is nothing but a mere prejudice, from an inadvertent customary use of words, in a meaning that is not clearly understood, nor carefully reflected upon. Let the objector reflect again, if he has candour and patience enough, and does not scorn to be at the trouble of close attention in the affair. He would have a man's volition be from himself. Let it be from himself, most primarily and originally of any way conceivable ; that is, from his own choice : how will that help the matter, as to his being justly blamed or praised, unless that choice itself be blame or praise-worthy ? And how is the choice itself (an ill choice, for instance,) blame-worthy, according to these principles, unless that be from himself too, in the same manner ; that is, from his own choice ? But the original and first-determining choice in the affair is not from his choice : his choice is not the cause of it. And if it be from himself some other way, and not from his

faculties, and the manner of their operation. But then one has as good right to allege his experience as another. As to my own experience, I find that in innumerable things I can do as I will; that the motions of my body, in many respects, instantaneously follow the acts of my will concerning those motions; and that my will has some command of my thoughts; and that the acts of my will are my own, *i. e.* that they are acts of my will, the volitions of my own mind : or, in other words, that what I will, I will. Which I presume is the sum of what others experience in this affair. But as to finding by experience that my will is originally determined by itself; or that, my will first choosing what volition there shall be, the chosen volition accordingly follows, and that this is the first rise of the determination of my will in any affair, or that any volition rises in my mind contingently ; I declare I know nothing in myself by experience of this nature; and nothing that ever I experienced carries the least appearance or shadow of any such thing, or gives me any more reason to suppose or suspect any such thing, than to suppose that my volitions existed twenty years before they existed. It is true, I find myself possessed of my volitions before I can see the effectual power of any cause to produce them, (for the power and efficacy of the cause is not seen but by the effect) ; and this, for aught I know, may make some imagine that volition has no cause, or that it produces itself. But I have no more reason from hence to determine any such thing, than I have to determine that I gave myself my own being, or that I came into being accidentally without a cause, because I first found myself possessed of being, before I had knowledge of a cause of my being.

choice, surely that will not help the matter. If it be not from himself of choice, then it is not from himself voluntarily ; and if so, he is surely no more to blame, than if it were not from himself at all. It is a vanity to pretend it is a sufficient answer to this to say, that it is nothing but metaphysical refinement and subtlety, and so attended with obscurity and uncertainty.

If it be the natural sense of our minds, that what is blameworthy in a man must be from himself, then it doubtless is also, that it must be from something bad in himself, a bad choice, or bad disposition. But then our natural sense is, that this bad choice or disposition is evil in itself, and the man blameworthy for it, on its own account, without taking into our notion of its blame-worthiness another bad choice, or disposition going before this, from whence this arises : for that is a ridiculous absurdity, running us into an immediate contradiction, which our natural sense of blameworthiness has nothing to do with, and never comes into the mind, nor is sup-posed in the judgment we naturally make of the affair. As was demonstrated before, natural sense does not place the moral evil of volitions and dispositions in the cause of them, but the nature of them. An evil thing's be-ing *from* a man, or from something antecedent in him, is not essential to the original notion we have of blame-worthiness : but it is its being the choice of the heart: as appears by this, that if a thing be from us, and not from our choice, it has not the nature of blameworthiness or ill-desert, according to our natural sense. When a thing is from a man, in that sense, that it is from his will or choice, he is to blame for it, because his will is *in it :* so far as the will is in it, blame is in it, and no further. Neither do we go any further in our notion of blame, to inquire whether the bad will be from a bad will : there is no consideration of the original of that bad will : because, according to our natural apprehen-sion, blame originally consists in it. Therefore a thing's being from a man is a secondary consideration in the notion of blame or ill-desert. Because those things, in

iu our external actions, are most properly said to be from
us, which are from our choice ; and no other external
actions, but those that are from us in this sense, have
the nature of blame ; and they, indeed, not so properly
because they are from us, as because we are in them,
i. e. our wills are in them ; not so much because they
are from some property of ours, as because they are our
properties.

However, all these external actions being truly from
us, as their cause, and we being so used, in ordinary
speech, and in the common affairs of life, to speak of
men's actions and conduct that we see, and that affect human society, as deserving ill or well, as worthy of blame or
praise ; hence it is come to pass, that philosophers have
incautiously taken all their measures of good and evil,
praise and blame, from the dictates of common sense,
about these overt acts of men ; to the running of every
thing into the most lamentable and dreadful confusion.

And therefore I observe :

III. It is so far from being true (whatever may be
pretended) that the proof of the doctrine which has been
maintained depends on certain abstruse, unintelligible,
metaphysical terms and notions, that the Arminian
scheme, without needing such clouds and darkness for
its defence, is supported by the plain dictates of common
sense, that the very reverse is most certainly true, and
that to a great degree. It is fact that they, and not we
have confounded things with metaphysical, unintelligible
notions and phrases, and have drawn them from the
light of plain truth into the gross darkness of abstruse
metaphysical propositions, and words without a meaning. Their pretended demonstrations depend very much
on such unintelligible metaphysical phrases, as self-determination and sovereignty of the will; and the metaphysical sense they put on such terms as necessity,
contingency, action, agency, &c. quite diverse from their
meaning as used in common speech; and which, as they use
them, are without any consistent meaning, or any manner of distinct consistent ideas; as far from it as any of

the abstruse terms and perplexed phrases of the peripatetic philosophers, or the most unintelligible jargon of the schools, or the cant of the wildest fanatics. Yea, we may be bold to say, these metaphysical terms, on which they build so much, are what they use without knowing what they mean themselves; they are pure metaphysical sounds, without any ideas whatsoever in their minds to answer them; inasmuch as it has been demonstrated, that there cannot be any notion in the mind consistent with these expressions, as they pretend to explain them, because their explanations destroy themselves. No such notions as imply self-contradiction and self-abolition, and this a great many ways, can subsist in the mind; as there can be no idea of a whole which is less than any of its parts, or of solid extension without dimensions, or of an effect which is before its cause. Arminians improve these terms as terms of art, and in their metaphysical meaning, to advance and establish those things which are contrary to common sense, in a high degree. Thus, instead of the plain, vulgar notion of liberty, which all mankind, in every part of the face of the earth, and in all ages, have, consisting in opportunity to do as one pleases, they have introduced a new, strange liberty, consisting in indifference, contingence, and self-determination, by which they involve themselves and others in great obscurity and manifold gross inconsistence. So, instead of placing virtue and vice, as common sense places them very much, in fixed bias and inclination, and greater virtue and vice in stronger and more established inclination; these, through their refinings and abstruse notions, suppose a liberty consisting in indifference, to be essential to all virtue and vice. So they have reasoned themselves, not by metaphysical distinctions, but metaphysical confusion, into many principles about moral agency, blame, praise, reward and punishment, which are, as has been shown, exceeding contrary to the common sense of mankind, and perhaps to their own sense, which governs them in common life.

x

CONCLUSION.

WHETHER the things which have been alleged are liable to any tolerable answer, in the ways of calm, intelligible, and strict reasoning, I must leave others to judge; but I am sensible they are liable to one sort of answer. It is not unlikely, that some, who value themselves on the supposed rational and generous principles of the modern fashionable divinity, will have their indignation and disdain raised at the sight of this discourse, and on perceiving what things are pretended to be proved in it. And if they think it worthy of being read, or of so much notice as to say much about it, they may probably renew the usual exclamations, with additional vehemence and contempt, about the fate of the heathen, Hobbes's necessity, and making men mere machines; accumulating the terrible epithets of fatal, unfrustrable, inevitable, irresistible, &c., and it may be, with the addition of horrid and blasphemous; and perhaps much skill may be used to set forth things, which have been said, in colours which shall be shocking to the imaginations, and moving to the passions, of those who have either too little capacity, or too much confidence of the opinions they have imbibed, and contempt of the contrary, to try the matter by any serious and circumspect examination.* Or, difficulties may be started and insist-

---

* A writer of the present age, whom I have several times had occasion to mention, speaks once and again of those who hold the doctrine of necessity, as scarcely worthy of the name of philosophers. I do not know whether he has respect to any particular notion of necessity, that some may have main-

ed on, which do not belong to the controversy; because let them be more or less real, and hard to be resolved, they are not what are owing to any thing distinguishing of this scheme from that of the Arminians, and would not be removed nor diminished by renouncing the former, and adhering to the latter. Or, some particular things may be picked out, which they may think will sound harshest in the ears of the generality; and these may be glossed and descanted on, with tart and contemptuous words; and from thence, the whole treated with triumph and insult.

It is easy to see how the decision of most of the points in controversy between Calvinists and Arminians depends on the determination of this grand article concerning the freedom of the will requisite to moral agency; and that by clearing and establishing the Calvinistic doctrine in this point, the chief arguments are obviated by which Arminian doctrines in general are supported, and the contrary doctrines demonstratively confirmed. Hereby it becomes manifest, that God's moral government over mankind, his treating them as moral agents, making them the objects of his commands, counsels, calls, warnings, expostulations, promises, threatenings, rewards, and punishments, is not inconsistent with a determining disposal of all events, of every kind, throughout the universe, in his providence, either by positive efficiency or permission. Indeed, such a universal determining providence infers some kind of necessity of all events, such a necessity as implies an infallible previous fixedness of the futurity of the event; but no other ne-

tained; and, if so, what doctrine of necessity it is that he means. Whether I am worthy of the name of a philosopher, or not, would be a question little to the present purpose. If any, and ever so many, should deny it, I should not think it worth the while to enter into a dispute on that question: though, at the same time, I might expect some better answer should be given to the arguments brought for the truth of the doctrine I maintain; and I might further reasonably desire, that it might be considered, whether it does not become those who are truly worthy of the name of philosophers, to be sensible that there is a difference between argument and contempt; yea, and a difference between the contemptibleness of the person that argues, and the inconclusiveness of the arguments he offers.

cessity of moral events, or volitions of intelligent agents, is needful in order to this, than moral necessity; which does as much ascertain the futurity of the event as any other necessity. But, as has been demonstrated, such a necessity is not at all repugnant to moral agency, and a reasonable use of commands, calls, rewards, punishments, &c. Yea, not only are objections of this kind against the doctrine of a universal determining Providence removed by what has been said, but the truth of such a doctrine is demonstrated. As it has been demonstrated, that the futurity of all future events is established by previous necessity, either natural or moral, so it is manifest, that the sovereign Creator and Disposer of the world has ordered this necessity, by ordering his own conduct, either in designedly acting, or forbearing to act. For, as the being of the world is from God, so the circumstances in which it had its being at first, both negative and positive, must be ordered by him, in one of these ways; and all the necessary consequences of these circumstances must be ordered by him. And God's active and positive interpositions, after the world was created, and the consequences of these interpositions, also every instance of his forbearing to interpose, and the sure consequences of this forbearance, must all be determined according to his pleasure. And therefore every event, which is the consequence of any thing whatsoever, or that is connected with any foregoing thing or circumstance, either positive or negative, as the ground or reason of its existence, must be ordered of God, either by a designing efficiency and interposition, or a designed forbearing to operate or interpose. But, as has been proved, all events whatsoever are necessarily connected with something foregoing, either positive or negative, which is the ground of its existence. It follows, therefore, that the whole series of events is thus connected with something in the state of things, either positive or negative, which is *original* in the series, *i. e.* something which is connected with nothing preceding that, but God's own immediate conduct, either his acting or forbearing to act. From whence it follows, that as God designedly orders his own conduct, and its connected consequences, it must necessarily be, that he designedly orders all things.

The things which have been said, obviate some of the chief objections of Arminians against the Calvinistic doctrine of the total depravity and corruption of man's nature, whereby his heart is wholly under the power of sin, and he is utterly unable, without the interposition of sovereign grace, savingly to love God, believe in Christ, or do any thing that is truly good and acceptable in God's sight. For the main objection against this doctrine is, that it is inconsistent with the freedom of man's will, consisting in indifference and self-determining power; because it supposes man to be under a necessity of sinning, and that God requires things of him, in order to his avoiding eternal damnation, which he is unable to do; and that this doctrine is wholly inconsistent with the sincerity of counsels, invitations, &c. Now, this doctrine supposes no other necessity of sinning, than a moral necessity, which, as has been shown, does not at all excuse sin, and supposes no other inability to obey any command, or perform any duty, even the most spiritual and exalted, but a moral inability, which, as has been proved, does not excuse persons in the nonperformance of any good thing, or make them not to be the proper objects of commands, counsels, and invitations. And, moreover, it has been shown, that there is not, and never can be, either in existence, or so much as in idea, any such freedom of will, consisting in indifference and self-determination, for the sake of which, this doctrine of original sin is cast out; and that no such freedom is necessary, in order to the nature of sin, and a just desert of punishment.

The things which have been observed do also take off the main objections of Arminians against the doctrine of efficacious grace, and, at the same time, prove the grace of God in a sinner's conversion (if there be any grace or

Divine influence in the affair, to be efficacious, yea, and irresistible too; if by irresistible is meant, that which is attended with a moral necessity, which it is impossible should ever be violated by any resistance. The main objection of Arminians against this doctrine is, that it is inconsistent with their self-determining freedom of will, and that it is repugnant to the nature of virtue, that it should be wrought in the heart by the determining efficacy and power of another, instead of its being owing to a self-moving power; that, in that case, the good which is wrought, would not be *our* virtue, but rather *God's* virtue; because it is not the person in whom it is wrought, that is the determining author of it, but God that wrought it in him. But the things which are the foundation of these objections have been considered; and it has been demonstrated, that the liberty of moral agents does not consist in self-determining power, and that there is no need of any such liberty, in order to the nature of virtue; nor does it at all hinder, but that the state or act of the will may be the virtue of the subject, though it be not from self-determination, but the determination of an intrinsic cause, even so as to cause the event to be morally necessary to the subject of it. And as it has been proved, that nothing in the state or acts of the will of man is contingent, but that, on the contrary, every event of this kind is necessary by a moral necessity, and has also been now demonstrated, that the doctrine of a universal determining Providence follows from that doctrine of necessity which was proved before; and so, that God does decisively, in his providence, order all the volitions of moral agents, either by positive influence or permission; and it being allowed, on all hands, that what God does in the affair of man's virtuous volitions, whether it be more or less, is by some positive influence, and not by mere permission, as in the affair of a sinful volition: if we put these things together, it will follow, that God's assistance or influence must be determining and decisive, or must be attended with a moral necessity of the event; and so that God gives virtue, holiness, and conversion to sinners, by an influence which determines the effect, in such a manner, that the effect will infallibly follow by a moral necessity, which is what Calvinists mean by efficacious and irresistible grace.

The things which have been said do likewise answer the chief objections against the doctrine of God's universal and absolute decree, and afford infallible proof of this doctrine, and of the doctrine of absolute, eternal, personal election, in particular. The main objections against these doctrines are, that they infer a necessity of the volitions of moral agents, and of the future moral state and acts of men, and so are not consistent with those eternal rewards and punishments, which are connected with conversion and impenitence, nor can be made to agree with the reasonableness and sincerity of the precepts, calls, counsels, warnings, and expostulations of the word of God, or with the various methods and means of grace which God uses with sinners to bring them to repentance, and the whole of that moral government which God exercises towards mankind: and that they infer an inconsistence between the secret and revealed will of God, and make God the author of sin. But all these things have been obviated in the preceding discourse. And the certain truth of these doctrines concerning God's eternal purposes, will follow from what was just now observed concerning God's universal providence; how it infallibly follows from what has been proved, that God orders all events, and the volitions of moral agents amongst others, by such a decisive disposal, that the events are infallibly connected with his disposal. For if God disposes all events, so that the infallible existence of the events is decided by his providence, then he, doubtless, thus orders and decides things knowingly, and on design. God does not do what he does, nor order what he orders, accidentally and unawares, either without or beside his intention. And if there be a foregoing design of doing and ordering as he does, this is the same with a purpose or decree. And as

it has been shown that nothing is new to God, in any
respect, but all things are perfectly and equally in his
view from eternity, hence it will follow, that his designs
or purposes are not things formed anew, founded on any
new views or appearances, but are all eternal purposes.
And as it has been now shown how the doctrine of determining efficacious grace certainly follows from things
proved in the foregoing discourse, hence will necessarily
follow the doctrine of particular, eternal, absolute election.   For if men are made true saints no otherwise
than as God makes them so, and distinguishes them from
others, by an efficacious power and influence of his, that
decides and fixes the event; and God thus makes some
saints, and not others, on design and purpose, and (as
has been now observed) no designs of God are new; it
follows, that God thus distinguished from others, all that
ever become true saints, by his eternal design or decree.
I might also show how God's certain foreknowledge
must suppose an absolute decree, and how such a decree
can be proved to be a demonstration from it; but that
this discourse may not be lengthened out too much, that
must be omitted for the present.

   From these things it will inevitably follow, that however Christ in some sense may be said to die for all, and
to redeem all visible Christians, yea, the whole world,
by his death; yet there must be something particular in
the design of his death, with respect to such as he intended should actually be saved thereby.   As appears
by what has been now shown, God has the actual salvation or redemption of a certain number in his proper absolute design, and of a certain number only; and therefore such a design only can be prosecuted in anything
God does, in order to the salvation of men.   God pursues a proper design of the salvation of the elect in giving Christ to die, and prosecutes such a design with respect to no other, most strictly speaking; for it is impossible that God should prosecute any other design
than only such as he has; he certainly does not, in the
highest propriety and strictness of speech, pursue a de-

sign that he has not. And, indeed, such a particularity and limitation of redemption will as infallibly follow, from the doctrine of God's foreknowledge, as from that of the decree. For it is as impossible, in strictness of speech, that God should prosecute a design, or aim at a thing, which he at the same time most perfectly knows will not be accomplished, as that he should use endeavours for that which is beside his decree.

By the things which have been proved, are obviated some of the main objections against the doctrine of the infallible and necessary perseverance of saints, and some of the main foundations of this doctrine are established. The main prejudices of Arminians against this doctrine seem to be these: they suppose such a necessary, infallible perseverance, to be repugnant to the freedom of the will; that it must be owing to man's own self-determining power, that he first becomes virtuous and holy; and so, in like manner, it must be left a thing contingent, to be determined by the same freedom of will, whether he will persevere in virtue and holiness; and that otherwise his continuing steadfast in faith and obedience would not be his virtue, or at all praiseworthy and rewardable; nor could his perseverance be properly the matter of Divine commands, counsels, and promises, nor his apostacy be properly threatened, and men warned against it. Whereas, we find all these things in Scripture: there we find steadfastness and perseverance in true Christianity represented as the virtue of the saints, spoken of as praiseworthy in them, and glorious rewards promised to it; and also find, that God makes it the subject of his commands, counsels, and promises; and the contrary, of threatenings and warnings. But the foundation of these objections has been removed, in its being shown that moral necessity and infallible certainty of events is not inconsistent with these things; and that as to freedom of will lying in the power of the will to determine itself, there neither is any such thing, nor any need of it, in order to virtue, reward, commands, counsels, &c.

And as the doctrines of efficacious grace and absolute election do certainly follow from things which have been proved in the preceding discourse; so some of the main foundations of the doctrine of perseverance are thereby established. If the beginning of true faith and holiness, and a man's becoming a true saint at first, does not depend on the self-determining power of will, but on the determining efficacious grace of God; it may well be argued, that it is also with respect to men's being continued saints, or persevering in faith and holiness. The conversion of a sinner being not owing to a man's self-determination, but to God's determination, and eternal election, which is absolute, and depending on the sovereign will of God, and not on the free will of man, as is evident from what has been said; and it being very evident, from the Scriptures, that the eternal election which there is of saints to faith and holiness, is also an election of them to eternal salvation: hence their appointment to salvation must also be absolute, and not depending on their contingent, self-determining will. From all which it follows, that it is absolutely fixed in God's decree, that all true saints shall persevere to actual eternal salvation.

But I must leave all these things to the consideration of the fair and impartial reader ; and when he has maturely weighed them, I would propose it to his consideration, whether many of the first reformers, and others that succeeded them, whom God in their day made the chief pillars of his church, and greatest instruments of their deliverance from error and darkness, and of the support of the cause of piety among them, have not been injured, in the contempt with which they have been treated by many late writers, for their teachng and maintaining such doctrines as are commonly called *Calvinistic.* Indeed, some of these new writers, at the same time that they have represented the doctrines of these ancient and eminent divines as in the highest degree ridiculous, and contrary to common sense, in an ostentation of a very generous charity, have al-

lowed that they were honest, well-meaning men: yea,
it may be, some of them, as though it were in great
condescension and compassion to them, have allowed,
that they did pretty well for the day which they lived
in, and considering the great disadvantages they laboured
under: when, at the same time, their manner of speaking has naturally and plainly suggested to the minds of
their readers, that they were persons, who through the
lowness of their genius, and greatness of the bigotry
with which their minds were shackled and thoughts
confined, living in the gloomy caves of superstition,
fondly embraced, and demurely and zealously taught,
the most absurd, silly, and monstrous opinions, worthy
of the greatest contempt of gentlemen possessed of that
noble and generous freedom of thought which happily
prevails in this age of light and inquiry,—when, indeed,
such is the case, that we might, if so disposed, speak as
big words as they, and on far better grounds. And
really, all the Arminians on earth might be challenged,
without arrogance or vanity, to make these principles
of theirs, wherein they mainly differ from their fathers,
whom they so much despise, consistent with common
sense: yea, and perhaps to produce any doctrine ever
embraced by the blindest bigot of the Church of Rome,
or the most ignorant Mussulman, or extravagant en-
thusiast, that might be reduced to more demonstrable
inconsistencies, and repugnances to common sense and
to themselves; though their inconsistencies indeed may
not lie so deep, or be so artfully veiled by a deceitful
ambiguity of words, and an indeterminate signification
of phrases. I will not deny, that these gentlemen, many
of them, are men of great abilities, and have been helped
to higher attainments in philosophy than those ancient
divines, and have done great service to the church of
God in some respects: but I humbly conceive, that their
differing from their fathers, with such magisterial assurance, in these points in divinity, must be owing to
some other cause than superior wisdom.

It may also be worthy of consideration, whether the

great alteration which has been made in the state of
things in our nation, and some other parts of the Pro-
testant world, in this and the past age, by the exploding
so generally Calvinistic doctrines, that is so often spoken
of as worthy to be greatly rejoiced in by the friends of
truth, learning, and virtue, as an instance of the great
increase of light in the Christian church; I say, it may
be worthy to be considered, whether this be indeed a
happy change, owing to any such cause as an increase
of true knowledge and understanding in things of religion; or whether there is not reason to fear, that it may
be owing to some worse cause.

And I desire it may be considered, whether the boldness of some writers may not be worthy to be reflected
on, who have not scrupled to say, that if these and
those things are true (which yet appear to be the demonstrable dictates of reason, as well as the certain dictates of the mouth of the Most High), then God is unjust and cruel, and guilty of manifest deceit and double
dealing, and the like. Yea, some have gone so far, as
confidently to assert, that if any book which pretends
to be Scripture, teaches such doctrines, that alone is
sufficient warrant for mankind to reject it, as what cannot be the word of God. Some, who have not gone so
far, have said, that if the Scripture seems to teach any
such doctrines, so contrary to reason, we are obliged to
find out some other interpretation of those texts where
such doctrines seem to be exhibited. Others express
themselves yet more modestly : they express a tenderness and religious fear, lest they should receive and
teach any thing that should seem to reflect on
God's moral character, or be a disparagement to his
methods of administration, in his moral government;
and therefore express themselves as not daring to embrace some doctrines, though they seem to be delivered
in Scripture, according to the more obvious and natural
construction of the words. But indeed it would show
a truer modesty and humility, if they would more en-

tirely rely on God's wisdom and discerning, who knows infinitely better than we what is agreeable to his own perfections, and never intended to leave these matters to the decision of the wisdom and discerning of men : but by his own unerring instruction, to determine for us what the truth is, knowing how little our judgment is to be depended on, and how extremely prone vain and blind men are to err in such matters.

The truth of the case is, that if the Scripture plainly taught the opposite doctrines to those that are so much stumbled at, viz. the Arminian doctrine of free-will, and others depending thereon, it would be the greatest of all difficulties that attend the Scriptures, incomparably greater than its containing any, even the most mysterious of those doctrines of the first reformers, which our late free-thinkers have so superciliously exploded.—Indeed, it is a glorious argument of the divinity of the holy Scriptures, that they teach such doctrines, which in one age and another, through the blindness of men's minds, and strong prejudices of their hearts, are rejected as most absurd and unreasonable by the wise and great men of the world; which yet, when they are most carefully and strictly examined, appear to be exactly agreeable to the most demonstrable, certain, and natural dictates of reason. By such things it appears, that the *foolishness of God is wiser than men;* and God does, as is said in 1 Cor. i. 19, 20 : " For it is written, I will destroy the wisdom of the wise, and will bring to nothing the understanding of the prudent. Where is the wise? where is the scribe? where is the disputer of this world? hath not God made foolish the wisdom of this world?" And as it is used to be in time past, so it is probable it will be in time to come, as it is there written, in ver. 27—29. " But God hath chosen the foolish things of the world, to confound the wise; and God hath chosen the weak things of the world, to confound the things that are mighty; and base things of the world, and things which are despised, hath God chosen, yea, and things which are not, to bring to nought things that are; that no flesh should glory in his presence." Amen.

REMARKS

ON

LORD KAMES' ESSAYS ON THE PRINCIPLES OF MORALITY AND NATURAL RELIGION:

IN A LETTER TO A MINISTER OF THE CHURCH OF SCOTLAND.

BY THE

REV. MR JONATHAN EDWARDS.

REV. SIR,

The intimations you have given me of the use which has, by some, been made of what I have written on the " Freedom of the Will," &c. to vindicate what is said on the subject of liberty and necessity by the author of the Essays on the principles of Morality and Natural Religion, has occasioned my reading this author's essay on that subject with particular care and attention. And I think it must be evident to every one that has read both his Essay and my Inquiry, that our schemes are exceeding reverse from each other. The wide difference appears particularly in the following things.

This author supposes, that such a necessity takes place with respect to all men's actions, as is inconsistent with liberty, and plainly denies that men have any liberty in acting. Thus, in p. 168, after he had been speaking of the necessity of our determinations, as connected with motives, he concludes with saying, " In short, if motives are not under our power or direction, which is confessedly the fact, we can at bottom have NO LIBERTY." Whereas I have abundantly expressed it as my mind, that man, in his moral actions, has true liberty ; and that the moral necessity, which universally takes place, is not in the least inconsistent with anything that is properly called liberty, and with the utmost liberty that can be desired, or that can possibly exist or be conceived of.

I find that some are apt to think, that in that kind of moral necessity of men's volitions, which I suppose to be universal, at least some degree of liberty is denied ; that though it be true I allow a sort of liberty, yet those who maintain a self-determining power in the will, and a liberty of contingence and indifference, hold a higher sort of freedom than I do : but I think this is certainly a great mistake.

Liberty, as I have explained it, in various places, is the power, opportunity, or advantage, that any one has to do as he pleases, or conducting in any respect, according to his pleasure; without considering how his pleasure comes to be as it is. It is demonstrable, and I think has been demonstrated, that no necessity of men's volitions that I maintain is inconsistent with this liberty: and I think it is impossible for any one to rise higher in his conceptions of liberty than this. If any imagine they desire higher, and that they conceive of a higher and greater liberty than this, they are deceived, and delude themselves with confused and ambiguous words instead of ideas. If any one should here say, "Yes, I conceive of freedom above and beyond the liberty a man has of conducting in any respect as he pleases, viz. a liberty of *choosing* as he pleases :" Such a one, if he reflected, would either blush or laugh at his own instance. For, is not choosing as he pleases, conductting, IN SOME RESPECT, according to his pleasure, and still without determining how he came by that pleasure? If he says, " Yes, I came by that pleasure by my own choice." If he be a man of common sense, by this time he will see his own absurdity: for he must needs see that his notion or conception, even of this liberty, does not contain any judgment or conception how he comes by that choice which first determines his pleasure, or which originally fixed his own will respecting the affair. Or if any shall say, " That a man exercises liberty in this, even in determining his own choice, but not as he pleases, or not in consequence of any choice, preference, or inclination of his own, but by a determination arising contingently ont of a state of absolute indifference;" this is not rising higher in his conception of liberty; as such a determination of the will would not be a voluntary determination of it. Surely, he that places liberty in a power of doing something not according to his own choice or from his choice, has not a higher notion of it, than he that places it in doing as he pleases, or acting from his own election. If there were a power in the mind to determine itself, but not by its choice or according to its pleasure, what advantage would it give ; and what liberty worth contending for would be exercised in it? Therefore, no Arminian, Pelagian, or Epicurean, can rise higher in his conceptions of liberty than the notion of it which I have explained : which notion is, apparently, perfectly consistent with the whole of that necessity of men's actions which I suppose takes place. And I scruple not to say, it is beyond all their wits to invent a higher notion, or form a higher imagination of liberty : let them talk of sovereignty of the will, self-determining power, self-motion, self-direction, arbitrary decision, liberty *ad utrumvis*, power of choosing differently in given cases, &c. as long as they will. It is apparent that these men, in their strenuous affirmation, and dispute about these things, aim at they know not what, fighting for something they have no conception of, substituting a number of confused, unmeaning words instead of things and instead of thoughts. They may be challenged clearly to explain what they would have : they never can answer the challenge.

The author of the Essays, through his whole essay on liberty and necessity, goes on that supposition, that in order to the being of real liberty, a man must have a freedom that is opposed to moral necessity: and yet he supposes p. 175, that "such a liberty must signify a power in the mind of acting without and against motives, a power of acting without any view, purpose, or design, and even of acting in contradiction to our own desires and aversions, and to all our principles of action, and is an absurdity altogether inconsistent with a rational nature." Now, who ever imagined such a liberty as this, a higher sort or degree of freedom, than a liberty of following one's own views and purposes, and acting agreeable to his own inclinations and passions? Who will ever reasonably suppose that liberty, which is an absurdity altogether inconsistent with a rational nature, to be a kind of liberty above that which is consistent with the nature of a rational, intelligent, designing agent?

The author of the Essays seems to suppose such a necessity to take place as is inconsistent with some supposable POWER OF ARBITRARY CHOICE; or that there is some liberty conceivable, whereby men's own actions might be more PROPERLY IN THEIR POWER, and by which events might be more DEPENDENT ON OURSELVES; contrary to what I suppose to be evident, in my Inquiry. What way can be imagined, of our actions being more in our power, from ourselves, or dependent on ourselves, than their being from our power to fulfil our own choice, to act from our own inclination, pursue our own views, and execute our own designs? Certainly, to be able to act thus, is as properly having our actions in our power, and dependent on ourselves, as a being liable to be the subjects of acts and events, contingently and fortuitously, without desire, view, purpose, or design, or any principle of action, within ourselves; as we must be, according to this author's own declared sense, if our actions are performed with that liberty that is opposed to moral necessity.

This author seems everywhere to suppose, that necessity, most properly so called, attends all men's actions; and that the terms *necessary, unavoidable, impossible,* &c. are equally applicable to the case of moral and natural necessity. In p. 173, he says, "The idea of *necessary* and *unavoidable* equally agrees, both to moral and physical necessity." And in p. 184, " All things that fall out in the natural and moral world are alike necessary." P. 174, " This inclination and choice is unavoidably caused or occasioned by the prevailing motive. In this lies the necessity of our actions, that, in such circumstances, it was *impossible* we *could* act otherwise." He often expresses himself in like manner elsewhere, speaking in strong terms of men's actions as unavoidable, what they cannot forbear, having no power over their own actions, the order of them being unalterably fixed, and inseparably linked together, &c.

On the contrary, I have largely declared, that the connexion between antecedent things and consequent ones, which takes place with regard to the acts of men's wills, which is called moral necessity, is called by the name of necessity improperly; and that all such terms as *must, cannot, impossible, unable, irresistible, unavoidable, invincible, &c.*, when applied here, are not applied in their proper signification, and are either used nonsensically, and with perfect insignificance, or in a sense quite diverse from their original and proper meaning, and their use in common speech: and that such a necessity as attends the acts of men's wills, is more properly called *certainty* than *necessity;* it being no other than the certain connexion between the subject and predicate of the proposition which affirms their existence.

Agreeable to what is observed in my Inquiry, I think it is evidently owing to a strong prejudice in persons' minds, arising from an insensible habitual perversion and misapplication of such-like terms as *necessary, impossible, unable, unavoidable, invincible,* &c., that they are ready to think, that to suppose a certain connexion of men's volitions, without any foregoing motives or inclinations, or any preceding moral influence whatsoever, is truly and properly to suppose such a strong irrefragable chain of causes and effects, as stands in the way of, and makes utterly vain, opposite desires and endeavours, like immoveable and impenetrable mountains of brass ; and impedes our liberty like walls of adamant, gates of brass, and bars of iron: whereas, all such representations suggest ideas as far from the truth as the east is from the west. Nothing that I maintain, supposes that men are at all hindered by any fatal necessity, from doing, and even willing and choosing, as they please, with full freedom ; yea, with the highest degree of liberty that ever was thought of, or that ever could possibly enter into the heart of any man to conceive. I know it is in vain to endeavour to make some persons believe this, or at least fully and steadily to believe it; for if it be demonstrated to them, still the old prejudice remains which has been fixed by the use of the terms *necessary, must, cannot, impossible,* &c.; the association with these terms of certain ideas inconsistent with liberty, is not broken, and the judgment is powerfully warped by it, as a thing that has been long bent and grown stiff, if it be straightened, will return to its former curvity again and again.

The author of the Essays most manifestly supposes, that if men had the truth concerning the real necessity of all their actions clearly in view, they would not appear to themselves, or one another, as at all praiseworthy or culpable, or under any moral obligation, or accountable for their actions: which supposes that men are not to be blamed or praised for any of their actions, and are not under any obligations, nor are truly accountable for any thing they do, by reason of this necessity; which is very contrary to what I have endeavoured to prove throughout the third part of my Inquiry. I humbly conceive it is there shown, that this is so far from the truth, that the moral necessity of men's actions, which truly take place, is requisite to the being of virtue and vice, or any thing praiseworthy or culpable,—that the liberty of indifference and contingence, which is advanced in opposition to that necessity, is inconsistent with the being of these; as it would suppose that men are not determined in what they do by any virtuous or vicious principles, nor act from any motives, intentions, or aims whatsoever; or have any end, either good or bad, in acting. And is it not remarkable, that this author should suppose, that, in order to men's actions truly having any desert, they must be performed without any view, purpose, design, or desire, or any principle of action, or any thing agreeable to a rational nature? As it will appear that he does, if we compare pp. 206 and 207 with p. 175.

The author of the Essays supposes, that God has deeply implanted in man's nature a strong and invincible apprehension, or feeling, as he calls it, of a liberty, and contingence of his own actions, opposite to that necessity which truly attends them; and which in truth does not agree with real fact, is not agreeable to strict philosophic truth, is contradictory to the truth of things, and which truth contradicts, not tallying with the real plan: and that, therefore, such feelings are deceitful, are in reality of the delusive kind. He speaks of them as a wise delusion, as nice artificial feelings, merely that conscience may have a commanding power: meaning plainly, that these feelings are a cunning artifice of the Author of nature, to make men believe they are free, when they are not. He supposes that, by these feelings, the moral world has a disguised appearance. And other things of this kind he says. He supposes, that all self-approbation, and all remorse of conscience, all commendation or condemnation of ourselves or others, all sense of desert, and all that is connected with this way of thinking, all the ideas which at present are suggested by the words *ought, should,* arise from this delusion, and would entirely vanish without it.

All which is very contrary to what I have abundantly insisted on and endeavoured to demonstrate in my Inquiry; where I have largely shown, that it is agreeable to the natural sense of mankind, that the moral necessity or certainty that attends men's actions is consistent with praise and blame, reward and punishment;* and that it is agreeable to our natural notions, that moral evil, with its desert of dislike and abhorrence, and all

* Inquiry, Part IV. sect. iv. throughout.

its other ill deservings, consists in a certain deformity in the nature of the dispositions and acts of the heart, and not in the evil of something else, diverse from these, supposed to be their cause or occasion.*

I might well ask here, whether any one is to be found in the world of mankind, who is conscious to a sense or feeling, naturally and deeply rooted in his mind, that in order to a man's performing any action that is praise or blame-worthy, he must exercise a liberty that implies and signifies a power of acting without any motive, view, design, desire, or principle of action? For such a liberty, this author supposes, that must be which is opposed to moral necessity, as I have already observed once and again. Supposing a man should actually do good, independent of desire, aim, inducement, principle, or end; is it a dictate of invincible natural sense, that his act is more meritorious or praiseworthy, than if he had performed it for some good end, and had been governed in it by good principles and motives? and so I might ask, on the contrary, with respect to evil actions.†

The authorh of the Essays supposes that the liberty without necessity, which we have a natural feeling of, implies contingence: and, speaking of this contingence, he sometimes calls it by the name of *chance*. And it is evident, that his notion of it, or rather what he says about it, implies things happening loosely, fortuitously, by accident, and without a cause. Now, I conceive the slightest reflection may be sufficient to satisfy any one, that such a contingence of men's actions, according to our natural sense, is so far from being essential to the morality or merit of those actions, that it would destroy it; and that, on the contrary, the dependence of our actions on such causes, as inward inclinations, incitements, and ends, is essential to the being of it. Natural sense teaches men, when they see anything done by others of a good or evil tendency, to inquire what their intention

* Inquiry, Part IV. sect. i. throughout.
‡ See this matter illustrated in my Inquiry, Part IV. sect. iv.

was; what principles and views they were moved by, in order to judge how far they are to be justified or condemned; and not to determine, that, in order to their being approved or blamed at all, the action must be performed altogether fortuitously, proceeding from nothing, arising from no cause. Concerning this matter, I have fully expressed my mind in the Inquiry.

If the liberty, which we have a natural sense of as necessary to desert, consists in the mind's self-determination, without being determined by previous inclination or motive, then indifference is essential to it, yea, absolute indifference; as is observed in my Inquiry. But men naturally have no notion of any such liberty as this, as essential to the morality or demerit of their actions; but, on the contrary, such a liberty, if it were possible, would be inconsistent with our natural notions of desert, as is largely shown in the Inquiry.* If it be agreeable to natural sense, that men must be indifferent in determining their own actions; then, according to the same, the more they are determined by inclination, either good or bad, the less they have of desert: the more good actions are performed from good disposition, the less praiseworthy; and the more evil deeds are from evil dispositions, the less culpable; and in general, the more men's actions are from their hearts, the less they are to be commended or condemned: which all must know is very contrary to natural sense.

Moral necessity is owing to the power and government of the inclination of the heart, either habitual or occasional, excited by motive; but, according to natural and common sense, the more a man does anything with full inclination of heart, the more is it to be charged to his account for his condemnation, if it be an ill action, and the more to be ascribed to him for his praise, if it be good.

If the mind were determined to evil actions by contingence, from a state of indifference, then, either there would be no fault in them, or else the fault would be in being so

* Especially in Part III. sect. vi. and vii.

perfectly indifferent, that the mind was equally liable to a bad or good determination. And if this indifference be liberty, then the very essence of the blame or fault would lie in the liberty itself, or the wickedness would, primarily and summarily, lie in being a free agent. If there were no fault in being indifferent, then there would be no fault in the determination's being agreeable to such a state of indifference: that is, there could no fault be reasonably found with this, viz. that opposite determinations actually happen to take place *indifferently*, sometimes good and sometimes bad, as contingence governs and decides. And if it be a fault to be indifferent to good and evil, then such indifference is no indifference to good and evil, but is a determination to evil, or to a fault; and such an indifferent disposition would be an evil, faulty disposition, tendency, or determination of mind. So inconsistent are these notions of liberty, as essential to praise or blame.

The author of the Essays supposes men's natural delusive sense of a liberty of contingence, to be in truth the foundation of all the labour, care, and industry of mankind; and that if men's practical ideas had been formed on the plan of universal necessity, the *ignava ratio*, the inactive doctrine of the Stoics, would have followed; and that there would have been no room for forethought about futurity, or any sort of industry and care; plainly implying that in this case men would see and know that all their industry and care signified nothing, was in vain, and to no purpose, or of no benefit; events being fixed in an irrefragable chain, and not at all DEPENDING on their care and endeavour; as he explains himself particularly, in the instance of men's use of means to prolong life: not only very contrary to what I largely maintain in my Inquiry,* but also very inconsistently with his own scheme, in what he supposes of the ends for which God has so deeply implanted this deceitful feeling in man's nature: in which he manifestly supposes men's

---

* Especially Part IV. sect. v.

care and industry not to be in vain and of no benefit, but of great use, yea, of absolute necessity, in order to the obtaining the most important ends and necessary purposes of human life, and to fulfil the ends of action to the BEST ADVANTAGE : as he largely declares. Now, how shall these things be reconciled? That, if men had a clear view of real truth, they would see that there was no ROOM for their care and industry, because they would see it to be in vain, and of no benefit ; and yet that God, by having a clear view of real truth, sees that their being excited to care and industry, will be of excellent use to mankind, and greatly for the benefit of the world, yea, absolutely necessary in order to it : and that therefore the great wisdom and goodness of God to men appears, in artfully contriving to put them on care and industry for their good, which good could not be obtained without them ; and yet both these things are maintained at once, and in the same sentences and words by this author. The very reason he gives, why God has put this deceitful feeling into men, contradicts and destroys itself ; that God in his great goodness to men gave them such a deceitful feeling, because it was very useful and necessary for them, and greatly for their benefit, or excites them to care and industry for their own good, which care and industry is useful and necessary to that end ; and yet the very thing that this great benefit of care and industry is given as a reason for, is God's deceiving men in this very point, in making them think their care and industry to be of great benefit to them, when indeed it is of none at all ; and if they saw the real truth, they would see all their endeavours to be wholly useless, that there was NO ROOM for them, and that the event does not at all DEPEND upon them.

And besides, what this author says, plainly implies (as appears by what has been already observed), that it is necessary men should be deceived, by being made to believe that future events are contingent, and their own future actions free, with such a freedom as signifies that their actions are not the fruit of their own desires, or designs; but altogether contingent, fortuitous, and without a cause. But how should a notion of liberty, consisting in accident or loose chance, encourage care and industry? I should think it would rather entirely discourage every thing of this nature. For surely, if our actions do not depend on our desires and designs, then they do not depend on our endeavours, flowing from our desires and designs. This author himself seems to suppose, that if men had indeed such a liberty of contingence, it would render all endeavours to determine or move men's future volitions in vain : he says, that, in this case, to exhort, to instruct, to promise, or to threaten, would be to no purpose. Why? Because (as he himself gives the reason) "then our will would be capricious and arbitrary, and we should be thrown loose altogether, and our arbitrary power could do us good or ill only by accident." But if such a loose fortuitous state would render vain others' endeavours upon us, for the same reason would it make useless our endeavours on ourselves ; for events that are truly contingent and accidental, and altogether loose from and independent of all foregoing causes, are independent on every foregoing cause within ourselves, as well as in others.

I suppose that it is so far from being true, that our minds are naturally possessed with a notion of such liberty as this, so strongly that it is impossible to root it out, that indeed men have no such notion of liberty at all, and that it is utterly impossible, by any means whatsoever, to implant or introduce such a notion into the mind. As no such notions as imply self-contradiction and self-abolition can subsist in the mind, as I have shown in my Inquiry, I think a mature, sensible consideration of the matter, sufficient to satisfy any one, that even the greatest and most learned advocates themselves for liberty of indifference and self-determination, have no such notion ; and that indeed they mean something wholly inconsistent with, and directly subversive of, what they strenuously affirm, and earnestly contend for.

By a man's having a power of determining his own will, they plainly mean a power of determining his will as he pleases, or as he chooses ; which supposes that the mind has a choice, prior to its going about to confirm any action or determination to it. And if they mean that they determine even the original or prime choice by their own pleasure or choice, as the thing that causes and directs it, I scruple not most boldly to affirm, that they speak they know not what, and that of which they have no manner of idea ; because no such contradictory notion can come into, or have a moment's subsistence in, the mind of any man living, as an original or first choice being caused, or brought into being, by choice. After all they say, they have no higher or other conception of liberty than that vulgar notion of it which I contend for, viz., a man's having power or opportunity to do as he chooses ; or if they had a notion that every act of choice was determined by choice, yet it would destroy their notion of the contingence of choice ; for then no one act of choice would arise contingently, or from a state of indifference, but every individual act, in all the series, would arise from foregoing bias or preference, and from a cause pre-determining and fixing its existence ; which introduces at once such a chain of causes and effects, each preceding link decisively fixing the following, as they would by all means avoid.

And such kind of delusion and self-contradiction as this, does not arise in men's minds by nature ; it is not owing to any natural feeling which God has strongly fixed in the mind and nature of man, but to false philosophy, and strong prejudice, from a deceitful abuse of words. It is artificial; not in the sense of the author of the Essays, supposing it to be a deceitful artifice of God; but artificial as opposed to natural, and as owing to an artificial, deceitful management of terms, to darken and confound the mind. Men have no such thing when they first begin to exercise reason; but must have a great deal of time to blind themselves with metaphysical confusion, before they can embrace and rest in such definitions of liberty as are given, and imagine they understand them.

On the whole, I humbly conceive, that whosoever will give himself the trouble of weighing what I have offered to consideration in my Inquiry, must be sensible, that such a moral necessity of men's actions as I maintain, is not at all inconsistent with any liberty that any creature has, or can have, as a free, accountable, moral agent, and subject of moral government ; and that this moral necessity is so far from being inconsistent with praise and blame, and the benefit and use of men's own care and labour, that, on the contrary, it implies the very ground and reason why men's actions are to be ascribed to them as their own, in that manner as to infer desert, praise and blame, approbation and remorse of conscience, reward and punishment ; and that it establishes the moral system of the universe, and God's moral government, in every respect, with the proper use of motives, exhortations, commands, counsels, promises, and threatenings; and the use and benefit of endeavour, care, and industry : and that therefore there is no need that the strict philosophic truth should be at all concealed from men; no danger in *contemplation* and *profound discovery* in these things. So far from this, that the truth in this matter is of vast importance, and extremely needful to be known ; and that the more clearly and perfectly the real fact is known, and the more constantly it is in view, the better ; and, particularly, that the clear and full knowledge of that which is the true system of the universe in these respects, would greatly establish the doctrines which teach the true Christian scheme of Divine administration in the city of God, and the gospel of Jesus Christ, in its most important articles : and that these things never can be well established, and the opposite errors, so subversive of the whole gospel, which at this day so greatly and generally prevail, be well confuted, or the arguments by which they are maintained answered, till these points are settled : while this is not done, it is, to me, beyond doubt, that the friends of those great gospel truths will but poorly maintain their controversy with the adversaries of those truths : they will be obliged often to dodge, shuffle, hide, and turn their backs ; and that the latter will have a strong fort, from whence they never can be driven, and weapons to use, which those whom they oppose will find no shield to screen themselves from; and they will always puzzle, confound, and keep under the friends of sound doctrine, and glory and vaunt themselves in their advantage over them ; and carry their affairs with a high hand, as they have done already for a long time past.

I conclude, Sir, with asking your pardon for troubling you with so much said in vindication of myself from the imputation of advancing a scheme of necessity, of a like nature with that of the author of the " Essays on the Principles of Morality and Natural Religion." Considering that what I have said is not only in vindication of myself, but, as I think, of the most important articles of moral philosophy and religion; I trust in what I know of your candour, that you will excuse

Your obliged friend and brother,

J. EDWARDS.

Stockbridge, *July* 25, 1757.

ANDREW JACK, PRINTER.